2-19-22

CHINESE
COOKING FOR EVERYONE

CHINESE
COOKING FOR EVERYONE

**With more than 350 authentic and
easy-to-follow recipes illustrated in full color**

edited by Emma Callery

CRESCENT BOOKS
New York

A QUINTET BOOK

This 1991 edition published by Crescent Books, distributed by Outlet Book Company, Inc., a
Random House Company, 225 Park Avenue South, New York, New York 10003.

ISBN 0-517-07004-9

8   7   6   5   4   3   2   1

This book was designed and produced by
Quintet Publishing Ltd, 6 Blundell Street, London N7 9BH

Designer: Miranda Snow
Project Editor: Laura Sandelson
Editor: Emma Callery
Photographers: Ian Howes and Michael Freeman

Typeset in Great Britain by En to En Typesetters, Tunbridge Wells
Manufactured in Hong Kong by Regent Publishing Services Limited
Printed in Hong Kong by Leefung-Asco Printers Limited

The material in this publication previously appeared in *Chinese Regional Cooking, Classic
Chinese and Oriental Cooking, Chinese Cookery Masterclass* and *Chinese Vegetarian Cooking*.

PICTURE CREDITS

All the pictures in this book, except those
mentioned below, were taken by Michael
Freeman, Ian Howes and Jon Wyand.

p6 Tim Megarry; pp41 and 46 Xinhua News
Agency; p98 Richard and Sally Greenhill; p123
Francis Wood and pp172-3 Deh-Ta Hsiung.

CONTENTS

INTRODUCTION

The Regional Cooking Styles of China

Looking at a map of China, it is not difficult to understand why there should be such a large variety of different cooking styles throughout the country. The Chinese attach great importance to the use of fresh meat and tender young vegetables, so, because it was difficult to transport food and keep it fresh, each region was forced to make the best use of its own products. Every district has its own specialty, yet all these different forms and styles of cooking can be grouped under four main "schools": Peking, Shanghai, Sichuan and Guangzhou (Canton).

PEKING (Northern School)

Besides the local cooking of Hebei (in which province Peking is situated), Peking cuisine embraces the cooking styles of Shandong, Henan and Shanxi, as well as the Chinese Moslem cooking of Inner Mongolia and Xinjiang. Also, being the capital of China for many centuries, it became the culinary center, drawing inspiration from all the different regional styles.
Specialties: Peking duck, Mongolian hot pot.

SHANGHAI (Eastern School)

Also known as the Huaiyang School of the Yangtse River delta, with Shanghai as its culinary center. This region covers the fertile lands of Anhui, Jiangsu and Fujian. (Fujian forms a school of its own, but sometimes is linked with the Southern School.)

The two provinces of Hubei and Jiangxi are sometimes grouped here because they both belong to China's "Lands of Fish and Rice."
Specialties: white-cut pork, lions' heads, squirrel fish.

SICHUAN (Western School)

The "red basin" of Sichuan is one of the richest lands of China. Owing to its geographical position, it was practically inaccessible from the rest of China until recently, therefore it developed a very distinct style of cooking. Its richly flavored and piquant food has influenced its neighboring provinces of Hunan and Guizhou, although the last two have a style of their own.

Sichuan food has only comparatively recently been introduced to the outside world but now has a strong following in many Western countries.
Specialties: tea-smoked duck, chili dishes, eggplant in "fish sauce".

CANTON (Southern School)

The Pearl River delta, with Canton as the capital of Guangdong, is undoubtedly the home of the most famous of all Chinese cooking styles as it also embraces Hong Kong. Unfortunately its reputation has been damaged by a great number of so-called "chop-suey" houses outside China. Authentic Cantonese food has no rival and has a greater variety of dishes than any other School. Because Canton was the first Chinese port opened for trade, foreign influences are particularly strong in its cooking.
Specialties: *cha shao*, roast suckling pig. Also famous for its *dim sum* (snacks).

▲ *Planting rice in the paddy fields of the Yangtse delta.*

▲ *Fresh squid in a Chinese market; squid are a Cantonese speciality.*

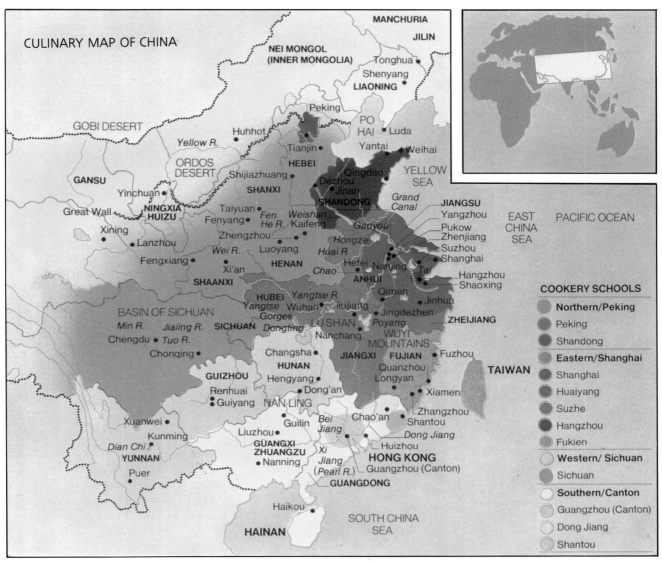

CULINARY MAP OF CHINA

MANCHURIA
JILIN
NEI MONGOL
(INNER MONGOLIA)
Tonghua
Shenyang
LIAONING
GOBI DESERT
Peking
Huhhot
PO HAI
Luda
Yellow R.
Tianjin
Yantai
Weihai
ORDOS DESERT
HEBEI
Qingdao
YELLOW SEA
GANSU
Shijiazhuang
Dezhou
Jinan
SHANXI
SHANDONG
Yinchuan
Grand Canal
JIANGSU
EAST CHINA SEA
PACIFIC OCEAN
Great Wall
NINGXIA HUIZU
Taiyuan
Fen He R.
Weishan
Yangzhou
Fenyang
Kaifeng
Gaoyou
Pukow
Zhenjiang
Xining
Zhengzhou
Hongze
Suzhou
Lanzhou
Wei R.
Luoyang
Huai R.
Hefei
Shanghai
Fengxiang
Xi'an
HENAN
Chao
Nanjing
Tai
Hangzhou
Shaoxing
SHAANXI
HUBEI
Yangtse R.
Qimen
Yangtse
Wuhan
Jiujiang
Jinhua
BASIN OF SICHUAN
Gorges
LU SHAN
Jingdezhen
ZHEJIANG
Min R.
Jialing R.
SICHUAN
Dongting
Poyang
WUYI MOUNTAINS
Chengdu
Tuo R.
Nanchang
Chonqing
Changsha
JIANGXI
FUJIAN
Fuzhou
HUNAN
Quanzhou
TAIWAN
GUIZHOU
Hengyang
Longyan
Renhuai
Dong'an
Xiamen
Guiyang
NAN LING
Zhangzhou
Xuanwei
Chao'an
Shantou
Kunming
Liuzhou
Guilin
Bei Jiang
Dong Jiang
Dian Chi
GUANGXI ZHUANGZU
Xi Jiang
Huizhou
YUNNAN
Nanning
(Pearl R.)
HONG KONG
Puer
Guangzhou (Canton)
GUANGDONG
Haikou
SOUTH CHINA SEA
HAINAN

COOKERY SCHOOLS

Northern/Peking
Peking
Shandong
Eastern/Shanghai
Shanghai
Huaiyang
Suzhe
Hangzhou
Fukien
Western/ Sichuan
Sichuan
Southern/Canton
Guangzhou (Canton)
Dong Jiang
Shantou

▲ *A vegetable market in Peking.*

▲ *Tea-pickers in Yunnan.*

▲ *This culinary map of China gives a vivid impression of the sheer scale and variety of the country, from the harsh continental climate of the north to the subtropical regions of the south. With such a range of climates and geography, it is hard to talk in general terms about Chinese cooking. There are no formal divisions between the great schools of Peking (north), Shanghai (east) Canton (south) or Sichuan (west), but rather shifts of emphasis and perspective.*

The Elements of Taste

"Everyone eats and drinks," said Confucius, "but few can appreciate taste." Since taste is a very personal thing (just as "beauty is in the eye of the beholder"), one's palate has to be developed both physically and intellectually. Few people in the West, however, are aware that, for centuries, Chinese scholars discussed, analyzed and wrote down their thoughts on food and drink, and that some of them developed an extensive knowledge of the nature of food and the physiology of taste based on Taoist and Confucianist teachings.

No one would disagree that the essence of the art of cooking lies in the taste of food. The Chinese believe the most important elements that help us to appreciate the taste are color, aroma, flavor and texture. All these elements have to be well balanced to form a harmonious whole and this is the central principle of culinary art.

Any wine connoisseur will immediately recognize the parallel with wine tasting: first you examine the color, then smell the bouquet, next you taste the flavor and, finally, you judge its body and aftertaste. This may sound very elementary to the expert, but how many uneducated palates can truly appreciate the subtleties of all these elements when they are combined in one single dish?

COLOR

Each ingredient has its own color, some items change their color when cooked, and others only show off their true color well when supplemented with different colored ingredients in contrast.

AROMA

Aroma and flavor are very closely related to each other, and they both form an essential element in the taste experience. The agents a Chinese cook most often uses in order to bring out the true aroma of a certain ingredient are: scallions, root ginger, garlic and wine – the four essential flavors.

FLAVOR

Each region has its own classification of flavors, but out of scores of subtle taste experiences, the Chinese have isolated five primary flavors: sweet, sour, salty, bitter and piquant. They have also learned how to combine some of these flavors to create an entirely new flavor - sweet and sour, for instance, make an interesting pair, but not sweet and piquant nor sour and bitter.

TEXTURE

This is another vital element in Chinese cooking. A dish should have one or several textures: tenderness, crispness, crunchiness, smoothness and softness. The selection of different textures in one single dish is as important as the blending of different flavors and the contrast of complementary colors.

The different flavors and textures so important in Chinese cooking, including Chinese chives ▲, some of the many varieties of Chinese cabbage ▼ and succulent Peking ducks prepared for deep-frying ▶.

HARMONY

Very few Chinese dishes consist of only one single ingredient; as it offers no contrast it therefore lacks harmony. This is the basic Taoist philosophy of *yin* and *yang*. So, with few exceptions, all Chinese dishes consist of a main ingredient (be it pork, beef, chicken or fish) with one or several supplementary ingredients (usually vegetables) in order to give the dish the desired harmonious balance of color, aroma, flavor and texture.

For instance, if the main ingredient is pork, which is pale pink in color and tender in texture, one would use either celery (pale green and crunchy) or green peppers (dark green and crisp) as the supplementary ingredient; or one might choose mushrooms (Chinese mushrooms are much darker in color with a soft texture) or bamboo shoots (pale yellow and crunchy when fresh), or a combination of both to give the dish an extra dimension.

This principle of harmonious contrast is carried all the way through a meal. No Chinese would serve just one single dish on his table, however humble his circumstances might be. The order in which different dishes are served, either singly or in pairs (often in fours), is strictly governed by the same principles: avoid monotony and do not serve similar types of food one after another or together, but use contrasts to create a perfect harmony.

Vegetarian cooking has a long history in China. Traditionally the Chinese have always been highly aware of, indeed one would almost say obsessed by, the link between food and health, whether physical or spiritual. Consequently many Chinese follow a vegetarian diet on health rather than economical grounds, although many are Buddhists who abhor the killing of any living creature and would certainly never dream of eating meat or fish in any form.

The close associations between Buddhists and the non-believer vegetarians are deep-rooted. One interesting point to note here is that despite their continual introduction, milk and dairy products are, to date, not prominent in Chinese cuisine. Therefore, unlike their counterparts in the West, Chinese vegetarians will not use butter, cheese or milk in their cooking, and a true Buddhist will eat neither eggs nor fish.

The art of cooking vegetables has been perfected by the Chinese - the vegetables are almost always done lightly and simply. Obviously, different types of vegetables should be treated differently: a few require longer cooking time; others need to be cooked with more than one ingredient in order to gain the correct "cross-blending" of flavors.

▼ *Eggplant*   ▲ *Tofu*

9

Special Ingredients

BAMBOO SHOOTS

There are several kinds of bamboo shoots available in the West - all in cans only, which is a pity since they lose much of their crispy texture and flavor. Try to obtain winter bamboo shoots; they are dug up from the cracked earth before the shoots grow to any great length or size, therefore they are extra tender and tasty. Spring bamboo shoots are much larger; they sometimes may reach several feet in length and 3-4in in diameter. Once the can is opened, the shoots may be kept in a covered jar of water in the refrigerator for several days. Braised bamboo shoots in cans should be eaten cold without any further cooking.

TOFU

Made from soaked yellow soy beans ground with water. A coagulant is added after some of the water is strained through cheesecloth, causing the ground beans to curdle and become firm tofu. Usually sold in squares about $2\frac{1}{2} \times 2\frac{1}{2}$in, $\frac{1}{4}$in thick. Will keep a few days if submerged in water in a container and placed in the coldest part of the refrigerator. **Dried tofu skin** is usually sold either in thick sticks or thin sheets. It should be soaked in cold water overnight or in warm water for at least an hour before use.

BEAN SPROUTS

Two kinds are available: yellow soy bean sprouts, only to be found in Chinese provision stores, and green mung bean sprouts, which can be bought from almost every large city supermarket. (Never use canned bean sprouts; they do not have the crunchy texture which is the main characteristic of bean sprouts.) They can be kept in the refrigerator for two or three days if bought fresh. See also mung beans.

BLACK BEAN SAUCE

Sometimes called **crushed bean sauce**, this thick sauce is made from black beans, flour and salt. It is sold in cans and, once opened, must be transferred into a screw-top jar and then it will keep in a refrigerator for months. It has a distinctive salty taste.

CELLOPHANE OR TRANSPARENT PAPER AND NOODLES

Made from mung beans. They are sold in dried form, the noodles tied into bundles weighing from 2oz to 1lb. Soak in warm water for five minutes before use.

CHILI PASTE

Also called **chili purée**. Is made of chili, soy bean, salt, sugar and flour. Sold in jars and will keep almost indefinitely.

CHILI SAUCE

Hot, red sauce made from chilis, vinegar, plums, salt and sesame.

CHINESE CABBAGE

There are innumerable varieties of cabbage grown in China, of which only two or three types are available in the West. The one most commonly seen is known as celery cabbage or

Chinese leaves: it has a pale green color and tightly wrapped elongated head, two thirds of the vegetable is stem which has a crunchy texture; another variety has a shorter and fatter head with curlier, pale yellow leaves. Then there is the dark green-leaved variety, also with white stems, and the bright green-leaved variety with pale green stems, sometimes with a sprig of yellow flower in the center which is very much prized by the Chinese. These last two varieties are sold only in Chinese stores.

CHINESE DRIED MUSHROOMS

There are two main types of Chinese mushrooms: those that grow on trees, known as **fragrant or winter mushrooms**; and those cultivated on a bed of straw, known as **straw mushrooms**. Fragrant or winter mushrooms are sold dried; they are used in many dishes as a complementary vegetable for their flavor and aroma. Soak in warm water for 20-30 minutes, squeeze dry and discard the hard stalks before use. Straw mushrooms are available in cans, but are completely different in texture and flavor. The Western varieties of common or field mushrooms can be used as substitutes, but they do not impart as much flavor.

DRIED SHRIMPS

These are small to very small, and are sold cleaned, shelled and whole. They add a salty, savory seasoning to dishes.

FIVE-SPICE POWDER

A mixture of anise seed, fennel, cloves, cinnamon and pepper. It is very strongly piquant, so use a very small amount each time. It will keep for years if stored in a tightly covered container.

FRESH CORIANDER

Sometimes known as **Chinese parsley,** this plant is available in Oriental stores and large supermarkets. In Italian and Mexican groceries it is called *cilantro.*

GINGER ROOT

Sold by weight. Should be peeled and sliced or finely chopped before use. Will keep for weeks in a dry, cool place. Dried and powdered ginger is not a satisfactory substitute for fresh ginger.

GLUTEN

A high-gluten flour and water dough is soaked and kneaded in water to wash out the starch; the remaining gluten is porous like a sponge. It is cut into pieces to be used like dumplings to carry flavor and provide bulk in sauces.

GREEN HOT CHILI

Will keep fresh for a week or two in the vegetable compartment of the refrigerator in a plastic bag.

GREEN SEAWEED

This mosslike seaweed is dark green in color. It is sold dried, in wads or in matted chips. When deep-fried in oil, it is crisp and has a toasted fragrance. Dried green cabbage leaves can be used as a substitute.

HOISIN SAUCE

Also known as barbecue sauce. Made from soy beans, sugar, flour, vinegar, salt, garlic, chili and sesame.

KAO LIANG LIQUEUR

A spirit made from sorghum and millet. Brandy or vodka can be substituted.

MONOSODIUM GLUTAMATE (MSG)

This chemical compound, known as "taste essence," is often used to heighten the flavor of food. It is rather frowned upon by true gourmets as it can wipe out the subtle distinction of a dish when used to excess.

MUNG BEANS

A small green bean used for making mung bean noodles (see Cellophane noodles) or for sprouting. They are obtainable from Chinese groceries and many large supermarkets. Mung beans are easily sprouted at home in just a few days; they will have an excellent crunchy texture but will look smaller and curlier than shop-brought ones.

OYSTER SAUCE

A thick sauce made from oysters and soy sauce. Sold in bottles, will keep in the refrigerator indefinitely.

RED BEAN PASTE

A thick sauce made from fermented bean curd and salt. Sold in cans or jars, will keep indefinitely.

RICE WINE

Also known as **Shaoxing wine**, made from glutinous rice. Saké or pale (medium or dry) sherry can be substituted.

SALTED BLACK BEANS

Whole bean sauce, very salty.

1 *Shaoxing wine* 2 *Peanut oil* 3 *Vinegar*
4 *Monosodium glutamate* 5 *Sesame seed oil* 6 *Oyster sauce*

SESAME SEED OIL

Sold in bottles. Widely used in China as a garnish rather than for cooking. The refined yellow sesame oil sold in Middle Eastern stores has less flavor and therefore is not a very satisfactory substitute.

The most commonly used oils in China are vegetable oils such as soy bean, peanut or rape seed oils. The Chinese never use butter or meat dripping, although lard and chicken fat are used in some regional cooking, notably in the East.

SICHUAN PEPPERCORNS

Reddish-brown peppercorns, much stronger then either black or white peppercorns of the West. Usually sold in plastic bags. Will keep indefinitely in a tightly sealed container.

SOY SAUCE

Sold in bottles or cans, this liquid ranges from light to dark brown in color. The darker colored sauces are strongest, and more often used in cooking, whereas the lighter is used at the table.

GOLDEN NEEDLES (dried Tiger Lily buds)

The buds of a special type of lily. Sold in dried form, should be soaked in warm water for 10-20 minutes and the hard stems removed. They are often used in combination with wood ears (see below).

TOMATO SAUCE

Quite different from Western tomato ketchup. Italian tomato paste may be substituted when fresh tomatoes are not available.

WATER CHESTNUTS

Strictly speaking, water chestnuts do not belong to the chestnut family, they are the roots of a vegetable. Also known as "horse's hooves" in China on account of their appearance before the skin is peeled off. They are available fresh or in cans. Canned water chestnuts retain only part of the texture and flavor of fresh ones. Will keep for about a month in a refrigerator in a covered jar.

WATER CHESTNUT FLOUR OR POWDER

A flour made from water chestnuts. Cornstarch is a good substitute.

WHITE NUTS

Also known as **ginkgo nuts,** they are the stones or nuts of the fruits from the ginkgo tree. Available canned, they are very popular with Chinese vegetarians.

1 Hoi sin sauce   2 Salted black beans   3 Light soy sauce
4 Dark soy sauce   5 Red bean-curd sauce
6 Crushed yellow bean sauce   7 Yellow bean sauce

WOOD EARS

Also known as **cloud ears** or **tree fungus.** Sold in dried form, should be soaked in warm water for 20 minutes; discard any hard stems and rinse in fresh water before use. They have a crunchy texture and a mild but subtle flavor. According to the Chinese, wood ears contain protein, calcium, phosphorus, iron and carbohydrates.

YELLOW BEAN SAUCE

This thick sauce is made from crushed yellow beans, flour and salt. It is sold in cans or jars; once opened, it should be transferred into a screw-top jar. It will keep in the refrigerator for months.

K*itchen* U*tensils*

An average Chinese kitchen has far less equipment and tools than one in the West. To start with, very few Chinese kitchens are equipped with an oven. Most stoves are not suitable for baking or roasting; a great majority of families have to make do with a small brazier, burning either charcoal or firewood. But then, over the years, the Chinese have been refining their utensils to achieve a maximum efficiency and usefulness.

The wok and cleaver are two tools in point: with these two basic pieces of equipment, a Chinese cook can work wonders with whatever ingredients he or she is given.

The principal implements found in a Chinese kitchen include woks (two or three different sizes and types), cleavers (two or three different weights), a chopping block, bamboo steamers (two types), a strainer, scooper, spatula and sand pots (casseroles).

▲ *Chinese bamboo steamer with lid and ornate wooden cooking chopsticks.*

CLEAVERS AND CHOPPING BOARDS

The ingredients in Chinese cooking are frequently prepared by using a knife or sharp cleaver. Many recipes are prepared by the "cut-and-cook" method, which requires that equal attention is paid to both the cutting and the cooking. Whether you are preparing ingredients by cutting them into chunky pieces, or by slicing, thick shredding, fine shredding, dicing into cubes or grinding, you must always ensure that everything is of equal size. If you do not, then the quality of the cooking will be affected because of the uneven heating that will result. The secret for beginners is to avoid cutting horizontally. Instead, use your whole hand on the top of the blade, rather than chopping from the handle, and slice carefully into the ingredients at an angle. This is risk-free and easy, thanks to the sharpness of the blade.

For safe and effective chopping you need a good heavy chopping board. Any good quality Chinese chopper will be more than adequate, and a traditional chopping board made of solid wood 5-6in thick is much better than the skimpy modern ones.

WOKS

The wok is cone shaped with a rounded bottom. The advantage of the wok is that because of its shape, the heat is evenly spread to all parts of the wok; therefore only a short cooking time is required. The ingredients naturally return to the center of the wok however vigorously you stir them. The traditional wok is made of iron, and thus it retains a steady and intense heat.

A new wok should be seasoned before use. First, wash it in hot water and dry it by placing it over a moderate heat. Then wipe the inside with a pad of paper towels soaked in cooking oil until clean. After each use, wash it under hot or cold water. Never use any detergents, but scrape off any food that has stuck to the bottom with a hard brush or scourer. Dry the wok thoroughly over a moderate heat before putting it away, otherwise it will rust.

Besides stir-frying, the wok can also be used for deep-frying, shallow-frying, steaming, braising and boiling and so on. The type with a single handle is best suited for stir-frying; the two-handled type is better suited for all other purposes as it is more stable on top of a stove. The ordinary wok is not really suitable for an electric stove. Only gas provides the instant control and very high heat that is often called upon in Chinese cooking, but flat-bottomed woks are available for cooking on electric stoves and ranges, and there are also electric woks for sale.

▲ *Chinese earthenware cooking pot with basket ladle, and a Mongolian hot pot with long-handled wire baskets for cooking.*

OTHER USEFUL UTENSILS

Much Chinese food is steamed at some stage of its preparation, and a selection of steamers in different sizes is convenient. Ordinary metal steamers work well, but the advantage of the bamboo steamer over a conventional metal one is that the bamboo lid is not absolutely airtight, thus allowing a certain amount of evaporation which prevents condensation forming inside the lid.

The scoops and strainers required for Chinese cooking are usually already part of the equipment in the average Western kitchen, although those stocked in Chinese stores are often larger than average, making the work of dealing with whole fish or batches of deep-fried food easier.

Likewise, Chinese casseroles are not very different from Western ones except sometimes in appearance. It is nice to have one or two which are attractive enough to serve from.

1 Scoopers   2 Spatula   3 Woks   4 Strainers
5 Bamboo steamer   6 Chopsticks   7 Chopping block
8 Cleavers   9 Sand pot

There is one Chinese cooking pot, however, which is quite distinctive and, while not essential, definitely adds an Oriental touch to a Chinese meal prepared at home. Mongolian hot pots, or fire-pots, heat stock or soup at the table from glowing charcoal under and in the middle of the pot. Small long-handled wire baskets or bamboo sieves or chopsticks are used to add and remove ingredients from the liquid.

Mongolian hot pots are becoming increasingly available in stores specializing in kitchen equipment, where they go under a variety of names, including Japanese steamboats. There are several recipes in the book which use Mongolian hot pots; a fondue set makes a perfectly adequate substitute.

Preparation and Techniques

SLICING

This is probably the most common form of cutting in Chinese cooking. The ingredients are cut into very thin slices, not much bigger than an oblong stamp, and as thin as cardboard. When slicing meat, always cut across the grain - this makes it more tender when cooked.

1 Slicing meat across the grain.

2 To preserve vitamins, always wash vegetables before cutting.

SHREDDING

The ingredients are first cut into thin slices, then shredded into thin strips as small as matches but twice as long.

1 Meat is shredded into thin strips.

2 Shredding bamboo shoots.

PREPARING SHRIMP

The large Pacific or King varieties should be deveined before cooking.

1 Remove the shell.

2 Use a sharp knife to make a shallow incision on the back of the shrimp, then remove the black intestinal parts.

CHOPPING

The normal method of cutting a fowl is to do it in sections. Starting on the outside with the wings and working towards the breast on the inside, the pieces are finally reassembled.

1 Remove the two wings.

2 Remove both the legs and thighs.

3 Separate the breast from the backbone.

4 Divide the breast into two sections.

5 Cut each breast into 3-4 pieces.

6 Cut each wing into 3 pieces and each leg into 5 pieces. Reassemble neatly.

DIAGONAL CUTTING

Carrots, celery, zucchini and asparagus are normally cut into diamond-shaped pieces.

1 Carrots are cut diagonally.

2 Sweet peppers are cut into diamond-shaped pieces.

DICING

The ingredients are first cut into coarse strips about the size of French fries, then diced into small cubes.

1 Chicken breast is cut into strips.

2 Then cut crosswise into small cubes.

GRINDING

Finely chop up the ingredients into small bits. Although it is much easier to use a grinder, the flavor is not quite the same.

1 Slices of pork are finely shredded and then coarsely chopped.

2 "Grinding" with a cleaver.

STEAMING FISH

The Chinese steam almost all types of food including bread and dim sum, but they prize whole steamed fish above all. Served on its cooking dish, the fish juices blend with the seasonings and any marinade flavorings.

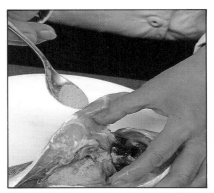

1 Sprinkle the seasoning mixture inside the fish.

2 Rub seasoning well inside the slits, and leave for the flavor to develop.

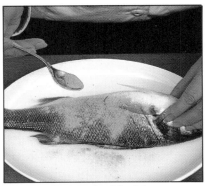

3 Season the outside of the fish.

4 Spread the scallion and ginger garnish over the steamed fish.

5 Pour soy sauce over the fish. Repeat the process with dry wine or sherry. Finally, pour smoking hot oil over the fish to finish cooking.

TEMPERATURES

The temperature of the cooking oil will also have to be varied according to the ingredients used and the dishes to be produced.

Hot pan with cold oil: Heat the pan until very hot, then add the cold oil. Put in the ingredients before the oil gets really hot and remove the ingredients after deep frying for a short time. This method requires the temperature of the oil to be 175-210°. When you add the ingredients, there should be no smoke from the oil and no hissing sound. This method is used to prepare good cuts of meat as it helps to retain their natural flavor and preserves the tenderness of the meat.

Hot pan with hot oil: Heat the pan until very hot, then add the oil and heat it to a temperature of 350-450°. The oil should start to smoke, and it will hiss if you stir it. This method is used to prepare seafood and food that requires a crunchy covering (often battered foods).

Medium heat with hot oil: Heat the pan until very hot, then heat the oil until it reaches a temperature of 225-330°. A small amount of smoke will begin to come off the surface of the oil. This method is used for frying large pieces of meat, whole fish, chicken or duck.

STIR-FRYING

The ability to stir-fry is an important part of any Cantonese chef's skill. It is essential to heat the pan over maximum gas or electricity until it is extremely hot. Then add the necessary quantity of oil. When that is hot, add ground or finely chopped garlic, ginger and scallions. As the mixture begins to cook, add the other ingredients, stir-fry and turn them to cook everything quickly and evenly. Sprinkle wine and sesame seed oil at the end to produce a fragrant aroma.

SHALLOW FRYING

For shallow frying, heat the pan until it is extremely hot and then add oil. Lower the ingredient into the pan and, when it is slightly brown, reduce the heat to a minimum. Use this method to fry fish. It will stop the skin sticking to the pan and ensure an attractive appearance when it is served.

DEEP FRYING

This is a popular technique in Chinese cooking. Strictly speaking, blanching the ingredients in oil can be regarded as deep frying. To deep fry you need, in most cases, adequate heat and hot oil to make the ingredients crunchy and tender. Be careful, however, with ingredients that are coated in batter: keep the temperature somewhat lower, otherwise you will overcook the outside of the food while the inside is still raw. In these cases, it might be better to use the "soak-fry" method. Heat the oil, add the ingredients and turn off the heat. Let them soak for a while in the hot oil and then take them out. Re-heat the oil until it reaches a temperature of 350-425° and then deep fry the ingredients for a second time, until done. This method is also known as double deep frying.

▲ *A Chinese housewife prepares a meal.*

STEAMING

There are two kinds of steaming. Short steaming, requiring high heat, and long steaming, requiring low heat. Some other Chinese cook books may call long steaming "double boiling" because the foods are contained in a closed receptacle. In some recipes, those calling for the steaming of a duck, chicken or a large piece of meat for example, you should use the low, medium heat until the ingredients are tender.

BOILING

This is a very simple method of cooking. Simply add water to cook the ingredients, exactly as you would cook soup, rice or porridge. If you want to make a bowl of clear meat soup, you must blanch the meat with boiling water first, then rinse it under cold water. Heat a bowlful of water in a pan and, when the water is boiling, put the ingredients into it. You should use the maximum heat at the start, reducing to medium heat and finally ending with low heat. This kind of soup is delicious once you have mastered the timing and the amount of water to add.

BRAISING

Cook ingredients over moderate heat with sufficient liquid to cover them. Reduce the liquid to 15 percent of the original and add seasonings to make a sauce.

STEWING

Add more water or stock and use low heat to cook the ingredients until they are soft and tender. Once the liquid has nearly all evaporated - or reduced to 10-20 percent - add seasonings, ingredients and flavoring to make the sauce.

MARINATING

After cutting, the next stage in the preparation of food before actual cooking is marinating, sometimes called "coating" or "blending" in Chinese. The basic method is to marinate meat, fish or chicken in salt, egg-white and starch - usually water-chestnut flour, but cornstarch is a good substitute. Sometimes sugar, soy sauce and wine are added. The purpose of this "coating" is to preserve the vitamins and protein content in meat after it is finely cut up, while retaining its tenderness and delicacy.

POULTRY

Stir-Fried Chicken with Garlic and Cucumber Cubes

INGREDIENTS *serves 5-6*
about ½ chicken breast
1 medium cucumber
1 tsp salt
pepper to taste
4 tsp cornstarch
½ egg white
2 cloves garlic
1 tbsp lard
2 tbsp good stock
2 scallions
3 tbsp vegetable oil
2 slices fresh ginger root
½ tsp salt
1½ tbsp rice wine or dry sherry
1 tbsp light soy sauce
½ tsp sesame seed oil

METHOD
Cut the chicken into ½in cubes. Cut the cucumber into similar-sized cubes. Sprinkle and rub the chicken evenly with 1 tsp of salt, pepper and half the cornstarch, then wet with egg white. Crush the garlic. Chop the lard. Blend the remaining cornstarch with the 2 tbsp of stock. Cut the scallions into 1½in sections.

Heat the vegetable oil in a wok or frying pan. When hot, stir in ginger slices for 15 seconds to flavour the oil. Remove and discard the ginger. Add the chicken cubes to the pan and stir-fry over medium to high heat for 45 seconds. Remove and drain. Add the lard and garlic to the wok or pan and stir over medium heat for 15 seconds. Add the cucumber cubes and sprinkle with the ½ tsp of salt and pepper. Stir-fry for 1 minute. Add the rice wine or sherry, soy sauce and scallions. Return the chicken to the pan and stir-fry for 1 minute. Add the blended flour and sesame seed oil and stir-fry for 10 seconds. Serve.

Hot Tossed Shredded Chicken in Red Chili Oil

INGREDIENTS *serves 4-6*
½ medium chicken
1 medium onion
3 tsp salt
3 slices fresh ginger root
1 medium cucumber

SAUCE
1½ tbsp chili sauce or red chili oil
1 tbsp chopped garlic
1 tbsp chopped fresh root ginger
1 tbsp peanut butter
1 tbsp chopped scallion
2 tsp sesame seed oil
1½ tbsp vegetable oil
4 tbsp good stock
½ tsp salt

METHOD
Bring about 5 cups water to a boil in a pan. Add the chicken and simmer for about 10 minutes. Peel and slice the onion. Pour away a quarter of the water and add the salt, ginger and onion. Cook for another 35 minutes. Cut the cucumber into shreds, leaving the skin on. Remove the chicken and cool. Shred the meat into pieces of similar size to the cucumber shreds.

Place all the sauce ingredients in a bowl and mix well. Arrange the cucumber on a plate and pile the chicken on top. Pour over the sauce.

Quickly Braised Chicken with Chili, Green Peppers and Black Beans

INGREDIENTS *serves 4-6*
2lb chicken
3 green peppers
2 fresh red chilies
1 small piece dried orange peel
2 cups peanut oil
2 tbsp fermented, salted soy beans
1 tsp chopped garlic
3oz shallots, chopped
2 tsp rice wine

SEASONINGS
3 tsp stock
1 tsp salt
1 tsp monosodium glutamate (optional)
1 tsp sugar
2 tsp dark soy sauce
1 tbsp cornstarch blended with 3 tbsp water

METHOD
Chop the chicken through the bones into large, bite-sized pieces and dust with cornstarch.

Cut the peppers and chilies into slices, and soak the dried orange peel before shredding it.

Heat the pan until it is very hot. Pour in the peanut oil and fry the chicken until it starts to turn brown.

Heat a clay pot or casserole until it is very hot. Pour 2 tbsp peanut oil into it and add the chilies, peppers, fermented beans, chopped garlic and shallots to sauté, stirring them together until fragrant.

Add the chicken pieces and sprinkle with rice wine. Sauté for a further 30 seconds.

Blend the seasonings and add to the pot. Stir and cover the container to cook for 1½ minutes over a high heat. Keep the container covered until ready to serve.

Golden Chicken with Shrimp Paste

INGREDIENTS *serves 6-8*
3-3½lb fresh chicken
2-3 tbsp shrimp paste (fresh shrimps, finely ground)
3 cups peanut oil

MARINADE
3 tbsp cornstarch
1 tbsp rice wine or dry sherry
2 tsp ginger juice
1 tsp sugar
few drops sesame seed oil

METHOD
Chop the chicken into large, bite-sized pieces and pat them dry.

Mix the shrimp paste with the marinade ingredients, and marinate the chicken with the mixture for 20 minutes.

Heat the peanut oil in a pan until it is very hot. Put in the chicken pieces and fry them for 2 minutes over a low heat. Remove the chicken and set the pieces aside while you re-heat the oil to boiling point. Fry them again for 1½ minutes and serve.

▲ *Quickly Braised Chicken With Chilies, Green Peppers and Black Beans: a rich and very tasty dish distinguished by the unique taste of black beans.*

▼ *As in all fried chicken dishes, the chicken in Golden Chicken with Shrimp Paste should be juicy inside and crispy outside. Careful heat control is the key.*

◄ *Multi-Flavored Chicken: the particular flavor of this dish comes from the addition of sesame oil to the sauce during cooking.*

Crispy "Five Spiced" Chicken Legs

INGREDIENTS *serves 4-6*
8 chicken drumsticks
2½tsp salt
pepper to taste
1 tsp ground ginger
vegetable oil for deep-frying

SAUCE
1¼ cups good stock
1½ tbsp hoisin sauce
1½ tbsp yellow bean paste
¾ tsp pepper
1½ tbsp mixed five-spice pieces

METHOD
Rub the chicken drumsticks with a mixture of the salt, pepper and ground ginger. Leave to season for 30 minutes. Bring a pan of water to a boil, add the drumsticks and cook for 3 minutes. Drain and cool.

Place the sauce ingredients in a wok or pan and bring to a boil. Add the drumsticks and simmer for about 15 minutes. Leave the drumsticks to cool in the sauce for 15 minutes, then remove and drain thoroughly. Heat the oil in a wok or deep-fryer. When hot, gently fry the chicken for about 5 minutes until golden-brown.

Remove the knuckle from the drumstick and put a cutlet frill on the exposed bone. Arrange on a heated plate and serve.

Multi-Flavored Chicken

INGREDIENTS *serves 8-10*
4-5lb fresh chicken

SAUCE
2 tbsp sesame oil
1 tsp brown vinegar
1 tsp sugar
1 tbsp chili sauce
1 tbsp chopped garlic
1 tsp ground peppercorns
3 tbsp shredded scallions
1½ tsp salt
8 tbsp stock

METHOD
Clean the chicken thoroughly.

Put 6 cups water into a pan and bring to a boil. Add the chicken and simmer for 10 minutes over low heat. Remove the chicken and rinse under the tap for 2 minutes. Return the chicken to the water and boil for a further 5 minutes. Rinse with cold water again.

Remove the bones from the chicken and hand-shred the meat, arranging the shredded chicken on a plate.

Blend together the ingredients for the sauce. Pour it over the chicken on the dish and serve.

Red-Cooked Chicken

INGREDIENTS *serves 6-8*
3-4lb chicken
1¼ cups good stock
1 chicken bouillon cube
4 slices fresh ginger root
¼ tsp salt
1½ tbsp sugar
pepper to taste
5-6 tbsp light soy sauce
2 pieces star anise

METHOD
Bring a large pan of water to a boil, add the chicken and simmer for about 8 minutes. Remove and drain thoroughly. Place the bird in a flameproof casserole, add the stock, crumbled bouillon cube, ginger, salt, sugar, pepper, soy sauce and star anise. Bring to a boil.

Cover and place the casserole in a pre-heated oven at 400°F, and cook for 30 minutes. Turn the bird over, reduce the oven temperature to 350°F, and cook for a further 25 minutes. Turn the bird over again and continue to cook for a final 25 minutes.

► *Shanghai Quick-Braised Chicken on the Bone: where meat is left on the bone in Chinese recipes it is not carved, but usually chopped with a heavy cleaver into bite-sized pieces that are easy to pick up with chopsticks.*

Shanghai Quick-braised Chicken on the Bone

INGREDIENTS *serves 6-8*
3-4lb chicken
1 tbsp cornstarch
4 tbsp vegetable oil
5 slices fresh ginger root
2 tbsp sugar
3 tbsp light soy sauce
3 tbsp dark soy sauce
1 tbsp hoisin sauce
1 tbsp oyster sauce
4 tbsp rice wine or dry sherry
2 cups good stock
scallions to garnish

METHOD
Chop the chicken through the bone into about 30 bite-sized pieces. Bring a large pan of water to a boil, add the chicken and simmer for about 5 minutes. Remove and drain thoroughly. Blend the cornstarch with 3 tbsp of water.

Heat the oil in a wok or pan. When hot, stir in the ginger for about 1½ minutes. Add the chicken pieces and stir-fry for about 3 minutes. Put in the sugar, soy sauces, hoisin sauce, oyster sauce, wine or sherry and stock. Bring to a boil and continue to stir over the highest heat until the sauce begins to thicken and reduce. Add the blended flour and stir until the sauce is thick and coats the chicken pieces. Garnish with the scallions, shredded or decoratively cut.

Stir-Fried Chicken and Celery on Rice

INGREDIENTS *serves 4-6*

2-3 medium dried Chinese mushrooms
1 chicken breast
1 celery stalk
⅓ cup canned bamboo shoots, drained
2 slices fresh ginger root
2 scallions
3 tbsp vegetable oil
salt and pepper to taste
2 tbsp good stock
2 tbsp rice wine or dry sherry
1 tbsp light soy sauce
1 cup boiled rice

METHOD
Soak the dried mushrooms in hot water to cover for 25 minutes. Drain and discard the tough stalks. Cut the mushroom caps into small cubes. Dice the chicken into small cubes. Dice the celery and bamboo shoots into similar-sized cubes. Finely chop the ginger. Chop the scallions.

Heat the oil in a wok or frying pan. When hot, stir-fry the ginger, scallions, mushrooms, celery and bamboo shoots over high heat for 1 minute. Add the chicken and stir-fry for 1 minute. Sprinkle with salt and pepper to taste. Add the stock, rice wine or sherry and soy sauce, toss and turn for a further minute.

Serve on boiled rice. If liked, wrap spoonfuls of chicken and rice in lettuce leaves to eat with the fingers.

Melon Chicken

INGREDIENTS *serves 6 - 8*
3 large dried Chinese mushrooms
2 tbsp dried shrimps
1 large melon, approximately 8in in
   diameter
3oz ham
$\frac{1}{2}$ cup canned bamboo shoots, drained
2$\frac{1}{2}$-3lb chicken
2 tbsp vegetable oil
2 slices fresh ginger root
3oz button mushrooms
1 tsp salt
pepper to taste
1$\frac{1}{4}$ cups good stock
2 tbsp dry sherry

METHOD

Soak the dried mushrooms and dried shrimps separately in hot water to cover for 25 minutes. Slice the top of the melon off and reserve for a lid. Scrape out most of the flesh and reserve about a quarter for cooking with the chicken. Drain and discard the tough mushroom stalks. Cut the mushroom caps into quarters. Cut the ham and bamboo shoots into cubes.

Place the chicken in a steamer and steam for about 1 hour. Leave to cool. When cool enough to handle, remove the meat from the bones and cut into cubes. Heat the oil in a wok or large skillet. When hot, stir-fry the ginger, dried shrimps and dried mushrooms over high heat for about 2 minutes. Add the ham, half of the chicken, the bamboo shoots, reserved melon, fresh mushrooms, salt and pepper. Stir-fry for a further 3 minutes. Pack all the stir-fried ingredients into the melon. Add any excess to the remaining chicken. Mix the crumbled stock cube with the stock and sherry and pour on to the melon to the brim. Replace melon lid and fasten with a few wooden cocktail sticks. Place on a heatproof plate, steam for 30 minutes.

Bring the whole melon to the table to serve. This is a pretty dish and the different savory flavors in the chicken-ham-mushroom stuffing and the sweetness of the melon give it a unique appeal.

White-Cut Chicken

This famous Cantonese dish is about the simplest way of cooking a chicken. It is always served cold.

INGREDIENTS *serves 6 - 8*
3lb young chicken
2 slices ginger root
2 scallions

SAUCE
1 tsp salt
2 tbsp soy sauce
1 tsp sugar
1 clove garlic, crushed
1 slice ginger root, peeled
1 scallion
$\frac{1}{2}$ tbsp sesame seed oil

METHOD

Clean the chicken, place it in a large pot with enough water to cover. Add the ginger root and scallions; cover the pot with a tight-fitting lid and bring it to a boil. Simmer for 5 minutes, then turn off the heat and let the chicken cook gently in the hot water for 3-4 hours. Do *not* lift the lid while you wait for it to cool.

▲ *Melon Chicken: an attractive and unusual presentation.*

▼ *White-Cut Chicken makes an ideal starter or part of a buffet meal.*

To serve, remove the chicken and drain. Chop it into 20-24 pieces, then reassemble on a long dish.

Finely chop the garlic, ginger root and scallion; mix with salt, sugar, soy sauce, sesame seed oil and a little stock. Either pour it all over the chicken or use as a dip.

Bright Moon and Red Pine Chicken

INGREDIENTS *serves 4-6*

1 chicken leg, boned but with skin attached
1 egg
3oz snow peas
½oz cooked ham
scant ¼lb pork
3 tbsp lard
1½ tbsp soy sauce
1 tsp salt
1 tbsp rice wine or dry sherry
1 tbsp sugar
1 tbsp cornstarch
1 slice fresh ginger root, finely chopped

METHOD

Break the egg into a bowl; cut the ends off a few snow peas and place them halfway round the egg to resemble the leaves of a flower. Finely shred the ham and arrange the shreds in the middle to make it look like a chrysanthemum. Warm up 1tbsp lard in a wok or skillet and with one swift movement empty the bowl into the wok to be fried on one side until the egg just sets; lift the "chrysanthemum" out.

Finely chop the pork and mix it with ½tbsp rice wine or sherry, ½tsp salt, 1 tsp sugar and 1 tsp cornstarch.

Spread the chicken leg out flat with the skin side down, score the meat with a criss-cross pattern (not too deep), then press the pork hard on top. Make sure it is stuck firmly to the chicken, and add a little more cornstarch to bind them together.

Heat another tbsp lard; fry the chicken-pork piece on both sides until golden; add rice wine or sherry, 1tsp sugar, soy sauce, finely chopped ginger root and a little water. Bring it to a boil, then reduce heat and simmer for about 40 minutes. Remove and cut it into 3 strips with the pork side up; place them on a serving dish.

Now steam the egg "chrysanthemum" for 2 minutes. In the meantime, stir-fry the rest of the snow peas with the remaining lard, salt and sugar. Arrange the snow peas around the chicken-pork pieces, and place the egg higher up in the midle. The egg is the "bright moon" and the chicken-pork is the "red pine."

Steamed Chicken and Frogs' Legs Wrapped in Lotus Leaves

INGREDIENTS *serves 4-6*

1lb chicken legs
½lb frogs' legs

MARINADE

1 egg white
1 tsp salt
1 tbsp light soy sauce
1 tsp dark soy sauce
1 tsp sugar
2 tsp Chinese yellow wine
1 tbsp cornstarch
½ tsp sesame seed oil
¼lb fresh straw mushrooms
2 scallions
1-2 lotus leaves (depending on their size)
1oz ham, sliced
6 slices fresh ginger root

METHOD

Chop the chicken legs into bite-sized pieces and cut the frogs' legs in half, discarding the lower leg. Marinate the chicken and frogs' legs and set aside. Cut the straw mushrooms in half and cut the onions into 1½in sections.

Blanch the dry lotus leaves in about 4 cups boiling water until they are soft. Remove, rinse under the tap and pat dry. Put all the ingredients in an even layer on the lotus leaves, wrapping them up firmly and neatly. Place the parcel on a heatproof plate and steam over medium heat for 35 minutes. Unwrap the parcel and trim the lotus leaves to fit the plate. Serve.

▼ *Steamed Chicken and Frogs' Legs Wrapped in Lotus Leaves: a great summer dish distinguished by the refreshing fragrance of lotus leaves. The colors – jade green, ivory and ruby red – suggest a Chinese painting.*

▲ *Purse Chicken: an apposite name, for a variety of ingredients are wrapped in a thin omelet which is gathered up to look like a drawstring purse.*

Purse Chicken

INGREDIENTS *makes about 20 "purses"*

9oz broccoli
2 medium black mushrooms
$\frac{1}{3}$ cup bamboo shoots
$\frac{1}{2}$ cup water chestnuts
1 tbsp salt
5 tbsp peanut oil
3 scallions
5oz chicken breast
2 tsp egg white
$\frac{1}{2}$ tbsp cornstarch
1 tbsp fresh coriander, stem and leaf, chopped
strands of scallion
2 tbsp crab roe

PANCAKES
3 egg whites
2 tsp cornstarch
3 tbsp chicken stock

SAUCE
$\frac{3}{4}$ cup chicken stock
1 tsp sesame oil
2 tsp Chinese yellow wine
1 tsp salt

METHOD

Cut the broccoli into shavings, wash in salted water and set aside.

Soak the black mushrooms in hot water for 30 minutes. Remove and discard the stems, finely chop the caps and set aside.

Finely chop the bamboo shoots and water chestnuts and set aside. Bring 1 cup water to a boil, add 1tbsp salt and 1 tbsp oil and cook the broccoli spears for 5 minutes. Blanch the scallions for 30 seconds. Remove and set aside.

Dice the chicken finely and mix it with 2 tsp egg white and $\frac{1}{2}$ tsp cornstarch. Set aside.

Heat 2 tbsp oil in pan. Add the black mushrooms, water chestnuts, bamboo shoots, coriander and the chicken mixture. Stir and cook for $1\frac{1}{2}$ minutes over a low heat. Remove, drain and set aside.

Mix together the pancake ingredients. Heat the pan and grease the bottom with oil. Spoon 1 tbsp of the pancake mixture into the center of pan and make a thin pancake over low heat. Repeat this process until all mixture is used up.

Take one pancake and spoon 1 tbsp of the chicken and vegetable filling into the center, gather up the edges and tie the top of the bundle with a strand of scallion (use the green part only). Put $\frac{1}{2}$ tsp crab roe on top in the center of the bundle.

Arrange the purses in the center of a plate, sprinkle with broccoli and steam over medium heat for 5 minutes.

Heat 2 tbsp oil in a pan and add the sauce ingredients. Bring the sauce to a boil, stir and pour it over the chicken purses before serving.

Drunken Chicken

INGREDIENTS *serves 4-6*
2lb chicken
1 tbsp salt
2 scallions
4oz fresh ginger root
1 cup Chinese yellow wine

METHOD

Clean the chicken thoroughly. Bring 10 cups water to the boil, turn off the heat, place the chicken in the hot water and turn it over. Poach the chicken for 1 minute, remove, drain and pat it dry with absorbent paper towels.

Rub ½ tbsp salt over the skin and spoon ½ tbsp salt into the cavity. Finely shred the scallions and ginger and stuff them into the cavity. Finally, pour the Chinese yellow wine into the cavity.

Steam the chicken over medium heat for 20 minutes in a shallow basin. Remove it and chop it into bite-sized pieces. Return the chicken pieces to the wine in the basin, soak overnight and transfer to a plate to serve.

Tangerine Peel Chicken

INGREDIENTS *serves 4-6*
1lb chicken meat, boned
2 slices fresh ginger root
1 scallion
1½ tbsp rice wine or dry sherry
1 tsp salt
2 tsp soy sauce
1 tbsp sugar
1 tbsp vinegar
3-4 dried chilies
½ tsp Sichuan pepper
1 tsp dried tangerine peel
oil for deep-frying
½ tsp sesame seed oil

METHOD

Cut the chicken meat into small pieces and crush the ginger root and scallion; add them to the chicken meat together with salt, rice wine or sherry and 1 tbsp soy sauce. Let it marinate for a while.

Mix the remaining soy sauce with the sugar and vinegar in a bowl to make sweet and sour sauce.

Heat up the oil; discard the ginger root and onion; deep-fry the chicken until golden; remove and drain.

Pour off the excess oil leaving about 2 tbsp in the wok; put in the dried red chilies, Sichuan pepper and tangerine peel. Add chicken, stir a few times, then add the sweet and sour sauce; blend well and serve hot.

When eating, savor each mouthful slowly. After the initial hot taste is passed, you will be able to distinguish all the other different flavors, with the subtle fragrance of tangerine peel.

▲ *Drunken Chicken: served principally as a cold appetizer, the chicken is lightly boiled, then immersed in wine for a period which may be a few hours or a few days. The chicken used should be a free-range fowl for choice; if not, the chicken should be marinated overnight to improve its flavor.*

Stir-Fried Chicken Kung-Po Style

INGREDIENTS *serves 4-6*
1¼lb chicken breast
4 tbsp peanut oil
1 tsp peppercorns
1 tsp dried red chili pepper, cut in rings
1 tsp Chinese yellow wine or dry sherry
3 slices ginger root
1 tsp garlic, chopped
2 tsp scallion, chopped
4oz roasted peanuts

SEASONING
1 tsp sugar
1 tbsp dark soy sauce
1 tbsp cornstarch

SAUCE
1 tsp sugar
2 tsp vinegar
1 tbsp dark soy sauce
3 tbsp stock
2 tsp cornstarch

METHOD
Cut the chicken into ½in cubes and mix the meat with the seasoning ingredients.

In a separate bowl, blend together the ingredients for the sauce and set it to one side.

Heat the oil in a pan, add the peppercorns and dried red chili peppers and when the chili peppers darken in color, pour the oil into a bowl through a strainer. Discard the peppercorns.

Return the oil and the dried red chili peppers to the pan, and add the chicken. Stir-fry for 1 minute, add the yellow wine, then the ginger, garlic and scallions. Keep on stirring and turning the ingredients. Add the sauce ingredients, stir well, then add the roast peanuts. Stir and serve.

▶ *Stir-Fried Chicken Kung-Po Style: Chicken is diced into cubes, coated in cornstarch and stir-fried, first in very hot oil, then with the oil drained off. Kung-po style means the dish is colored pink with a combination of soy sauce and red oil, which gives it a distinctive flavor and appearance.*

Chicken in Vinegar Sauce

INGREDIENTS *serves 4-6*
½lb chicken breast meat
⅔ cup bamboo shoots
1 egg white
1 tbsp rice wine or dry sherry
1 tsp salt
1 tbsp cornstarch
3-4 dried red chili peppers, soaked
3 tbsp oil

VINEGAR SAUCE
1 tbsp vinegar
1 tbsp soy sauce
1 tbsp sugar
1 slice ginger root, peeled and finely chopped
1 clove garlic, finely chopped
1 scallion, finely chopped
3 tbsp stock
1 tbsp cornstarch

METHOD
Score the skinless surface of the chicken in a criss-cross pattern; cut it into oblong pieces about the size of a stamp. Marinate it with the egg white, wine or sherry, salt and cornstarch.

Cut the bamboo shoots to roughly the same size as the chicken; finely chop the soaked red chili peppers.

Finely chop the ginger root, garlic and scallion; mix the sauce in a bowl.

Warm up the oil and stir-fry the chicken pieces for about 2 minutes; add chili peppers and bamboo shoots, stir a few times more then add the sauce. Blend well; serve as soon as the sauce thickens.

Chicken, Bamboo Shoots and Black Mushroom Casserole

INGREDIENTS *serves 4-6*
1½lb chicken pieces
6-8 medium black mushrooms
2 cups peanut oil
⅔ cup sliced bamboo shoots
4 slices fresh ginger root
1 scallion, cut into 2in lengths
1 tsp sesame oil
1 tsp Chinese yellow wine
1 tbsp cornstarch blended with 2 tbsp water

SEASONING
2 tsp salt
1 tsp sesame oil
½ tsp pepper
2 tsp Chinese yellow wine or dry sherry
1 tbsp cornstarch

SAUCE
1 tbsp oyster sauce
1 tbsp soy sauce
1 tsp sugar
4 tbsp chicken stock

METHOD

Cut the chicken into bite-sized pieces. Mix the seasonings together thoroughly and add the chicken pieces. Mix and set aside.

Soak the black mushrooms in warm water for 30 minutes until they are soft; remove the stems.

Heat the oil and deep fry the chicken for 1¼ minutes over a moderate heat. Drain

bsp oil in a casserole, add the
, bamboo shoots, ginger,
the chicken and stir-fry over a
or 1¼ minutes.

sauce ingredients and add the
the casserole. Bring to a boil and
15 minutes over a moderate to

dd the sesame oil, yellow wine
cornstarch, stir well and serve
role.

▲ *Chicken, Bamboo Shoots and Black Mushroom Casserole: in spite of its exotic name, this is a simple, tasty casserole cooked the Chinese way.*

Chicken Fu-Yung

INGREDIENTS *serves 4-6*
4 chicken breasts
4 tbsp chicken stock
6 egg whites
1 tbsp cornstarch
1 tsp salt
1 cup peanut oil
2 slices fresh ginger root
1 clove garlic
2 tsp ham, ground
2 tsp fresh coriander leaves, finely
    chopped

SAUCE
¼ cup chicken stock
½ tsp salt
1 tbsp cornstarch
2 tsp Chinese yellow wine

METHOD
Pound the chicken breasts with the back of a cleaver and grind the chicken meat finely. Add 2 tbsp chicken stock to the meat and force the mixture through a strainer. Add 1 tbsp egg white to the strained meat and stir well.

Blend 1 tbsp cornstarch with 2 tbsp chicken stock. Mix the egg whites, salt and ground chicken together, stirring with a fork

▲ *Chicken Fu-Yung: shredded or ground chicken breast is deep-fried with beaten egg white. The bite-sized pieces are drained then cooked in thickened stock. Wine may be added to the sauce.*

in one direction only, and add the blended cornstarch, continuing to stir and mix the ingredients thoroughly.

Heat a pan until it is very hot and add the peanut oil. When the oil is warm, add tablespoonfuls of the egg white and ground chicken mixture. Reduce the heat to low and use a spatula to push the egg mixture to and fro in the pan. When it begins to set into snowflake-like pieces, remove them with a perforated spoon, drain and set them aside on a plate to keep warm.

Heat 2 tbsp oil in the pan. Add the ginger and garlic, but remove and discard them when they have turned brown.

Blend together the ingredients for the sauce, add to the pan and bring to a boil. Stir and pour over the egg white mixture.

Sprinkle the ground ham over the sauce and garnish with the chopped coriander leaves before serving.

Chili Chicken Cubes

INGREDIENTS *serves 4-6*
½lb chicken breast meat, boned
1 egg white
½ tsp salt
1½ tbsp cornstarch
1 slice ginger root, peeled
1 clove garlic
2 scallions, white parts only
1 small green pepper
1 small red pepper
1 tbsp rice wine or sherry
1 tbsp soy sauce
3 tbsp stock
oil for deep-frying
1 tbsp chili paste
½ tsp sesame seed oil

METHOD
Dice the chicken into ½in cubes, mix with the egg white, salt and ½ tbsp cornstarch.

Cut the ginger root and garlic into thin slices; cut the scallions diagonally into short lengths. Cut the green and red peppers into small squares roughly the same size as the chicken cubes.

Mix together the rice wine or sherry, soy sauce, stock and the remaining cornstarch in a bowl.

Heat up the oil and deep-fry the chicken cubes until pale golden; scoop out and drain.

Pour off the excess oil, leaving about 1 tbsp in the wok; toss in the ginger root, garlic, scallions, green and red peppers, the chicken and chili paste. Stir a few times.

Now add the sauce mixture to the wok; blend well; add the sesame seed oil just before serving.

Chicken "Sauce"

INGREDIENTS *serves 4-6*
1½lb young chicken
1½ tbsp rice wine or sherry
2 tbsp soy sauce
1 tbsp sugar
1¾ cups stock
2 tbsp lard
1 tbsp cornstarch
2 scallions, cut into 1in lengths

METHOD
Cut off the wings and parson's nose of the chicken, then chop it into about 20 pieces with the bone still attached.

Heat up the lard over a high heat; stir-fry the chicken pieces for about 30 seconds; add wine or sherry, soy sauce and sugar; stir until the chicken turns brown, then add the stock. Bring it to a boil, reduce heat to simmer for 10 minutes or until the stock is reduced by a third; now increase the heat, add the cornstarch mixed in a little water, blend well. When the juice is further reduced by half add the scallions and serve.

Each chicken piece should be wrapped in a dark, thickish sauce, hence the name of this dish.

▲ *Chili Chicken Cubes. This is another Sichuan dish that has gained nationwide popularity. It is reputed to have been one of the late Chairman Mao's favorites.*

Steamed Chicken

INGREDIENTS *serves 4-6*
2lb young chicken
4-5 Chinese dried mushrooms
²/₃ cup bamboo shoots
2oz cooked ham
1 cup broccoli stalks
2 scallions
2 slices ginger root, peeled
2 cups clear stock
3 tbsp rice wine or sherry
1 tsp salt
2 tbsp soy sauce

METHOD

Clean the chicken thoroughly; place it in a large pot, cover with cold water and boil for 25 minutes. Remove and cool it in cold water, then carefully remove the meat from the bones and carcass (but keep the skin on). Cut the meat into thin slices the size of a matchbox.

Soak the mushrooms in warm water for about 20 minutes, squeeze dry and discard the hard stalks, then cut them into slices as well. Cut the bamboo shoots and ham into pieces the same size as the chicken. Split the broccoli stalks in half lengthways, cut them into 2 dozen sticks, parboil for a few minutes and drain.

Place the bamboo shoots, mushrooms and ham slices in alternating rows in the bottom of a large bowl and arrange the chicken pieces on top with the skin side down. Place the broccoli stalks all around the chicken with the crushed carcass in the middle, add scallions cut into short lengths, ginger root, 1½ tbsp rice wine or sherry, ½ tsp salt, 1½ cups stock and steam vigorously for 1½ hours. Remove and discard the scallions and ginger root, then turn the bowl out into a large serving dish.

Heat up the remaining stock with the stock in which the chicken has been steamed and add soy sauce, the remaining salt and rice wine or sherry. When it starts to boil, skim off any scum; pour the stock over the chicken and serve.

▶ *Steamed Chicken – not so simple to make, but well worth the extra effort if you want to serve a special dish for your friends. It is both delicious and attractive.*

Watermelon Chicken

INGREDIENTS *serves 4-6*
2¹⁄₂lb young chicken (approximately)
3¹⁄₂lb watermelon (approximately)
2oz piece ham
¹⁄₃ cup bamboo shoots
2 tbsp rice wine or sherry
1 tbsp salt
2 slices of ginger root, peeled
3-4 Chinese dried mushrooms
2¹⁄₂-3pts water

METHOD
This is a very complicated method of serving a very simply cooked dish. It requires skill that far exceeds even that of a really good cook. You will have to be an artist of the first order if you are not going to make a mess of the whole thing.

Clean the chicken well; place it in a pot and add the water. Bring to a boil; take the chicken out and plunge it into cold water, then place it in a large bowl.

Add salt and rice wine or sherry to the water in which the chicken has been boiled; skim off any scum. Pour the liquid over the chicken in the bowl. Soak the dried mushrooms for 20 minutes, remove the hard stalks. Add the soaked mushrooms, the ham, bamboo shoots and ginger root to the bowl; place in a steamer and steam for 2 hours.

Slice off a piece across the top of the watermelon; scoop out the "flesh" from the lower part using a plastic or porcelain spoon, then carve some pretty pictures on the skin. Blanch the melon in boiling water, cool in cold water, then take it out and place it in a bowl.

Now place the steamed chicken inside the watermelon, breast side up. Cut the ham and bamboo shoots into small slices; place these and the mushrooms on top of the chicken; fill the melon with the chicken soup. Cut up the scooped-out melon; and add this to the soup. Place the "lid" on top, using tooth picks to secure it, then steam it for 10 minutes. Carefully carry the whole melon to the table; remove the tooth picks, take off the "lid" and serve.

If you can manage it, this is a real *pièce de resistance*.

Steamed Chicken with Chinese Mushrooms

INGREDIENTS *serves 4-6*
1lb chicken meat
3-4 Chinese dried mushrooms, soaked
2 slices ginger root, peeled
1 tsp salt
¹⁄₂ tsp monosodium glutamate
1 tbsp red wine or sherry
1 tsp sugar
1 tsp cornstarch
1 tsp sesame seed oil
freshly ground Sichuan pepper

METHOD
Use the breasts and thighs of a very young chicken; cut into small pieces and mix with salt, monosodium glutamate, rice wine or sherry, sugar and cornstarch.

Thinly shred the mushrooms and ginger root.

Grease a heat-proof plate with a little oil or lard, place the chicken pieces on it with the mushrooms and ginger root shreds on top, add ground pepper and all the sesame seed oil.

Steam vigorously for 20 minutes. Serve hot.

◀ *Steamed Chicken with Chinese Mushrooms: a favorite dish, always popular with family and friends.*

▼ *Dong'An Chicken: Dong'An is the small town in Hunan from which the dish originally came.*

Dong'An Chicken

INGREDIENTS *serves 4-6*

2lb young chicken
3-4 dried red chili peppers
2-3 Chinese dried mushrooms, soaked
2 slices ginger root, peeled
2 scallions
½ tsp Sichuan peppercorns
3 tbsp oil
2 tsp salt
1½ tbsp vinegar
1 tbsp soy sauce
1 tbsp Kao Liang spirit
1 tbsp cornstarch
1 tsp sesame seed oil

METHOD

Plunge the chicken into a pot of boiling water for 10 minutes, then rinse it in cold water and leave it to cool. Take the meat off the bone, and cut it into 1×½in strips.

Cut the mushrooms, dried red chili peppers, ginger root and scallions into shreds, crush the peppercorns.

Warm up the oil, first put in the chili peppers, ginger root, scallions and pepper, then add the chicken and mushrooms, stir for a few seconds. Now add salt, soy sauce, vinegar and spirit; when the juice starts to bubble, add the cornstarch mixed with a little water; blend well; add the sesame seed oil just before serving.

You may think this a Sichuan dish, but there is a subtle difference.

"Let a Hundred Flowers Bloom" Chicken

INGREDIENTS *serves 4-6*
1½lb young chicken
½lb shrimp, uncooked
¼ cup pork fat
¼ cup water chestnuts
¼ cup celery
1 egg white
2½ tsp salt
½ tsp oil
2 tsp cornstarch
1 tsp sesame seed oil
5 scallions
1 leek
1 green pepper

METHOD
Clean the chicken and boil in water for about 30-40 minutes; take out and discard the skin and bones.

Shell the shrimps, and finely grind them together with chicken and pork fat. Add egg white, mix well, next add water chestnuts, and then the celery finely chopped with 2 tsp salt.

Grease a dish with oil; spread out the chicken and shrimp mixture flat on it, about ½in thick; smooth the surface. Steam for 15 minutes; take out and cut into small pieces not much bigger than a stamp; arrange them on a serving dish in neat rows overlapping each other rather like a fish's scales.

Heat in a pan about ½ cup stock in which chicken has been cooked. Add ½ tsp salt, sesame seed oil and cornstarch, stir to make a smooth gravy, pour it all over the chicken.

Decorate the edge of the plate with the scallions, leek and green pepper cut into shapes of various flowers.

Oil-Braised Chicken

INGREDIENTS *serves 4-6*
1¼lb young chicken
2 tbsp soy sauce
2 tbsp rice wine or sherry
2 scallions, finely chopped
1 slice ginger root, peeled and finely chopped
½ tsp five-spice powder
oil for deep-frying

FOR THE DIP
chili sauce
Sichuan peppercorns, crushed

METHOD
Chop the chicken down the middle into two halves. Marinate with soy sauce, the wine or sherry, five-spice powder, finely chopped onions and ginger root. After 20-30 minutes, take the chicken halves out and pat them dry with paper towels.

Heat up the oil in a deep-fryer and, before the oil gets too hot, deep-fry the halves for about 5 minutes or until they start to turn golden, then take them out. Wait for the oil to get really hot, then fry the halves again until brown, take them out and chop them into small pieces; arrange on a plate.

Heat up the marinade; let it bubble for a while then pour it all over the chicken. Serve with chili sauce and Sichuan pepper as a dip.

The skin of the chicken should be crispy, and the meat very tender and highly aromatic.

▲ *Oil-Braised Chicken garnished with deep-fried shrimp crackers.*

Braised Chicken Breast

INGREDIENTS *serves 4-6*
10oz chicken breast meat, boned
1 egg
1 tbsp cornstarch
1 tbsp soy sauce
1 tbsp rice wine (or sherry)
1 tbsp tomato paste
1 tsp monosodium glutamate
½ tsp sesame seed oil
1 tsp sugar
a few shrimp crackers
lard for deep-frying

METHOD
Cut the chicken into small thin slices; mix with egg, soy sauce and cornstarch. Deep-fry the chicken pieces in lard for 2-3 minutes or until golden; remove and drain.

Pour off the excess lard; return the chicken pieces to the pan, followed by the rice wine or sherry, tomato paste, sugar, monosodium glutamate and sesame seed oil; blend well and place on a serving dish. Decorate the edge of the plate with shrimp crackers and serve.

Stir-Fried Chicken Cubes

INGREDIENTS *serves 4-6*

½lb chicken breast meat
1½ tsp salt
1 egg white
1½ tbsp cornstarch
2 scallions
1 small green pepper
1 small red pepper
1 tbsp rice wine (or sherry)
3 tbsp stock

METHOD

Cut the chicken meat into cubes the size of playing dice, mix them with a little salt, the egg white and 1 tbsp cornstarch, in that order which is very important.

Cut the scallions, green and red peppers to the same size as the chicken cubes.

Deep-fry the chicken cubes in oil on a medium heat for a few seconds only; scoop out and drain.

Pour off the excess oil leaving about 1 tbsp in the wok; put in the scallions, green and red peppers; stir and add the stock, wine or sherry, the remaining salt and cornstarch; mix well then add the chicken cubes; blend together and serve. A few drops of sesame seed oil can be added as garnish.

Salted Chicken

INGREDIENTS *serves 4-6*

2lb young chicken
2 tbsp soy sauce
4 slices ginger root, peeled
4 scallions
2 star anise
4 tbsp *mei kuei lu chiew* (rose petal wine) or fruit-based brandy
½ tbsp salt
18 cups rock salt

METHOD

Mei kuei lu chiew is fragrant liqueur used extensively in cooking. It is made from Kao Laing and specially grown rose petals, and it is very strong (96% proof!).

Clean the chicken; blanch for a short while. Remove and coat the whole chicken with soy sauce, then hang it up to dry.

Finely chop two slices ginger root and two scallions, crush the star anise; mix them with ½ tbsp salt and *mei kuei lu chiew*, and place this "marinade" inside the carcass of the chicken. Wrap it in a large sheet of aluminum foil.

In a large sand-pot or casserole, heat the rock salt over a high heat for a few minutes or until the salt is hot to the touch, then make a hole in the middle and place the foil-wrapped chicken in it. Cover with salt so that it is completely buried. Place the lid on and turn off the heat for 15 minutes. Remove the chicken (the salt can be kept for further use) and take it out of the foil. Chop it into small pieces and arrange on a serving dish.

Finely chop the remaining ginger root and scallions; mix with a little salt and stock as a dip.

▲ *Stir-frying the chicken cubes in a wok.*

37

▶ *Cantonese Fried Chicken: Cantonese chefs pride themselves on the fine presentation of their food; this photograph shows a particularly fine example.*

▼ *Chicken "Casserole": delicious and tender and good to look at.*

Cantonese Fried Chicken

INGREDIENTS *serves 4-6*
3lb young chicken
2 tbsp soy sauce
1 tbsp rice wine (or sherry)
oil for deep-frying

SAUCE
2 scallions, finely chopped
2 slices ginger root, peeled and finely
   chopped
1 tbsp sugar
1 tbsp vinegar

METHOD
Clean the chicken well; parboil in a large pot of boiling water for 2-3 minutes; remove and drain.

Marinate in soy sauce and rice wine or sherry for 20-30 minutes.

Heat up the oil in a deep-fryer; brown the chicken all over, basting constantly for 20-30 minutes. Leave it to cool before chopping into small pieces. Arrange neatly on a serving dish.

Heat up the remains of the marinade with the sauce mixture; either pour it over the chicken or use as a dip.

Chicken "Casserole"

INGREDIENTS *serves 4-6*
2½-3lb young chicken
1 tbsp five-spice powder
2 tbsp sugar
2½ cups soy sauce
1 slice ginger root
1 scallion
5 cups vegetable oil for deep-frying

METHOD
Use a fresh chicken, wash and dry it thoroughly.

Put the five-spice powder into a large pot or casserole, add sugar, soy sauce and about 5 cups water, bring it to the boil, then reduce the heat and simmer until it turns dark brown. This is the master sauce, which can be used over and over again; the flavor improves each time it is used, though after using it four or five times, you will have to add more five-spice powder.

Now parboil the chicken for 2 to 3 minutes, then place it in another pot of clean boiling water; add the ginger root and scallions; cook for about 40 minutes over a gentle heat; remove and let it cool for a short while. Cook the chicken in the "master sauce" for about 15 minutes, turning it over once or twice so that the entire chicken has become dark red. Remove the meat from the sauce and drain.

Heat up the oil over a high heat until smoking, then fry the chicken for about 15 minutes until the skin becomes dark brown but not quite burnt; remove. Chop up the chicken with a sharp cleaver and arrange it neatly on a plate and serve.

▶ *Chicken and Bamboo Shoots Assembly: usually served with rice at the end of a banquet, for those who still have some room left.*

Chicken and Bamboo Shoots Assembly

INGREDIENTS *serves 4-6*
6oz chicken breast meat
²/₃ cup bamboo shoots
1 egg white
1¹/₂ cups chicken stock
2 tbsp cornstarch
1 tbsp rice wine (or sherry)
1 slice ginger root, peeled
2 tbsp lard
1¹/₂ tsp salt
oil for deep-frying

METHOD
Cut the chicken into fine shreds about the size of matches and mix them with the egg white and ¹/₂ tbsp cornstarch. Cut the bamboo shoots into shreds roughly the same size as the chicken. Finely chop the ginger root.

Heat up the oil in a deep-fryer, fry the chicken shreds in oil over a moderate heat for about 10 seconds only. Separate the shreds, scoop them out and drain.

Heat up the lard in a wok or skillet, stir-fry the bamboo shoots, add ginger root, salt, wine or sherry and chicken stock. Bring it to a boil, then add the remaining cornstarch mixed with a little cold water; stir until the ingredients are well blended. When the gravy starts to thicken, add the chicken shreds, blend well and serve.

This is a semi-soup dish, ideal for serving with rice.

Chicken Cubes in Bean Sauce

INGREDIENTS *serves 4-6*
¹/₂lb chicken breast meat
1 egg white
2 tsp cornstarch
2¹/₂ cups oil for deep-frying
2 tbsp lard
2 tbsp crushed yellow bean sauce
1 tsp sugar
1 tbsp rice wine (or sherry)
1 slice ginger root, peeled and finely chopped

METHOD
Soak the chicken meat in cold water for 1 hour, separate the meat from the white tendon and membrane, then dice it into ¹/₃in cubes. Mix them with the egg white and cornstarch together with a little water - say 2 tsp.

Heat up the oil in a deep-fryer, lower the chicken cubes in and separate them with chopsticks or a fork. As soon as they start to turn golden, scoop them out with a perforated spoon and drain.

Meanwhile heat the lard in a wok or skillet, add the crushed bean sauce, stir until the sizzling noise dies down then add the sugar followed by wine (or sherry) and finely chopped ginger root. After about 10-15 seconds, it should have a smooth consistency. Now add the chicken cubes and stir well for 5 seconds so that each cube is coated with this bright reddish sauce. Serve.

This is a very popular dish, usually served during the early stages of a banquet.

Chicken Slices with Bamboo Shoots

INGREDIENTS *serves 4-6*
¹/₂lb chicken breast meat
¹/₂ tsp salt
1 egg white
2 tsp cornstarch
1 carrot
²/₃ cup bamboo shoots
3 dried Chinese mushrooms, soaked
2 scallions

SAUCE
1 tbsp soy sauce
1 tbsp sugar
1 tbsp vinegar
1¹/₂ tbsp cornstarch
2 tbsp water

METHOD
Cut the chicken into small slices not much bigger than the size of a postage stamp; mix with salt, egg white and cornstarch.

Slice the bamboo shoots, mushrooms and carrots; cut the scallions into short lengths; mix the sauce in a bowl.

Heat up the oil, stir-fry the chicken until its color changes; scoop out with a perforated spoon. Toss the bamboo shoots, mushrooms and carrots into the wok, stir a few times; put the chicken back, stir a few more times. Add the sauce with the crushed peanuts, blend well. As soon as the sauce thickens, dish out and serve.

Chicken Feet in Bean Paste Sauce

INGREDIENTS *serves 6*
approx 24 chicken feet
1 tsp oyster sauce
1 tsp light soy sauce
1 tsp dark soy sauce
1 tsp sesame seed oil
1/2 tsp five-spice powder
freshly ground pepper
oil for deep-frying
1 1/2 in piece fresh ginger root
3 cloves garlic
1 tbsp bean paste
2 tbsp oil
3-4 dried Chinese mushrooms, washed
    and soaked in 2 1/2 cups cold water for
    30 minutes
salt to taste
1 tbsp cornstarch

METHOD
Wash the chicken feet well, trimming off the nails. Put the feet into a pan of boiling, salted water until they become stiff; drain. Mix the oyster and both soy sauces, sesame seed oil, five-spice powder and pepper together. Pour this over the feet and mix well. Set aside for as long as possible, at least 1 hour.

Heat the oil in a wok, fry the feet until they are golden-brown and crisp. If the fat splutters and splashes a lot you can cover the wok with a lid. Lift out and immerse in cold water.

Meanwhile peel and slice the ginger and garlic. Set aside one-third of each for frying and finely pound the rest with the bean paste. First fry the ginger and garlic in oil to bring out the flavor. Add the pounded ingredients and fry over a brisk heat. Stir in 2 cups of the juice drained from the mushrooms and salt to taste. Place the drained chicken feet in an ovenproof casserole. Pop in the mushrooms and pour over the sauce. Cover and cook in a moderate oven (350°) for 30 minutes then reduce the heat to 300°, and cook for 3-4 hours or until the feet are tender. Mix the cornstarch into a paste with a little water, stir into the sauce to thicken just before serving.

Beggar's Chicken

INGREDIENTS *serves 6-8*
3-4lb chicken
1 large piece suet
2 pieces lotus leaf
5 cups all-purpose flour
2 cups water
1 large piece foil

MARINADE
2 tbsp dark soy sauce
4 tbsp Chinese yellow wine
1 tsp sesame oil
1 tsp sugar
1 tbsp salt

STUFFING
4-6 Chinese black mushrooms
1 1/4 lb pork
1/4 lb Sichuan preserved vegetables
2 1/2 cups bamboo shoots
2 tbsp peanut oil

METHOD
Blend together the ingredients for the marinade and use three-quarters of the mixture to rub over the inside and outside of the chicken. Set aside.

Prepare the stuffing by soaking the black mushrooms in hot water for 30 minutes. Discard the stems and shred the caps.

Shred the pork and mix it with the remaining quarter of the marinade.

Shred the Sichuan preserved vegetables into matchstick-sized pieces and soak them in water.

Shred the bamboo shoots into similar pieces and blanch them in boiling water for 2 minutes. (When using canned bamboo shoots this is not necessary.)

Heat a pan, add 2 tbsp peanut oil and stir-fry the pork for 1 minute.

Add the shredded black mushrooms, bamboo shoots and Sichuan preserved vegetables. Cook for 30 seconds and stuff the mixture generously into the cavity of the chicken.

Wrap the chicken in the piece of suet, trimming away any excess fat, and wrap the suet and chicken parcel in lotus leaves. (If you are using dried lotus leaves, soak them in hot water for 10 minutes first.)

Mix the flour and water and roll it out into a sheet. Encase the chicken parcel in the dough and wrap it all with foil.

Cook in a pre-heated oven at 450° for 1 hour. Reduce the temperature to 350° and bake for a further 45 minutes.

Remove the foil and crack the dough casing with a pestle. Carefully remove the lotus leaves and transfer the chicken to a serving platter.

▼ *Beggar's Chicken: this amusing barbecue dish should be cooked for several hours in the embers of a hot fire. The chicken, well marinated, is wrapped in lotus leaves then plastered with mud. The name of the dish indicates the Chinese admiration for the resourcefulness of the poor man – and suggests that the recipe should begin "First steal one chicken."*

Kou Shoa Deep-Fried Boneless Duck

INGREDIENTS *serves 6-8*
4-5lb duck
6 cups cooking sauce (see Aromatic and
   Crispy Duck recipe)
vegetable oil for deep-frying

BATTER
1 egg
5 tbsp cornstarch
2 tbsp self-rising flour

METHOD
Parboil the duck in a pan of boiling water for about 5 minutes, then drain. Mix the ingredients for the batter in a bowl until smooth.

Heat the cooking sauce in a heavy pan. Add the duck and simmer gently for about 45 minutes. Remove the duck and drain thoroughly. Allow the duck to cool for 30 minutes, then remove the meat from the bones, leaving the meat in large pieces if possible. Turn the meat in the batter mixture until evenly coated. Heat the oil in a wok or deep-fryer. When hot, fry the battered duck for about 5 minutes. Drain.

Place the large duck pieces on a chopping board, cutting each piece into 3-4 pieces, and serve.

▲ *The evocatively named Aromatic and Crispy Duck.*

▼ *Geese and duck flocks by a lakeside on a Chinese farm.*

Aromatic and Crispy Duck

INGREDIENTS *serves 6-8*
4-5lb duck
vegetable oil for deep-frying

COOKING SAUCE
6 cups good stock
6 tbsp sugar
6 slices fresh ginger root
10 tbsp soy sauce
4 tbsp yellow bean paste
6 tbsp rice wine or dry sherry
6 pieces star anise
$\frac{1}{2}$ tsp five-spice powder
$\frac{1}{4}$ tsp pepper

METHOD
Mix the ingredients for the cooking sauce together in a large saucepan. Clean the duck thoroughly and cut in half down the backbone. Place into the liquid and submerge.

Simmer the duck gently for 2 hours. Remove from the cooking liquid and leave to cool. When required, heat the oil in a wok or deep-fryer. When hot, place the duck gently in the oil and fry for 10-11 minutes. Drain well and serve.

Peking Duck

INGREDIENTS *serves 6-8*
5-6lb duck
40-50 Chinese pancakes (see next recipe, opposite)
6 scallions
½ cucumber, halved and seeded
1-2 red chili peppers

COATING
1 tbsp malt sugar, honey or molasses
1 tsp cornstarch
½ tsp vinegar

SAUCE
2 tbsp hoisin sauce
1 tbsp peanut butter
1 tbsp sesame oil
1 tbsp Chinese yellow wine

METHOD
Clean the duck, removing and discarding any excess fat in the cavity. Tie a piece of string around its neck. Pat dry.

Bring 25 cups water to boil and turn off the heat. Put the duck into the water and turn it backward and forward for about 1 minute. Remove. Bring the water to a boil again and repeat the previous step. Do this twice more (four times in all).

Hang the duck in a cool, draughty place for about 5 hours.

Mix the coating ingredients with 10tbsp hot water and brush the duck all over with the mixture. Hang to dry for a further 4 hours and apply a second layer of coating.

Pre-heat the oven to 450°. Put a roasting pan in the oven with a wire rack in it, making sure that there is a space of about 2in between the rack and the pan base.

Place the duck on the rack, breast side up, and roast for 8 minutes. Turn the duck over using a towel – not a fork – and roast for a further 8 minutes.

Reduce the temperature to 350° and turn the duck breast side up again. Roast for 20 minutes. Lower the temperature to 250° and roast for 10 minutes. Increase the heat again to 450° and roast the duck for about 10 minutes. At this point you have to watch carefully to make sure that the skin of the duck does not burn. Turn off the heat once the skin has turned a rich deep red.

While the duck is roasting prepare the Chinese pancakes (see next recipe). Cut the scallions into 2in lengths, shred the tip of each piece and put it in iced water for 10 minutes. Cut the cucumber into similar lengths. Decorate each piece with a red chili pepper ring.

Blend together the sauce ingredients over a low heat. Carve off the skin on the back of the duck. Hold the knife horizontally and carve the meat from the breast and legs, cutting at an angle of 15°. Arrange the skin and meat separately on a large plate and serve it with pancakes, scallions and cucumber and the sauce.

Diners help themselves. They place one pancake flat on a plate, put a piece of duck in the center, dip a scallion in the sauce and put it on top of the duck, wrap it up and eat it.

▶ *Peking Duck: scallions, cucumber, pancakes and sweet sauce surround the carefully separated skin and meat. Peking duck is eaten in a distinctive way. The diner assembles his own pancakes, with some crispy duck skin, some meat (skin and meat are served separately), some chive or scallion, and a generous dollop of sweet, plummy Peking duck sauce. The whole is then wrapped up. The contrast of textures and tastes is delicious.*

▲ *Diners prepare their own pancakes.*

▲ *Cucumber and scallions are dipped in the sauce and placed on the pancake.*

▲ *. . . together with some duck meat and skin.*

▲ *The rolled up pancake is ready to eat.*

▲ *A Chinese family enjoys a delicious dish of Peking duck.*

Chinese Pancakes

INGREDIENTS *makes about 40 pancakes*
4 cups all-purpose flour
1½ cups boiling water
1 tbsp sesame oil

METHOD
Place the unsifted flour in a mixing bowl. Make a well in the center and add the boiling water, stirring rapidly with a fork.

Knead the dough well on a lightly floured surface until it is smooth and firm. Return the dough to the mixing bowl, cover and leave to stand for 1 hour.

Knead the dough briefly on a lightly floured surface and roll into a sausage 1½in in diameter. Pull it apart with your fingers to make about 40 equal-sized pieces. Roll the pieces between your hands to make smooth balls, making sure that they are all the same size.

Lightly oil the fingers and palms of your hands and flatten each ball until it is ¼in thick. Brush the top with sesame oil.

Place one piece of dough on top of another, oiled sides facing, and roll out into a pancake about 5-7in across.

Heat the skillet and brush the bottom with sesame oil. Add the paired pancakes to the skillet one at a time. Cook over a medium heat for 30 seconds, turn and cook the other side for 30 seconds.

Pull the paired pancakes apart with your fingers to make two thin pancakes. Place them on a large piece of foil, one on top of the other, oiled side up.

Wrap them in the foil and steam for 30 minutes. Serve as an accompaniment to Peking Duck (see previous recipe). Any pancakes left over can be wrapped in foil and kept in the refrigerator for up to three days.

▲ *Fragrant and Crispy Duck surrounded by steamed buns. The buns can be made from the same dough as Cha Shao dumplings.*

Fragrant and Crispy Duck

INGREDIENTS *serves 3-4*
3lb duckling
1 tbsp salt
2 slices ginger root, crushed
2 cloves garlic, crushed
2 scallions, cut into short lengths
3 tbsp rice wine or dry sherry
2 tsp five-spice powder
1 tsp Sichuan peppercorns
oil for deep-frying

SERVING
4 scallions, cut into thin strips
6 tbsp hoisin sauce

METHOD
Clean the duck well and rub with salt inside and out. Place it in a deep dish; add ginger root, garlic, scallions, rice wine or sherry, five-spice powder and Sichuan peppercorns. Steam vigorously for at least 2½ hours; remove and discard the ginger root, garlic, scallions and Sichuan peppercorns. Turn the duck over and let it marinate in the juice. After about 2-3 hours take it out to cool until the skin is dry.

Heat up the oil and deep-fry the duck until golden and crispy.

To serve, either leave it whole or split it in half lengthways. It is eaten like Peking Duck (see page 42), wrapped in pancakes or steamed buns with strips of scallion and hoisin sauce.

Red-Cooked Duck

INGREDIENTS *serves 6-8*
4-5lb duck
3 scallions
4 slices fresh ginger root

SAUCE
½ tsp salt
6 tbsp soy sauce
2 tbsp yellow bean paste
2½ tsp sugar
4 tbsp rice wine or dry sherry

METHOD

Wipe the duck inside and out with a damp cloth. Place breast side up in a flameproof casserole and cover with water. Bring to the boil for 10 minutes, then pour out about a quarter of the water. Cut the scallions into 1½in sections.

Add the ginger, scallions, salt, soy sauce and yellow bean paste to the casserole. Bring to a boil, cover and simmer for about 1 hour, turning the duck over a couple of times during the cooking. Add the sugar and sherry and continue to cook, covered, for another 45 minutes.

Serve the duck whole, or chopped through the bone into bite-sized pieces. The remaining sauce can be reduced over high heat and thickened with a small amount of cornstarch mixed with a little water, if liked. Two tsp of sesame seed oil can also be added. Pour the sauce over the whole duck or pieces of duck arranged on a large heated plate.

Duckling and Salted Lime Clear Soup

INGREDIENTS *serves 4*
4-5lb duckling
4 cups chicken stock
1 salted lime
4 slices fresh ginger root

METHOD

Clean the duck, taking care to remove and discard any excess fat in the cavity and to remove the "parson's nose."

Boil 10 cups water and blanch the duck for 5 minutes. Remove the bird and set it aside.

Put 4 cups water and the chicken stock into a casserole with a lid. Add the duck, cutting it up if necessary. Then add the salted lime and ginger. Finally, cook the whole in the covered casserole over a low heat for between 3 and 4 hours. Serve immediately.

Duck Webs in Oyster Sauce

INGREDIENTS *serves 4-6*
5-6 duck webs
½lb broccoli or other greens
2-3 dried Chinese mushrooms, soaked
2 slices fresh ginger root
2 scallions
2 tbsp rice wine or dry sherry
1 tbsp soy sauce
½ tbsp sugar
1 tsp salt
1 star anise
2 tbsp oyster sauce
1 tsp sesame seed oil
1 tbsp cornstarch
4 tbsp oil

METHOD

Remove the outer skin of the duck webs; wash and clean well. Crush the ginger root and scallions.

Heat up 2tbsp oil; toss in the crushed ginger root and scallions, followed by the duck webs; stir a few times; add rice wine or sherry and soy sauce. After 5 minutes or so, transfer the entire contents to a sand-pot or casserole. Add sugar, a little salt, star anise and a little stock or water. Simmer gently for 3 hours.

Just before serving, stir-fry the broccoli or greens with the dried Chinese mushrooms, a little salt and sugar. Place them on a serving dish, then arrange the duck webs on top of that. Meanwhile heat a little oil in a saucepan, add oyster sauce and sesame seed oil. Thicken with cornstarch mixed with a little cold water; when it is smooth, pour it over the duck webs and serve.

▲ *Duckling and Salted Lime Clear Soup: The purpose of the salted lime is to counteract the richness of the duckling. A good deal of fat needs to be skimmed off the liquid before serving, but the flavor is interesting.*

▲ ▶ *Duck Webs in Oyster Sauce have a glutinous quality much prized in Chinese cuisine.*

▲ *Duck with rice.*

Duck with Rice

INGREDIENTS *serves 4*
1 roasted duck (rub with red food
  coloring before roasting), boned and
  cut into 2¹/₂×¹/₂in slices
4 cups cooked rice
4 tbsp thinly sliced pickled ginger root
4 tbsp thinly sliced sweet dill or pickled
  cucumber

COOKED SAUCE
2 cups chicken stock
1 tbsp sugar
¹/₂ tbsp white soya sauce
¹/₄ tbsp black soya sauce
1 tsp flour

SOYA CHILI SAUCE
scant ¹/₂ cup black soya sauce
3 fresh red chili peppers, sliced thinly
  into circles
1 tbsp sugar
¹/₂ tbsp vinegar

METHOD
Heat the ingredients for the cooked sauce
together in a pan and boil for 1 minute. Mix
the ingredients for the raw sauce in a bowl
and put to one side.

Warm the duck and rice in a 350° oven for
5 minutes. Then, divide the rice between 4
serving plates, and arrange the duck meat
over the top. Spoon the cooked sauce on top
of each, and place ginger and pickle slices
around the edges. Serve with the raw sauce
on the side.

▲ *The roasted duck is removed from the
oven. Barrel-shaped ovens like this one are
specially designed for cooking Peking
Duck (see page 42).*

▲ *Rows of Peking ducks hanging to dry
before cooking.*

Stir-Fried Shredded Roast Duck and Bean Sprouts

INGREDIENTS *serves 4-6*
12oz roast duck meat (from the back of
  the Peking duck)
4-6 medium black mushrooms
3 tbsp peanut oil
2 tsp chopped fresh ginger root
1¹/₂ tsp garlic, chopped
1¹/₄lb bean sprouts
1 tsp Chinese yellow wine

SAUCE
1 tsp salt
1 tbsp light soy sauce
1 tsp sesame oil
1 tsp sugar
1 tbsp cornstarch
4 tbsp stock
2-3 tbsp peanut oil

METHOD
Shred the roast duck meat.

Soak the black mushrooms in hot water
for 30 minutes. Remove and discard the
stems and cut the caps into shreds.

Heat 1 tbsp oil in a pan over a high heat
and add 1 tsp chopped ginger and ³/₄ tsp
chopped garlic.

Add the bean sprouts, stir-frying over
very high heat for 1 minute. Remove and set
aside.

Heat 2 tbsp oil in the pan. Add the
remaining ginger, garlic and the black
mushroom shreds. Stir-fry for 30 seconds,
add the roast duck and bean sprouts. Stir-
fry briefly. Add the sauce ingredients, and
stir rapidly over a very high heat for 30
seconds. Sprinkle with 1 tsp Chinese yellow
wine and serve.

Fried Duck Liver and Gizzard

INGREDIENTS *serves 4-6*
giblets from 1 duck (the liver and
  gizzard)
1lb duck fat (or lard) for deep-frying
salt and Sichuan pepper

METHOD

Clean and trim off all excess fat on the gizzard. Remove the gall bladder from the liver, making sure that it is not broken, otherwise it will leave a sharp, bitter taste. Now cut the gizzard into 6 small pieces, and the liver into 6 triangular pieces. Parboil the liver first – testing it by pressing with your finger to see it is still soft to the touch – remove and drain; parboil the gizzard for roughly the same length of time, then also remove and drain.

Heat up the fat until you can see blue smoke appearing, then fry the gizzard first for 3 minutes; remove and drain. Wait for the fat to produce more blue smoke, put both the liver and the gizzard into it and fry for another 3 minutes, then remove and drain. Serve with salt-pepper mixture as a dip (one part ground pepper mixed with 2 parts salt).

Braised Four Treasures

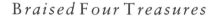

INGREDIENTS *serves 4-6*
6 duck webs
4 duck wings
10 duck tongues
5-6 duck kidneys
1 cup lard for deep-frying
1 scallion, finely chopped
1 slice fresh ginger root, finely chopped
1¼ cups chicken stock
2 tbsp rice wine or dry sherry
½ tsp monosodium glutamate (optional)
1 tbsp crushed bean sauce
2 tsp soy sauce

METHOD

Clean the duck webs in warm water and remove the outer coat of skin, then parboil for 20 minutes. Cool them in cold water and cut into small pieces about ½in in length.

Parboil the wings for 20 minutes. Cool them in cold water and cut into small pieces similar to the webs.

Clean the tongues in warm water and remove the outer layer of skin; parboil for 10 minutes, then cool in cold water.

Parboil the kidneys for 15 minutes and remove the outer layer of fat. Split each in half, cut each half in two, then marinate in a little soy sauce. Heat up the lard in a wok or pan until smoking; fry the kidney pieces for

5 minutes or until golden, then remove and drain.

Leaving about 2 tbsp of lard in the pan, first fry the finely chopped scallion and root ginger; add the chicken stock with wine or sherry, monosodium glutamate (if using), crushed bean sauce and the remaining soy sauce, stir and add the "four treasures." Bring to a boil, then reduce the heat and simmer for about 15 minutes. When the stock is reduced by half, increase the heat to high to thicken the gravy, and serve.

Smoked Duck Sichuan Style

INGREDIENTS *serves 4-6*
2lb duck
1½ tsp peppercorns
2 tbsp salt
2 tbsp jasmine tea
1 tbsp sugar
½ tsp pepper powder
2 tbsp Chinese yellow wine or dry sherry
4 cups peanut oil
1 tbsp sesame oil

METHOD

Clean the duck and soak it in 25 cups water with peppercorns and salt added for 4 hours.

Blanch the duck in boiling water for 5 minutes. Dry thoroughly.

Heat a dry pan over moderate heat, add the jasmine tea and sugar and cover with a lid. After 1 minute, place a wire rack in the pan and lay the duck on the rack. Replace the lid firmly and smoke the duck for about 10 minutes over low heat and then leave to stand in the smoke until it turns light golden brown.

Rub the duck all over with pepper powder and Chinese yellow wine and steam for 2 hours. Set aside.

Heat the peanut oil in a deep pan. When hot, add the duck and deep fry until the skin is rich golden brown in color and crispy.

Take the duck out of the pan and brush with sesame oil. Chop into bite-sized pieces and serve.

▲ *Smoked Duck Sichuan Style: smoke from sugar and tea burned together permeates the previously braised duck meat to flavor it. The whole duck is placed on a wire rack in a pot with a lid and the mixture is heated inside the pot until it smokes. After cooling, the duck can be deep-fried and eaten with a dipping sauce.*

Cantonese Roast Duck

INGREDIENTS *serves 4-6*
4¹/₂-5lb duckling
1 tsp salt

STUFFING
2 slices ginger root, peeled
2 scallions
2 tbsp sugar
2 tbsp rice wine (or sherry)
1 tbsp yellow bean sauce
1 tbsp hoisin sauce
¹/₂ tsp five-spice powder
1 tbsp oil

COATING
4 tbsp honey
1 tbsp vinegar
1 tsp "red powder" (or cochineal)
1¹/₂ cups water

METHOD
Clean the duck well; pat it dry with a cloth or paper towels inside and out. Rub both inside and out with salt, then tie the neck tightly with string so that no liquid will drip out when it is hanging head downward.

Heat up the oil in a saucepan, mix in the sugar, rice wine or sherry, bean sauce and hoisin sauce, five-spice powder and finely chopped ginger root and scallions. Bring it to a boil, pour it into the cavity of the duck and sew it up securely.

Plunge the whole duck into a large pot of boiling water for a few seconds only; take it out and baste it thoroughly with the "coating" mixture then hang it up to dry for at least 4-5 hours, ideally overnight in a well ventilated place.

Roast in a moderately hot oven – 400° hanging on a meat hook with its head down; place a tray of cold water in the bottom of the oven to catch the drippings. After 25 minutes or so, reduce the heat to 350°, roast for a further 30 minutes, basting once or twice during the cooking with the remaining coating mixture. When it is done let it cool for a while, then remove the strings and pour the liquid stuffing out. Use as the sauce when serving the duck.

▲ *Cantonese Roast Duck: usually served cold as an appetizer or a main course.*

Braised Five-Spice Duck

INGREDIENTS *serves 4-6*
4¹/₂lb duckling
2 slices ginger root, peeled
2 scallions
6-8 Chinese dried mushrooms, soaked
1 carrot
6 cups Chinese cabbage
4 tbsp soy sauce
4 tbsp rice wine (or sherry)
¹/₄ cup candy sugar
1 tsp five-spice powder

METHOD
Cut the duck into four pieces (two breasts, two legs and thighs). Place them in a large pot or casserole of boiling water; boil rapidly for 4-5 minutes, then discard two-thirds of the water and add ginger root, scallions, soy sauce, rice wine or sherry, candy sugar and five-spice powder. Bring it to a boil again, then put on the lid tightly and simmer gently for 1 hour.

Meanwhile cut the carrot into small slices, the cabbage into large chunks; add these and the mushrooms to the pot; continue cooking for 30 minutes. Serve with rice.

Soy Braised Duck

INGREDIENTS *serves 4-6*
3¹/₂lb duckling
3 tbsp rice wine (or sherry)
2 tbsp Wood Ears, soaked
2 tbsp sliced bamboo shoots
¹/₂ cup sliced carrots
2 slices ginger root, peeled and crushed
2 scallions, cut into short lengths
2 tbsp hoisin sauce
1 tbsp sugar
3 tbsp soy sauce
1 tbsp cornstarch
seasonal greens
oil for deep-frying

METHOD
Clean and parboil the duck, then rub it all over with rice wine or sherry.

Heat the oil and deep-fry the duck until golden; remove, chop it into halves lengthways.

Pour off the excess oil, leaving about 2 tbsp in the wok; add the ginger root, scallions, hoisin sauce, sugar, and soy sauce with the duck. Turn it over once or twice to cover it with the sauce. Take the duck out; place it on a plate and steam vigorously for 1-2 hours.

Braised Duck

INGREDIENTS *serves 4-6*
4½lb duckling
5½ tbsp red fermented rice
5½ tbsp sugar
1½ tbsp cornstarch
2 tbsp rice wine (or sherry)
¼ cup soy sauce
5½ tbsp crystal sugar, crushed
2 slices ginger root
2 scallions
1 tsp salt
2 tsp Chinese cinnamon bark
1 tsp fennel seeds

METHOD
Clean the duck thoroughly; place it in a large pot with its back facing upward; add enough water to cover it, then add red fermented rice, soy sauce, salt, rice wine or sherry, crystal sugar, cinnamon bark, fennel seeds, scallions and ginger root. Bring it to a rapid boil and keep the heat fairly high for 1 hour; turn the duck over and simmer gently for ½ hour; take it out to cool.

Leave about half the juice in the pan (keep the other half for future use), add sugar and when it is dissolved, pour through a strainer to get rid of the spices; mix the cornstarch with a little cold water to thicken the gravy, then leave to cool. Chop the duck into small pieces, pour the gravy over it and serve.

Meanwhile blanch the greens and place them on a large serving dish; put the duck on top of the greens.

Fry the Wood Ears, bamboo shoots and carrots in a little hot oil, add the sauce in which the duck was cooked, and the cornstarch mixed with a little water; when it is smooth pour it over the duck and serve.

▲ *Soy Braised Duck, served on a bed of lettuce – a favorite dish.*

Right ▼ *Braised Duck, crisp and tender, can be served cold as an appetizer, or hot as a main dish.*

▼ *Braised Five-Spice Duck.*

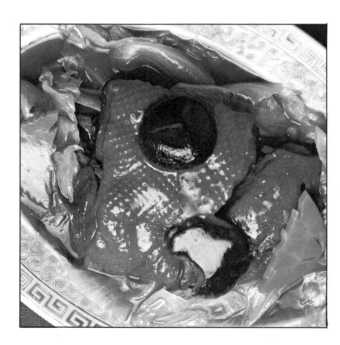

Oil-Soaked Duck

INGREDIENTS *serves 4-6*
3-3¹/₂lb duckling
3 tbsp rice wine (or sherry)
6 tbsp stock
3¹/₂ tbsp sugar
3 tbsp soy sauce
a few fennel seeds
1 slice ginger root
5 tbsp orange juice
oil for deep-frying

SERVING
2 tomatoes
6 scallions, white parts only
8oz Chinese pickled turnip (or radish)

METHOD
Clean the duck; discard the pinions (wing tips); blanch in a large pot of boiling water; place it on a long dish with its stomach side up. Mix 2 tbsp rice wine or sherry with 2 tbsp sugar, stock, soy sauce, fennel seeds and ginger root; pour it all over the duck; steam it vigorously for 15 minutes. Pierce the stomach with a sharp-pointed chopstick or knitting needle a dozen times or so; turn the bird over, steam for another 15 minutes, then turn it over once more and steam for a further 15 minutes. Now deep-fry it in hot oil until dark brown. Remove.

Pour off the excess oil, put in the remaining rice wine or sherry, sugar, orange juice and about one-third of the juice from the duck. Add the duck; turn it round a few times to make sure that the bird is well coated, then remove and chop it into small pieces. On a serving plate, rearrange it in the shape of the original duck; pour the juice over it.

Serve it with sliced tomato, shredded scallion and pickled turnip or radish. You can make your own pickle as follows: Cut some turnip or radish into thin slices; marinate with a little salt for a while, squeeze out the liquid, then in a jar mix it with sugar and vinegar and leave for several hours.

Tea-Smoked Duck

INGREDIENTS *serves 4-6*
3¹/₂-4lb duckling

MARINADE
¹/₂ tbsp salt
2 Sichuan peppercorns
¹/₂ tsp ground pepper
3 tbsp rice wine (or sherry)
2 tbsp hoisin sauce

SMOKING MATERIAL
2oz tea leaves
2oz camphor leaves
¹/₄lb saw dust
¹/₄lb cypress tree branch
oil for deep-frying

GARNISH
Chinese parsley (fresh coriander)
salt and pepper

METHOD
Make the marinade; rub it all over the duck both inside and out; leave to marinate for 12 hours, then let it dry in an airy place.

Mix the smoking materials together, then divide into three portions and put one portion in an earthenware bowl; place the bowl inside a large container such as a wine barrel sawn in half. Light a piece of charcoal until red; put it inside the bowl and place a sheet of wire netting on top. Lay the duck on the wire netting and place the other half of the wine barrel on top so that it keeps the smoke in. After 10 minutes, add the second portion of the smoking material to the bowl together with a new piece of burning charcoal, then turn the duck over and replace the lid. After 7 minutes add the last portion of the smoking material with another piece of burning charcoal, turn the duck over again and smoke for another 5 minutes. The duck should be nice and brown all over.

◄ *Oil-Soaked Duck: the tomatoes have been cut into flower shapes and decorated with green peas.*

Sunflower Duck

In China, the Cantonese have always been regarded as the people who really know how to enjoy themselves as far as good food is concerned. One of the Cantonese restaurants in Peking is called 'Food of Tan's Family' and was first opened by a Mr. Tan from Canton, whose father was a court official during the Manchu dynasty. Both father and son were gourmets and food from their family kitchen was much appreciated at the time, so other officials used to entertain at Tan's place and thus its reputation became widespread. Eventually Tan junior went into business and established this restaurant; here is one of their specialities:

INGREDIENTS *serves 4-6*
4lb duckling
1oz Chinese dried mushrooms
4oz cooked ham
1¼ cups good chicken and duck stock
2 tbsp soy sauce
1 tbsp sugar
1 tsp salt
1 tbsp cornstarch

METHOD
Clean the duck inside and out, then split it down the middle lengthwise with a cleaver. Place the two halves on a plate, skin side down, and steam vigorously for 2-3 hours. Remove and leave it to cool for a while with the skin side up.

Soak the mushrooms in warm water for 10 minutes, discard the stalks and cut the large ones into two to three pieces. Cut the ham into thin slices about the size of a matchbox.

Cut off the neck and wings of the duck, then very carefully remove the meat from the carcass and bones. Cut the meat into thin slices and neatly arange them on a plate in the shape of the duck with the skin side up, alternately overlapping each piece of meat with a piece of mushroom and a slice of ham. Then very carefully turn the meat out into a large, deep dish or bowl, pour in about a third of the chicken/duck stock, and steam vigorously for about 20 minutes, then turn it out back onto the plate and rearrange if necessary.

▲ *Sunflower Duck tastes particularly delicious when accompanied by wine.*

Warm up the rest of the stock, add soy sauce, salt, sugar and cornstarch mixed with a little cold water. Stir to make it into a smooth, thickish gravy; pour it all over the duck and serve.

Ground Duck with Croutons

INGREDIENTS *serves 4-6*
⅔ cup cooked duck meat
½ cup green peas
3 slices white bread
2½ cups stock
1 tsp salt
½ tsp monosodium glutamate
2 tsp rice wine (or sherry)
1 tbsp cornstarch mixed with 1tbsp water
1 tsp chicken fat
oil for frying the bread

METHOD
Finely grind the duck meat. Add it to the stock together with the peas, rice wine or sherry, salt and monosodium glutamate. Bring it to the boil over a high flame, then slowly pour in the cornstarch and water mixture. When it boils again, stir in the chicken fat, and remove.

Fry the bread cut into small cubes until they become golden and crispy; drain and place them on a soup plate, pour the ground duck all over them so they make a sizzling noise and serve at once before the fried bread croutons become soggy.

Roast Goose

INGREDIENTS *serves 6-8*
6lb young goose
1 tbsp soy bean paste
1 tsp five-spice powder
1 piece star anise
1 tbsp sugar
2 tbsp light soy sauce
2 tsp chopped garlic
1 tbsp Chinese yellow wine
6 cups boiling water
2 tbsp malt sugar
4 tbsp honey or corn syrup
4 tbsp vinegar
1 cup water

METHOD
Cut off the feet and wing tips of the goose.

Blend together the soy bean paste, five-spice powder, star anise, sugar, soy sauce, chopped garlic and yellow wine and rub the mixture all over the inside of the goose. Tightly fasten the neck and tail openings with skewers or string to ensure that the mixture does not run out when the goose is hung.

Place the goose on a rack, breast up, and pour half the boiling water over it. Turn the goose over and pour the remaining boiling water over it. Pat the goose dry and set it aside.

Heat the malt sugar, honey, vinegar and water together, stirring to mix well, and brush the mixture all over the goose. Tie a piece of string around the neck of the goose and hang it up in a draughty place for 1 hour to dry.

Preheat the oven to 450°. Place the goose on a rack in a deep 2in roasting pan and roast the goose, breast side up, for 12 minutes until golden. Turn the goose over with a towel (avoid using a fork) and roast for another 12 minutes.

Reduce the heat to 350° and, with the goose breast side up again, roast for 20 minutes. Reduce the heat to 300° and roast for a further 10 minutes, then reduce the heat to 250° and roast for a further 10 minutes. Finally, increase the heat to 450° again and roast for 10 minutes. You have to watch closely at this point to avoid burning the goose. Chop the goose into bite-sized pieces and serve.

Roast Goose Casserole with Bamboo Shoots

INGREDIENTS *serves 4-6*
³⁄₄lb roast goose
1¼ cups bamboo shoots
6 medium black mushrooms
¹⁄₃ whole piece of aged dried orange peel
1 tbsp peanut oil
6 slices fresh ginger root
2-3 cloves garlic, crushed
1 tbsp cornstarch
1 scallion, cut into 1½in lengths
1 tbsp chopped fresh coriander leaves

SAUCE
1 tbsp oyster sauce
1 tbsp light soy sauce
1 tbsp dark soy sauce
½ tsp sesame seed oil
2 tsp Chinese yellow wine
1 cup chicken stock

METHOD
Cut the roast goose into bite-sized pieces and the bamboo shoots into wedge shapes. Soak the black mushrooms and dried orange peel in hot water for 30 minutes. Remove and discard the mushroom stems. Finely shred orange peel. Set aside.

Blanch the bamboo shoots in boiling water for 5 minutes. Remove, rinse under the tap, drain and set aside.

Heat the peanut oil in a casserole and add the ginger and garlic. When the aroma rises add the roast goose, bamboo shoots, black mushrooms and orange peel, stir and cook for 1 minute.

Add the sauce ingredients to the pan and enough water to cover the ingredients. Bring to a boil, reduce the heat and simmer for 45 minutes. Thicken the sauce with 1 tbsp cornstarch mixed with an equal amount of water. Add the scallion and coriander and serve.

◀ *Carving the roasted goose. It is served in the same way as Peking Duck (see page 42).*

▼ *Roast Goose Casserole with Bamboo Shoots, a good way to use the stringier parts of the bird which might be tough if they weren't cut into small pieces.*

Stir-Fried Ground Goose with Lettuce

INGREDIENTS *serves 4-6*
4 medium dried Chinese mushrooms
1lb roast goose meat
²/₃ cup bamboo shoots
2 cloves garlic
2 slices fresh ginger root
4 water chestnuts
1 scallion
4 tbsp peanut oil
1 tsp salt
¼ tsp pepper
1 tbsp light soy sauce
½ tbsp yellow bean paste
½ tbsp hoisin sauce
½ tbsp sugar
1 tbsp rice wine or dry sherry
1½ tsp sesame seed oil
2 sprigs parsley to garnish
12 lettuce leaves

METHOD

Soak the mushrooms in hot water for 30 minutes. Remove and discard the stems and coarsely grind the caps.

Coarsely grind the goose meat, bamboo shoots, garlic, ginger, water chestnuts and scallion and arrange in piles.

Heat the oil in a pan or wok. When the oil is hot, add the ginger and mushrooms. Stir them in the hot oil for 30 seconds before adding the bamboo shoots, garlic and water chestnuts. Continue to stir and fry for 1 minute, then add the scallion and goose meat, together with the salt and pepper. Continue to stir all the ingredients for 2 minutes, turning them over to ensure that they are all thoroughly cooked.

Sprinkle the soy sauce, yellow bean paste, hoisin sauce, sugar and rice wine or sherry over the pan, and continue to stir, turn and fry, over a medium heat, for 3 minutes. Add the sesame seed oil and serve, garnished with sprigs of parsley.

Diners help themselves to a couple of spoonfuls of the goose mixture. They place the mixture on a lettuce leaf, wrap it up carefully and eat it with their fingers.

Squab in Dark Soy Sauce

INGREDIENTS *serves 4-6*
2 squab
5 cups water
1 stick cinnamon
2-3 slices liquorice root
3 slices fresh ginger root
4 shallots
1 cup dark soy sauce
¾ cup soy sauce
2 cups stock
2 tbsp Chinese yellow wine
1oz rock sugar

METHOD

Clean the squab. Boil the water and blanch the squab for 2 minutes. Remove the squab from the boiling water, drain and pat dry.

Place all the remaining ingredients in a casserole and bring to a boil. Allow to simmer over a low heat for 15 minutes before putting the squab into the pot to simmer in the sauce for a further 15 minutes. Let the squab color evenly by turning them over from time to time.

Cover the pot and turn off the heat, leaving the contents to sit for 30 minutes.

Dismember the squab and serve with the sauce from the cooking pot.

▲ *Stir-Fried Ground Goose with Lettuce: the use of lettuce leaves to wrap up ground poultry is very much a Hong Kong innovation. Traditionally, the wrapping would have been of pancake – but this is now regarded as altogether too heavy and filling when presented as a part of a Chinese dinner which may consist of more than a dozen dishes. This dish is often reproduced using chicken or squab.*

Salt-Baked Squab

INGREDIENTS *serves 4-6*
2 squab

MARINADE
1 crushed star anise
2 shallots
1 tbsp shredded scallion
1 tsp fresh ginger root, shredded
2 slices liquorice root
1 tsp Chinese yellow wine
1 tbsp dark soy sauce
1 tsp ginger juice
$\frac{1}{2}$ tsp sesame seed oil
5-6lb coarse salt
2 sheets waxed paper
2 sheets tin foil

METHOD
Clean the squab and dry them with absorbent kitchen paper. Mix together the star anise, shallots, scallion, ginger and liquorice and rub the skin and the inside of the squab with the mixture. Blend the yellow wine, soy sauce, ginger juice and sesame seed oil together, divide it and put it into the cavities of the squab.

Stir-fry the coarse salt over high heat for 2 minutes. Insert about one-third of the salt into the squab cavities, and cover the outside of the birds with the remaining salt. Wrap each bird first with a piece of waxed paper and then with foil. Bake the wrapped squab in an oven at 350° for 40 minutes.

Remove the paper and foil from the squab and shake them free of salt. To serve, cut the squab into bite-sized pieces.

Squab and Shark's Fin in a Casserole

INGREDIENTS *serves 2-3*
$\frac{1}{4}$lb soaked tiger shark's fin
1 king squab
3 tbsp shredded cooked ham
2 cups peanut oil (to fry squab)
3 slices fresh ginger root
2 stalks scallions
2 mushrooms
$\frac{1}{2}$ cup roast pork
3 cups unsalted stock

SEASONINGS
1$\frac{1}{2}$tsp salt
$\frac{1}{2}$tsp monosodium glutamate
1tsp sugar
1tbsp oyster sauce

METHOD
Soak the shark's fin in water overnight. Drain thoroughly.

Clean the squab and blanch it in boiling water for 1 minute. Drain thoroughly. Break up the shark's fin and insert the pieces and the shredded ham into the cavity of the bird. Close the cavity with a skewer.

Bring the peanut oil to high heat, add the squab and fry until the bird turns brown. Drain well.

Heat the casserole, and pour 2 tbsp peanut oil into it. Add the ginger, onion stalks, mushrooms and roast pork to sauté until fragrant (about 2 minutes). Add the squab, unsalted stock and the seasonings, and stew gently for 2$\frac{1}{2}$ hours. Serve in the casserole.

▲ *Salt-Baked Squab are tender yet crispy due to the thick salt crust which protects the birds while cooking.*

◄ *Squab and Shark's Fin compared to other casserole dishes, is well worth the expense.*

MEAT

Mustard and Red Chili Oil Beef with Leeks

INGREDIENTS *serves 4-6*
1lb beef steak, eg, rump, fillet or sirloin
1 tsp salt
1½ tbsp cornstarch
1 egg white
3 slices fresh ginger root
½lb leeks
4 tbsp vegetable oil
1oz lard
1 tbsp light soy sauce
2 tbsp good stock
1 tbsp prepared hot mustard
2 tsp red chili oil

METHOD
Cut the beef into very thin slices and rub with salt. Toss in the cornstarch and coat in the egg white. Shred the ginger. Clean the leeks thoroughly and cut slantwise into ¾in pieces.

Heat the vegetable oil in a wok or skillet. When hot, fry half the ginger for 30 seconds to flavor the oil. Add the leeks and stir-fry for 1½ minutes. Remove and set aside. Add the lard to the pan. When hot, stir-fry the beef for 1½ minutes. Add the soy sauce and remaining ginger, then return the leeks and stock to the pan. Toss together for another 30 seconds.

Transfer to a heated serving dish. Drizzle the mustard and red oil evenly over the dish.

Beef and Black Mushrooms

INGREDIENTS *serves 4-6*
¼lb pork fat
1¼lb ground beef
8 tbsp stock
1 tbsp cornstarch
1 tsp sesame seed oil
2½ tsp salt
12 small black mushrooms
1 tsp sugar
1 tbsp peanut oil

METHOD
Cut the pork fat into tiny cubes and blanch the pieces in boiling water for 1 minute. Rinse under the tap. Put the pork fat, ground beef, stock, cornstarch, sesame seed oil and 1½ tsp of salt in a mixing bowl and stir, in one direction only, with a fork until the mixture becomes sticky.

Soak the black mushrooms in hot water for 30 minutes, remove and discard the stems and place the caps in a bowl. Add 1tsp salt, the sugar and peanut oil and mix well. Steam the mushrooms over a medium heat for 5 minutes and set aside.

Divide the beef into 12 portions, molding each portion into an egg shape and place 1 mushroom on top of each "egg." Use 6 small dishes and place 2 of the beef and mushroom "eggs" in each dish. Steam over a high heat for 5 minutes and serve.

Cantonese Stir-Fried Beef in Oyster Sauce

INGREDIENTS *serves 4-6*
1lb beef steak, eg, rump or fillet
1 tsp salt
pepper to taste
2 tbsp cornstarch
1 egg white
3 slices fresh ginger root
¼lb snow peas or 3-4 scallions
4 tbsp vegetable oil
1 tsp lard
1½ tbsp good stock
1 tbsp soy sauce
1½ tbsp oyster sauce
1 tbsp rice wine or dry sherry

METHOD
Cut the beef into thin strips and mix with the salt and pepper. Toss in the cornstarch and coat in the egg white. Shred the ginger. Cut each snow pea slantwise in half or cut the onions slantwise in 1½in sections.

Heat the oil in a wok or skillet. When hot, stir-fry the ginger in the oil to flavor. Add the beef and stir-fry over high heat for about 1 minute. Remove and set aside. Add the lard to the pan. When hot, stir-fry the snow peas or scallions for 1-2 minutes. Add the stock and soy sauce, and continue to stir-fry for 30 seconds. Return the beef to the pan, add the oyster sauce and wine or sherry and stir-fry over high heat for 30 seconds.

▶ *Cantonese Stir-Fried Beef in Oyster Sauce: it is worth seeking out real oyster sauce, and not oyster-flavored sauce, to make this classic dish.*

Stir-Fried Beef Balls with Dried Fish and Chinese Kale

INGREDIENTS *serves 6-8*
1¼lb frozen beef balls (see below)
8-12oz dried fish (sole)
1¼lb Chinese kale
8 tbsp peanut oil
1 tsp fresh ginger root, chopped
4 tbsp chicken stock
1 tbsp fish or shrimp sauce
1 tsp sugar
1 tsp garlic, chopped
2 tsp Chinese yellow wine

METHOD
Defrost the beef balls and rinse them under the tap. Cut about a quarter of the way through each beef ball and set aside.

Remove and discard the bone of the dried fish and break the meat into bite-sized pieces. Fry the pieces in 8 tbsp oil until nicely browned. Remove, drain and set aside.

Cut the Chinese kale into lengths 1½×2in.

Heat 3 tbsp oil in a pan. Add the ginger and Chinese kale, stir-frying over a very high heat for 1 minute. Add 4 tbsp chicken stock, cover and continue to cook over a very high heat for a further minute.

Uncover the pan and add 1 tbsp fish or shrimp sauce and 1 tsp sugar. Stir rapidly over very high heat for 1 minute.

Add 2 tbsp oil, the garlic, beef balls and Chinese yellow wine, stir-frying for 2 minutes. Return the fried dried sole to the pan, stir for 30 seconds and serve.

If frozen beef balls are not available, you can make your own.

INGREDIENTS
1lb ground beef
1 egg white
4-5 tbsp water
1½ tbsp salt
1½ tbsp cornstarch
½ tbsp sesame oil
½ tsp ground pepper

METHOD
Put all the ingredients in a mixing bowl and use a fork to stir – in one direction only – until the mixture becomes sticky and firm. Make up to 20 small meat balls, about ¾in in diameter.

Bring about 4 cups water to a boil, add the beef balls and remove them when they float to the top. Set aside and follow the recipe above.

Stir-Fried Sliced Beef, Squid, Fresh Mushroom and Baby Corn

INGREDIENTS *serves 6-8*
5oz beef fillet
5oz squid
7oz straw mushrooms, fresh or canned
7oz baby corn cobs
1 cup peanut oil
1 tsp salt
½ tsp garlic, ground
3-4 slices fresh ginger root
2-3 slices scallion, cut into 1½in lengths
1½ tbsp Chinese yellow wine

SAUCE
2 tsp oyster sauce
2 tsp soy sauce
½ tsp salt
1 tsp sugar
¼ tsp pepper
1 tbsp cornstarch
6 tbsp stock
few drops sesame seed oil
1 tsp Chinese yellow wine
4 tbsp peanut oil

SEASONING FOR BEEF
2 tsp light soy sauce
½ tsp sesame seed oil
½ tsp pepper
½ tsp sugar
1 tbsp cornstarch

SEASONING FOR SQUID
1 tsp ginger juice
1 tsp Chinese yellow wine
½ tsp salt
½ tsp sesame seed oil
1 tbsp cornstarch

METHOD
Cut the beef fillet into very thin slices 2×3in.

Divide the squid into pieces ¾×2in, scoring the flesh on one side to form a diamond pattern. Cut the straw mushrooms and baby corns into halves.

Separately prepare the individual seasonings for the beef and the squid. Heat a pan, add the oil and heat for 1 minute over medium heat. Add the seasoned beef, stir to separate and remove with a perforated

spoon after 75 seconds.

Add the seasoned squid to the oil, removing it with a strainer when it curls up. Keep 1 tbsp oil in the pan. Add the baby corn cobs, straw mushrooms, 1tsp salt and stir well over a high heat for 30 seconds. Remove and set aside.

Heat the pan, this time over a very high heat and add 2 tbsp oil, the garlic and sliced ginger. When the aroma rises, add the beef, squid and onions, sprinkle 1 tbsp Chinese yellow wine over them and stir rapidly for 30 seconds. Add the baby corn cobs and straw mushrooms. Stir for 30 seconds.

Blend together the sauce ingredients and add them to the pan. Stir for 10 seconds, sprinkle with ½ tbsp wine and serve.

▲ *Stir-Fried Sliced Beef, Squid, Fresh Mushroom and Baby Corn Cobs: the success of this dish depends on presenting the four main ingredients almost separately, so that the different flavors, colors and textures remain distinct.*

◀ *Stir-Fried Beef Balls with Dried Fish and Chinese Kale: because the meat is ground, the beef balls need cooking only briefly. This recipe calls for Chinese kale, but spinach would do equally well. Sometimes water chestnuts are used for crunchiness and the dish may be flavored with soy bean paste, sugar and ginger.*

Stir-Fried Shredded Beef with Pickled Mustard Green, Green Pepper and Red Chilies

INGREDIENTS *serves 4-6*
¾lb fillet of beef
¾lb pickled mustard green
¾lb green peppers
2 red chili peppers
2 tsp sugar
3 tbsp peanut oil
1 tsp salt
1 cup peanut oil
1oz rice vermicelli
1 tsp fresh ginger root, chopped
1 tsp garlic, chopped

MARINADE
½ egg white
1 tsp cornstarch
½ tsp sesame oil
1 tsp Chinese yellow wine
1 tbsp light soy sauce
½ tsp sugar

SAUCE
1 tbsp oyster sauce
1 tbsp light soy sauce
1 tsp dark soy sauce
1 tsp sesame oil
1 tsp sugar
1 tbsp cornstarch
¼ cup chicken stock

METHOD
Prepare the marinade ingredients in a separate bowl. Cut the fillet of beef into matchstick-sized shreds and marinate. Set aside.

Soak the pickled mustard green in water for 30 minutes. Chop into shreds and set aside. Shred the green pepper and red chili into "double matchstick-sized" pieces.

Heat a pan and add the chopped pickled mustard green, stirring to cook over a medium heat until quite dry. Add 2 tsp sugar and 1 tbsp oil, stir and cook for 30 seconds. Remove and set aside.

Heat 1 tbsp oil in the pan and add the green pepper and 1 tsp salt. Stir-fry for 2 minutes. Remove and set aside.

Heat 1 cup oil in a pan and add the beef, stirring to separate. Remove with a perforated spoon and set aside.

Heat the same oil for 15 seconds and add the rice vermicelli. It should expand and froth up immediately. Remove straight away and put on a plate to keep warm.

Heat 1 tbsp oil. Add the chopped ginger, garlic and red chili peppers and, when the aroma rises, return the beef, pickled mustard green and green pepper to the pan. Blend and add the sauce ingredients. Stir-fry over very high heat for 1 minute, place on top of the crispy rice vermicelli on the serving dish and serve.

Steamed Beef with Ground Rice

INGREDIENTS *serves 4-6*
1lb beef steak
1 tbsp salted black beans, crushed
2 tbsp soy sauce
1 tbsp chili paste
1 tbsp oil
2 tbsp rice wine or dry sherry
2 slices ginger root, peeled and finely chopped
½ tsp Sichuan pepper, freshly ground
⅔ cup/100g/4oz coarsely-ground rice (use 20 percent glutinous rice with 80 percent ordinary rice)

METHOD
Cut the beef into 2×¾in slices and ¼in thick; mix with crushed salted black beans, soy sauce, chili paste, oil, rice wine or sherry, ginger root and ground pepper. Marinate for 30 minutes, then coat each piece of beef carefully with ground rice.

Ideally, use small *dim sum* bamboo steamers as seen in Cantonese restaurants, otherwise any other type of steamer will do. Steam the beef vigorously for 30 minutes (if using the tenderest rump steak, then 15 minutes will do).

Serve hot, garnished with finely chopped onions or Chinese parsley (fresh coriander) if desired.

Shredded Beef with Celery

This dish originated in Sichuan and, like so many other dishes from that province, it has now become a national favorite.

INGREDIENTS *serves 4-6*
½lb beef steak
½ cup celery
½ cup leek or scallion
2 slices ginger root
1 tbsp chili paste
2 tbsp soy sauce
½ tsp salt
1 tsp sugar
1 tbsp rice wine (or sherry)
1 tsp vinegar
3 tbsp oil

METHOD
Shred the beef into thin strips about the size of matches. Shred the celery and leeks the same size (Chinese leeks are a cross between the Western leek and scallion with thin skin and green foliage). Peel the ginger root and cut it into thin shreds as well.

Heat up the wok or pan and put in the oil. When it starts to smoke, stir-fry the beef for a short while, add the chili paste, blend well, then add the celery, leek and ginger root, followed by the soy sauce, salt, sugar and wine. Stir for 1-2 minutes, then add vinegar and serve.

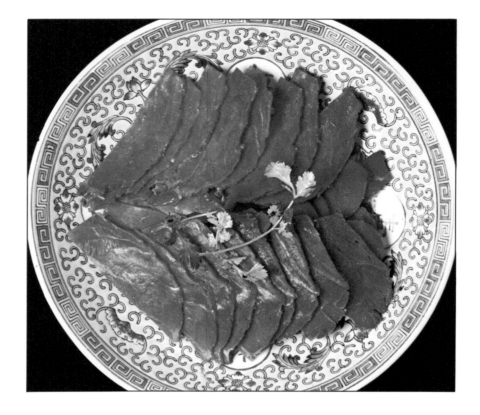

▲ *Stewed Beef – this is an ideal starter, thinly sliced and served cold on an attractive dish.*

▼ *Shredded Beef with Celery – a piquant dish typical of the Sichuan School, but highly popular in Peking.*

Stewed Beef

INGREDIENTS *serves 4-6*
2lb shin of beef
2 tbsp sugar
6 tbsp soy sauce
2 tbsp rice wine (or sherry)
1 tsp five-spice powder
3-4 scallions
2-3 slices ginger root
2 tbsp oil

METHOD
This dish makes excellent use of a cheap cut of meat. It is cooked slowly so that the meat becomes really tender.

Cut the beef into 1in cubes. Cut the onions into 1in lengths.

Heat up the oil and brown the beef before blanching it in a pot of boiling water for a few seconds. Pour the water away and cover with fresh cold water, add scallions, ginger root, five-spice powder, sugar, soy sauce and rice wine or sherry, and place a tightly fitting lid over the pan. Bring it to a boil over a high heat, then reduce the heat and simmer gently for 3-4 hours, after which there should be very little juice left. Serve hot or cold.

Rapidly-Fried Beef Steak

INGREDIENTS *serves 4-6*

½lb best beef steak

1½ tbsp soy sauce

1 tbsp cornstarch

2 cloves garlic, finely chopped

2 scallions, white parts only, cut into ½in lengths

1 tsp vinegar

2 tsp rice wine (or sherry)

oil for deep-frying

METHOD

Cut the beef into thin slices and marinate with 1 tbsp soy sauce and cornstarch.

Heat up the oil until smoking, deep-fry the beef slices for about 30 seconds only, stir with chopsticks to separate them, then quickly scoop them out with a perforated spoon.

Now heat up about 1 tbsp oil in a wok and toss in the onions and garlic. When they start to turn golden, put in the beef slices, add vinegar, rice wine (or sherry) and the remaining soy sauce, stir-fry for about 30 seconds, then it is done.

A simple dish, but the quality of the beef steak, the degree of heat and the timing all must be right.

wine or sherry, soy sauce, cornstarch and a little oil; leave to marinate for 10 minutes.

Cut the bamboo shoots and carrot into slices the same size as the beef, cut the broccoli into small flowerets.

Deep-fry the beef in warm oil for 1½ minutes; remove and drain.

Pour off the excess oil leaving about 2tbsp oil in the wok. Wait until it smokes, toss in the ginger root, broccoli, bamboo shoots, carrot and mushrooms; add salt, stir a few times then add the beef with oyster sauce and stock; cook together for 1 minute. Serve hot.

▲ *Rapidly-Fried Beef Steak: the degree of heat is very important.*

▼ *Stir-Fried Beef with Vegetables, cooked with oyster sauce.*

Stir-Fried Beef with Vegetables

INGREDIENTS *serves 4-6*

¾lb beef steak

1 cup broccoli

⅔ cup bamboo shoots

3-4 Chinese dried mushrooms, soaked

2 slices ginger root, peeled

1 carrot

1 tsp salt

1 tbsp rice wine (or sherry)

2 tbsp oyster sauce

1 tbsp soy sauce

1 tbsp cornstarch

3 tbsp stock

oil for deep-frying

METHOD

Cut the beef across the grain into thickish slices the size of matchboxes; mix with rice

Dry-Fried Beef, Flavored with Aged Orange Peel

INGREDIENTS *serves 4-6*
1½lb lean beef (topside, tenderloin, etc)
1 dried, aged orange or tangerine peel
3 slices fresh ginger root
2 green chili peppers
2 dried red chili peppers
2 scallions
6 tbsp cornstarch
1 egg, lightly beaten
2½ cups peanut oil
½ tsp salt
1½ tbsp sugar
1½ tbsp dark soy sauce
1 tbsp hoisin sauce
2 tbsp good stock
2 tbsp rice wine or dry sherry
1½ tsp sesame seed oil

METHOD
Shred the beef into "double matchstick-sized" pieces. Wash and drain the pieces thoroughly.

Soak the dried orange or tangerine peel in warm water for 20 minutes and cut it into matchstick-sized shreds. Cut the ginger and the green and red chili peppers into similar-sized pieces and the scallion into 2in sections.

Mix together the cornstarch and lightly beaten egg and coat the shredded beef, making sure that each piece is evenly covered.

Heat the oil in a pan or wok and, when a crumb dropped into the oil sizzles, add the beef. Using a fork or wooden chopstick to separate the shreds, stir-fry the beef over a medium heat for 6-7 minutes. Remove the beef from the pan with a perforated spoon and set it aside to drain. Meanwhile, allow the oil in the pan to increase in temperature until it is smoking. Return the beef and stir-fry for a further 2 minutes. Remove the beef with a perforated spoon and drain thoroughly.

In a separate pan or wok heat 1tbsp oil. When the oil is hot, add the shredded ginger, orange or tangerine peel and green and red chili peppers and the onion slices. Stir-fry them together for 1 minute before adding the salt, sugar, soy sauce, hoisin sauce, stock and wine or sherry. Continue to stir and cook for another minute, by which time the liquid should have reduced by about half. Return the beef to the pan and stir well to mix the ingredients together for 1 minute. Sprinkle the sesame seed oil over the mixture and serve.

Muslim Long-Simmered Lamb

INGREDIENTS *serves 8-10*
4-5lb neck of lamb
3 medium onions
2 dried chili peppers
4 slices fresh ginger root
4 cloves garlic
7½ cups water
3 tsp salt

DIP SAUCE
9 tbsp soy sauce
2 tbsp garlic, finely chopped
2 tbsp finely chopped fresh ginger root
2 tbsp finely chopped scallions
2 tbsp finely chopped fresh coriander
1½ tbsp prepared English mustard
1½ tbsp wine vinegar
3 tbsp rice wine or dry sherry
1 tbsp sesame seed oil
1 tbsp vegetable oil

METHOD
Cut the lamb into slices 2×¾in and ¼in thick. Parboil in a pan of water for 3 minutes, then drain. Peel and slice the onions. Shred the chilies, discarding the seeds. Shred the ginger. Crush the garlic.

Place the lamb in a heavy flameproof casserole with a lid. Add the water, salt, onion, ginger, garlic and chili. Bring to the boil, reduce the heat and simmer slowly for 3 hours, turning the contents every 30 minutes. Add more water if the sauce becomes too thick. Meanwhile, mix the dip sauce ingredients together. Serve the casserole at the table. Eat the lamb with the dip sauce.

Braised Tripe

INGREDIENTS *serves 4-6*
2lb tripe
salt
2 slices fresh ginger root
2 scallions
2 tbsp rice wine or dry sherry
4 tbsp soy sauce
1 tbsp sugar
1 tsp five-spice powder
2 tbsp oil
1 tsp sesame seed oil

METHOD
Wash the tripe thoroughly, rub both sides with the salt several times and rinse well. Blanch it in boiling water for 20 minutes. Drain and discard the water.

Heat oil, brown the tripe lightly, add ginger root, scallions, rice wine or sherry, soy sauce, sugar and five-spice powder. Add 5 cups water and bring it to the boil, reduce heat and simmer gently under cover for 2 hours.

Remove the tripe and cut into small slices; garnish with sesame seed oil and serve hot or cold.

Tung-Po Mutton

INGREDIENTS *serves 4-6*
½lb stewing mutton or lamb
¼lb potato
¼lb carrot
oil for deep-frying
2 tbsp soy sauce
1 tbsp sugar
2 scallions
1 slice fresh ginger root
1 clove garlic, crushed
1 tsp five-spice powder
3 tbsp rice wine or dry sherry
½ tsp Sichuan pepper

METHOD
Cut the mutton into ¾in cubes, then score one side of each square halfway down. Peel the potato and carrot and cut them the same size and shape as the mutton.

Heat up quite a lot of oil in a wok or deep-fryer. When it is smoking, deep-fry the mutton for 5-6 seconds or until it turns golden; scoop out and drain, then fry the potato and carrot, also until golden.

Place the mutton in a pot or casserole, cover the meat with cold water, add soy sauce, sugar, onions, ginger root, garlic, pepper, five-spice powder and rice wine or sherry, and bring it to a boil. Then reduce the heat and simmer for 2-3 hours; add potato and carrot, cook together for about 5 minutes and serve.

▲ *Tung-Po Mutton, typical of the Moslem school of cooking, and a popular everyday family dish.*

63

Lamb in Sweet and Sour Sauce

It is believed that this dish originated from the Palace kitchen, though whether during the Mongol (Yuan) or Manchu dynasty, no-one seems to know.

INGREDIENTS *serves 4-6*
½lb fillet lamb
2 slices ginger root, peeled
1 tbsp crushed yellow bean sauce
2 tbsp cornstarch
1½ tbsp soy sauce
1 tbsp rice wine (or sherry)
1 tbsp vinegar
2 tbsp sugar
oil for deep-frying
½ tsp chicken fat or sesame seed oil

METHOD
Thinly slice the fillet lamb and finely chop the ginger root.

Mix the lamb with ½tbsp cornstarch, a little water and the crushed bean sauce.

Mix the remaining cornstarch with soy sauce, rice wine or sherry, vinegar, sugar and the finely chopped ginger root.

Heat up the oil in a wok or pan, fry the lamb slices for about 15 seconds and stir to separate them. When they turn pale, scoop them out and return the lamb slices to the wok over a high heat. Add the sauce mixture, stir and blend well for about 1 minute; add chicken fat or sesame seed oil, stir a few more times, then serve.

Diced Lamb with Scallions

INGREDIENTS *serves 4-6*
½lb fillet lamb
1⅓ cups chopped scallions
1½ tbsp cornstarch
1 tsp salt
2 tsp soy sauce
1 egg white
½ tbsp rice wine (or sherry)
oil for deep-frying
1 tsp sesame seed oil

METHOD
Dice the lamb into ½in cubes, marinate with ½tsp salt, egg white and ¾tbsp cornstarch. Cut the onions into 1cm/½in lengths.

Heat about 2½ cups oil in a wok. Before the oil gets too hot, add the lamb cubes, separate them with chopsticks or a fork, then scoop them out and drain.

Pour off the excess oil and leave about 2 tbsp in the wok. Put in the onions followed by the lamb cubes, salt, soy sauce, rice wine or sherry and the remaining cornstarch; stir for 1-2 minutes; add the sesame seed oil, stir a few more times, then serve.

▲ *Diced Lamb with Scallions – a popular dish of Moslem origin.*

Red-Cooked Lamb

However conservative the Chinese may be in their outlook on some aspects of life, they are quite open-minded about food, even daringly experimental. The following recipe for cooking lamb appears to be rather elaborate but, if followed correctly, it will taste like nothing on earth! If you tasted it blind-folded, you would never be able to guess what you were eating, but nevertheless you would marvel at the delicious flavor of this dish.

INGREDIENTS *serves 4-6*
1½lb lamb fillet in one piece
4-5 Chinese dried mushrooms, soaked
1½ tbsp Chinese dried dates, soaked
1 cup water chestnuts, peeled
½ tsp five-spice powder
2 slices ginger root, peeled
2 scallions, cut into short lengths
1 tsp salt
½ tsp Sichuan ground pepper
½ tsp sesame seed oil
2 tbsp soy sauce
2 tbsp rice wine (or sherry)
1 tbsp cornstarch
7½ cups stock
oil for deep-frying

METHOD
Wash the meat thoroughly; make a cut two-thirds the way through the piece of meat at ½in intervals. Blanch in boiling water for about 3 minutes; drain and coat with soy sauce.

Place the meat in a strainer and lower it into oil to deep-fry over a moderate heat for about 1½ minutes or until it turns red; remove and drain.

Pour off the excess oil; put the meat back with rice wine or sherry, salt, dates, water chestnuts, ginger root, onions, soy sauce, five-spice powder and stock; bring to a boil, then transfer into a sand-pot or casserole. Simmer gently for 1½ hours or until the stock is reduced by half; add the mushrooms and cook for another 10 minutes or so. Now remove the meat and cut it into ½in thick pieces. Place the water chestnuts, dates and mushrooms on a serving dish with the lamb pieces on top.

Remove the onions and ginger root from the gravy and discard them; warm up about 1 cup of the gravy in a small saucepan. Add sesame seed oil and thicken it with a little cornstarch; stir to make it smooth, then pour it over the lamb and serve.

You will find the strong odor of the lamb (which most Chinese dislike) has almost completely disappeared. Instead it has acquired a new aroma which is strange and difficult to describe, yet at once most attractive.

▼ *Red-Cooked Lamb, served with plum sauce as a dip.*

Peking Jelly of Lamb

INGREDIENTS *serves 6 - 8*
1½lb leg of lamb
½lb pork skin
2 scallions
3 cloves garlic
3 slices fresh ginger root
1½ tsp salt
pepper to taste
2½ cups good stock
3 tbsp white wine
1 tbsp light soy sauce

SAUCE
4 tbsp soy sauce
1 tbsp finely chopped ginger root
1 tbsp finely chopped garlic
1 tbsp finely chopped scallion

METHOD
Cut the lamb into 1½×2×¾in pieces. Cut the pork skin into smaller pieces. Parboil the lamb and pork skin in a pan of water for 2 minutes, then drain. Cut the scallions into 1¾in sections, keeping the green and white pieces separate. Thinly slice the garlic. Shred the ginger.

Place the pork skin on the bottom of a heavy casserole and cover with the lamb. Add the salt, pepper, white parts of the scallions and the ginger. Pour in the stock and about 1¼ cups water to cover the contents and bring to a boil. Reduce the heat to low, cover and simmer for 1¼ hours. Cool, then place in the refrigerator to encourage setting. The contents should be set after 3 hours. Remove the casserole from the refrigerator and peel away the pork fat and skin. Heat briefly to melt the jelly and then stir in the wine, soy sauce, garlic and green parts of the scallions. Pour the lamb mixture into a rectangular mold and leave in the refrigerator to set again. Mix the dip sauce ingredients together. Turn the mold out on to a serving dish and cut into ¼in slices. Serve with the dip sauce.

Mongolian Hot Pot

INGREDIENTS *serves 4 - 6*
2lb lamb
4 cakes tofu
4-6 Chinese dried mushrooms
1¼lb cabbage
1¼lb spinach
9oz bean-flour transparent noodles

SAUCE
sesame oil
sesame paste
shrimp sauce
soy sauce
Chinese yellow wine
wine vinegar
sugar
chili oil
fermented tofu cheese
1 bundle chives, chopped
coriander leaves, chopped
4 stalks scallions, chopped

METHOD
Cut the lamb into wafer-thin slices and arrange the slices on a large platter (or on several smaller plates to avoid stacking up slices of lamb). Cut each cake of tofu into eight or ten pieces.

Put plenty of water into the pot. Add the mushrooms and bring to a boil.

Diners are encouraged to mix their own sauce. One recipe would be to mix 1 tbsp each of sesame oil and sesame paste with 1tsp each of shrimp sauce, light soy sauce, Chinese yellow wine and wine vinegar and ½ tsp sugar.

The more adventurous might care to add 1tsp each of chili oil and fermented tofu cheese and chopped chives and stir in chopped coriander and scallion.

Mix the sauce in a bowl, sample it and correct it to taste.

Pick up one or two slices of lamb at a time with chopsticks or put them in a small, long-handled wire basket, designed especially for this purpose. Cook the lamb very briefly in the boiling water in the hot pot. Transfer to the sauce bowl and eat.

Add the vegetables and tofu halfway through, and the bean-flour noodles towards the end, when the boiling water has turned into a rich soup after all the meat has been cooked in it. The contents of the hot pot should then be spooned or ladled out into the individual diner's bowl and drunk as a soup.

▶ *and* ▼ *Mongolian Hot Pot: the essence of this dish is a very rich stock which is made by dipping bundles of thinly sliced lamb into boiling water or stock. The meat is eaten as it is cooked, each person making up his own dipping sauce from a selection. When the meat is finished, the stock, with cabbage and noodles added, is drunk from the dip bowls.*

Stir-Fried Shredded Lamb, Bamboo Shoots, Black Mushrooms and Green Pepper on Crispy Fried Rice Noodles

INGREDIENTS *serves 4-6*
1¼lb lamb fillet
4 medium black mushrooms
1¾ cups fresh bamboo shoots
1 green pepper
2 cups peanut oil
1oz dried rice vermicelli noodles
1½ tsp garlic, chopped
1½ tsp fresh ginger root, chopped

MARINADE
1 egg white
2 tsp cornstarch
1 tbsp light soy sauce
1 tsp sugar
1 tsp Chinese yellow wine
1 tsp sesame seed oil

SAUCE
1 tbsp oyster sauce
1 tbsp light soy sauce
½ tsp sugar
½ tsp sesame seed oil
1 tbsp Chinese yellow wine
½ cup chicken stock
1 tbsp cornstarch

1 tbsp lime leaves, finely shredded
1 tbsp fresh coriander, chopped

METHOD
Shred the lamb into matchstick-sized pieces and mix well with the marinade. Set aside.

Soak the black mushrooms in hot water for 30 minutes. Cut away and discard the stems and squeeze the mushrooms to remove any excess water. Shred the caps and set aside.

Finely chop the bamboo shoots and green pepper. Blanch the bamboo shoots in 4 cups boiling water for 2 minutes. Remove and rinse under tap. Drain and set aside.

Heat the oil in a pan. Add the lamb and, after 75 seconds, stir to separate. Remove and set aside.

Add the dried rice noodles to the hot oil, removing them as soon as they fluff up (it takes only an instant). Place them as a bed on a large platter and keep warm.

▲ *Stir-Fried Shredded Lamb, bamboo shoots, black mushrooms and green pepper on crispy fried rice noodles: here the flavor of the north, in the form of lamb, is combined with the texture of the south, in the form of rice noodles fried until they are almost as crispy as a bird's nest.*

▼ *Aromatic Mutton is marinated lamb or mutton steamed and cooled then deep-fried until somewhat crisp.*

Heat 3-4 tbsp of oil in the pan and add the garlic and ginger. When the aroma rises, add the black mushrooms, green pepper and bamboo shoots and sauté for 1 minute. Return the lamb and stir rapidly over a very high heat for 30 seconds.

Add the sauce ingredients and continue to stir over a very high heat for another 30 seconds. Transfer to the platter and place on top of the noodles. Add the lime leaves and coriander and serve.

Aromatic Mutton

INGREDIENTS *serves 4-6*
1½lb mutton or lamb fillet
11oz leeks
2 cups peanut oil
1 tsp garlic, chopped
1 tsp Chinese yellow wine

MARINADE
1 tbsp light soy sauce
1 tsp dark soy sauce
1 tsp sesame seed oil
2 tsp Chinese yellow wine
1 tbsp cornstarch

METHOD
Cut the mutton fillet into thin slices. Mix together the marinade ingredients, add the mutton slices and set to one side. Cut the leek into thin slices and set aside.

Heat a pan until it is very hot and add the oil. Heat the oil until it is warm and add the mutton (reserving the marinade in a separate bowl) and stir to separate. Remove, drain and set aside.

Heat 2 tbsp oil in the pan and add the chopped garlic and leek, stir and cook over a very high heat for 1 minute.

Return the mutton to the pan, stirring well. Add the reserved marinade, stirring vigorously over a very high heat for 15 seconds. Finally, add the Chinese yellow wine, stir for another 10 seconds and serve.

Braised Mutton in a Casserole

INGREDIENTS *serves 6 - 8*
3lb braising mutton or lamb (belly if possible)
20 cups water (for blanching mutton)
3oz tofu sticks
½ cup bamboo shoots
3-4 tbsp peanut oil
3½oz sliced fresh ginger root
3½oz leeks, cut into 1½in pieces
3 tbsp salted fermented soy bean paste
3 tbsp Chinese yellow wine
10 cups water (for braising mutton)
6-8 Chinese dried mushrooms
⅓ cup oyster sauce
2oz whole dried orange peel
3oz water chestnuts
4oz sugar cane
3 lemon leaves
3 tbsp oyster sauce
1 tsp salt

DIP
3 tbsp fermented tofu or tofu "cheese"
shredded lemon leaves
gravy from mutton in casserole — about 6 tbsp, enough to make one or two small dishes of dip

METHOD
Blanch the mutton in boiling water over a high heat for 10 minutes. Remove the mutton and chop it into large, bite-sized pieces.

Soak the tofu sticks in water for 1 hour. Fry the bamboo shoots for a short while until they turn bright yellow, which indicates that the water has been extracted from the shoots.

Heat the pan until it is very hot and pour 3-4 tbsp oil into the pan. Add the ginger, leeks and soy bean paste into the hot oil to release their aromatic flavors. Then add the mutton and pour in the Chinese yellow wine. Stir and turn for 10 minutes.

Transfer the ingredients from the pan to a casserole. Add all the remaining ingredients and the water for braising. Simmer the mutton for 1 hour over medium heat. Remove the sugar cane and lemon leaves and add the oyster sauce and salt to taste.

Mix the ingredients for the dip. The mutton is served with the dip, each piece of meat being dipped into the sauce before being eaten. The sauce or soup is excellent with rice.

▼ *Scrambling the "cassia" with chopsticks in a wok.*

Cassia Lamb

The cassia is a tiny, yellow four-petalled flower that blooms in the autumn; the dish is named from the similar color of the eggs.

INGREDIENTS *serves 4 - 6*
4oz lamb fillet
3 eggs
½ tsp monosodium glutamate (optional)
2 tsp rice wine or dry sherry
1 tsp salt
1 slice fresh root ginger root
2 tbsp chicken fat

METHOD
Cut the lamb into thin shreds. Finely chop the ginger root. Beat up the eggs and mix them with the lamb shreds and ginger root.

Heat up the chicken fat in a wok or pan, put in the egg mixture, stir and scramble for about 10 seconds and add salt, monosodium glutamate (if using) and rice wine or sherry. Stir and scramble for another 10 seconds. Serve.

◀ *Braised Mutton in a Casserole, a slow-cooked dish probably introduced to Canton from the north (Peking or Outer Mongolia), where mutton is more common. The meat is cooked in a simple way and is served with one or more stronger-tasting sauces for dipping.*

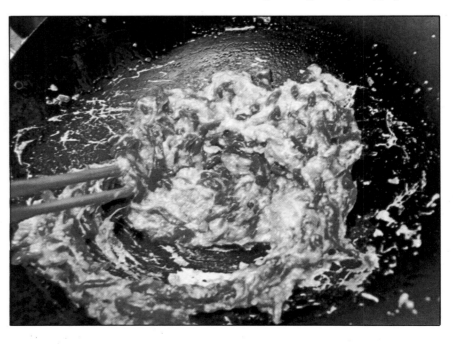

Three-Layer Shreds

INGREDIENTS *serves 4-6*
1/3 cup shredded cooked ham
1/3 cup shredded cooked chicken meat
2/3 cup shredded cooked pork (perhaps
    left over from white-cut pork)
1/3 cup bamboo shoots
1 large Chinese dried mushroom
2 tsp salt
1/2 tsp monosodium glutamate (optional)
1 tbsp lard
2 1/2 cups stock

METHOD
The ham, chicken, pork and bamboo shoots should be cut into match-sized shreds, but keep them separate. Discard the stalk of the mushroom after soaking it in warm water for 20 minutes. Place the mushroom smooth side down in the middle of a large bowl, and arrange the ham shreds around it in three neat rows, forming a triangle. Now arrange the chicken shreds on one of the outer edges and the bamboo shoots on the second edge with the pork on the third. Spread 1 tsp salt all over it, add about 4 tbsp stock and steam vigorously for 30 minutes. Remove and turn the bowl out into a deep serving dish without disarranging the contents. The success of this dish depends on the cutting and arranging, which must be done with skill and care.

Bring the remaining stock to a boil, add salt, monosodium glutamate (if using) and lard; let it bubble for a second or two then pour it all over the three-layer shreds and serve.

Crispy Five-Spice Pork

INGREDIENTS *serves 5-6*
1lb lean pork
1 tsp salt
1/2 tsp five-spice powder
1 1/2 tbsp cornstarch
2 slices fresh ginger root
2 cloves garlic
vegetable oil for deep-frying
1 1/2 tbsp soy sauce
1 tsp superfine sugar
2 tsp sea salt
1 1/2 tsp Sichuan peppercorns, pounded

METHOD
Cut the pork into thick strips. Sprinkle and rub with the salt, five-spice powder and cornstarch. Leave to season for 30 minutes. Finely chop the ginger and garlic.

Heat the oil in a wok or deep-fryer. When hot, fry half the pork strips over medium heat for 3 1/2 minutes. Drain and place in a bowl. Fry the remaining pork strips for 3 1/2 minutes, then drain and add to the bowl. Add the soy sauce and sugar to the pork, mixing well. Pour away the oil to use for other purposes, leaving 2 tbsp. Re-heat the wok or pan. When hot, stir in the ginger, garlic, sea salt and pepper over medium heat for 25 seconds. Pour the once-fried and seasoned pork into the pan. Turn and stir around quickly so that the pork is evenly coated by the spicy ingredients. Turn, toss and stir for 1 minute. Transfer to a heated serving dish.

◄ *Three-Layer Shreds, here seen garnished with cucumber slices, green peas and Chinese parsley (fresh coriander) to provide a contrast in color.*

Stir-Fried Ground Pork, Chili, Mushrooms and Black Olives

INGREDIENTS *serves 4-6*
9oz ground pork
¼lb button mushrooms
1 red chili pepper
1 tbsp black olives in sesame seed oil
1 tbsp peanut oil
1 tsp garlic, chopped

MARINADE
1 tsp cornstarch
2 tsp light soy sauce
1 tsp sugar
1 tsp Chinese yellow wine
2 tbsp peanut oil

METHOD
Prepare the marinade and marinate the ground pork. Set aside. Slice the button mushrooms and finely shred the red chili. Chop the black olives into small pieces.

Heat 1 tbsp oil in pan. Add the garlic and when the aroma rises, add the ground pork. Stir and cook over medium heat for 3 minutes. Add the black olives, button mushrooms and red chili and stir-fry over medium heat for 2 minutes.

White-Cut Pork

INGREDIENTS *serves 4-6*
2lb leg of pork (skinned and boned)

DIP
4 tbsp soy sauce
1 tbsp Kao Liang spirit (or brandy)
2 scallions, finely chopped
2 slices ginger root, peeled and finely chopped
1 tsp sesame seed oil
1 tsp chili sauce (optional)
8 cups water

METHOD
Place the pork (in one piece, tied together with string if necessary) in a large pot; add cold water, bring it to a rapid boil; skim off the scum. Cover and simmer gently for about 1 hour. Remove from the pot and leave it to cool under cover with the fat side up for 6-8 hours.

Just before serving, cut off any excess fat, leaving only a very thin layer, about ¹/₁₀in of fat on top, then cut the meat into small thin slices across the grain. Put any uneven bits and pieces in the center of a plate; arrange the well-cut slices in two neat rows, one on each side of the file, then neatly arrange a third row on top of the pile so that it resembles an arched bridge.

You can either pour the sauce mixture all over the pork and serve, or use the sauce as a dip.

Long-Steamed Knuckle of Pork

INGREDIENTS *serves 8-10*
1 knuckle of pork with skin on, about 5-6lb before boning, ask the butcher to remove the bone
2 tbsp dark soy sauce
vegetable oil for deep-frying
4 tbsp light soy sauce
3-4 slices fresh ginger root
2½ cups good stock
½ tsp salt
3 tbsp sugar
3 pieces star anise

METHOD
Bring a large pan of water to a boil. Add the knuckle of pork and boil for about 5 minutes, then remove and drain. Rub the skin and flesh with the dark soy sauce. Heat the oil in a wok or deep-fryer. When hot, fry the pork for about 5 minutes. Drain.

Place the knuckle of pork in a flameproof casserole and add the light soy sauce, ginger, stock, salt, sugar and star anise. Bring to a boil and simmer for about 5 minutes. Turn the knuckle over and put on the lid. Place the casserole into a steamer and cook for 2½ hours, turning the knuckle over every 30 minutes.

Serve the knuckle in a heated deep bowl with the sauce poured over the top. If liked, stir-fry about 1lb spinach, then arrange it around the knuckle. A knife may be used to carve off the meat into bite-sized pieces but usually the meat is tender enough to remove with a pair of chopsticks.

◄ *Stir-Fried Ground Pork, Chili, Mushrooms and Black Olives: this very unusual combination of olives and chili could only occur in Chiu Chow, which borders on olive-growing regions (olives are very rare in Chinese cooking) and is also influenced by the hotness of Sichuan and Hunan cooking.*

Top ► Ants Climbing Trees: the ground pork forms the "ants"; the transparent noodles the "trees."

► White-Cut pork: simplicity itself to make, but absolutely delicious.

Ants Climbing Trees

INGREDIENTS *serves 4-6*

1/2lb pork
2 tbsp soy sauce
1 tbsp sugar
1 tsp cornstarch
1/2 tsp chili paste
1 small red chili
2 scallions, chopped
1/4lb transparent noodles
3 tbsp oil
2/3 cup stock or water

METHOD

Grind the pork; mix it with the soy sauce, sugar, cornstarch and chili paste. Soak the noodles in warm water for 10 minutes.

Heat up the oil; first fry the chili and onions, then the pork. When the color of the meat starts to change, drain the noodles and add them to the pan. Blend well, then add the stock or water; continue cooking. When all the liquid is absorbed, it is ready to serve.

73

Crystal-Sugar Pork

INGREDIENTS *serves 4-6*
1 leg or hand (picnic shoulder) of pork, weighing about 2½-3lb
5 tbsp soy sauce
⅓ cup crystal sugar
4 tbsp rice wine or dry sherry
2 scallions
2 slices fresh ginger root

METHOD

Clean the skin or rind of pork well, making sure it is smooth and free of hairs; score an X mark down the middle as far as the bone; this will prevent the skin sticking to the pan.

Place the pork in a large pot with the skin side down, cover it with cold water, bring it to a rapid boil, skim off the scum; add all the other ingredients, place the lid on tightly, reduce heat and simmer for 30 minutes. Then turn the pork over, replace the lid and continue cooking for about 2 hours. The juice should by now be reduced to less than ⅔ cup. Turn the heat up for 5 minutes to thicken the gravy, then take the pork out and place it on a bowl or deep dish. Pour the gravy over it and serve. Like many casseroles this is even more delicious cooked in advance and then re-heated and served the following day.

Cha Shao (Roast Pork)

This famous Cantonese dish is very popular throughout the world, apart from those countries where religion prohibits the eating of pork.

INGREDIENTS *serves 4-6*
2lb pork fillet
2 tbsp Kao Liang spirit
3 tbsp sugar
2 tbsp light soy sauce
1 tbsp dark soy sauce
1 tbsp crushed yellow bean sauce
3 tbsp honey

METHOD

Cut the pork into thin strips lengthwise; marinate for about 45 minutes with Kao Liang spirit, sugar, soy sauce and bean sauce.

Roast it either suspended or on a rack in a moderately hot oven – 400° – for 30 minutes (place a pan of water at the bottom of the oven to catch the dripping). Take it out to cool for about 3 minutes, then coat each piece with honey and put it back in the oven to roast for a further 2 minutes or so.

Traditionally *cha shao* is served cold or it can be used for a number of dishes such as Cha Shao dumplings added to fried rice dishes.

Roasted Suckling Pig with Assorted Meat

Ask a Cantonese in exile what food back home he misses most, and the answer invariably will be roasted suckling pig. It is a dish normally served only at festivals and on other special occasions. It is not an ordinary suckling pig but a particular species reared specially for the table, only one month old and weighing not much more than 10lb.

Before cooking, the pig is coated with a mixture of red bean curd sauce, bean sauce, five-spice powder, salt and sugar. It can either be spit-roasted over a charcoal fire in a specially built kiln for about 50-60 minutes, or barbecued over an open fire (as often is the case in the countryside).

This is a dish of assorted cold meats neatly arranged with the roasted suckling pig as the centerpiece. When you have finished eating the suckling pig you will discover a layer of roast duck.

INGREDIENTS *serves 6-8*
¼lb *cha shao* (see previous recipe)
¼lb crystal-sugar pork
1 pig's tongue
½ roast duck
1lb roasted suckling pig
3 preserved eggs
plum sauce, bean sauce, mustard, salt and pepper

METHOD

Slice the *cha shao*, pork and tongue as thinly and as neatly as you can. Arrange them evenly on the edge of the serving dish. Cut up half of the duck for the center, then place the suckling pig pieces on top of the duck. Cut the preserved eggs in half; either use them as a garnish for the big dish, or serve on a separate dish.

◄ *Crystal-Sugar Pork.*

► *Roasted Suckling Pig, served here with various sauces and with preserved eggs, shelled and halved, in the foreground.*

Twice-Cooked Pork

INGREDIENTS *serves 6*
2lb belly of pork, rind and bones
   removed after weighing
4 tbsp canned black beans, rinsed
1 tbsp soy bean paste
2 tbsp soy sauce
1 tbsp tomato paste
1 tbsp hoisin sauce
2 tsp chili sauce
1 tbsp sugar
a little oil for frying
2 cloves garlic, peeled and finely crushed
½in fresh ginger root, finely chopped
¼ cup chicken stock
2 tbsp sherry
few drops sesame seed oil
few pieces bamboo shoot, finely sliced
scallion curls to garnish

METHOD
Place the pork into a pan of boiling water and cook for just over 30 minutes, or until tender. Lift out, drain, cool a little and cut into slices, a finger width, and then each slice into 4 pieces, and set aside. Drain the beans. Blend the soy bean paste with soy sauce, tomato paste, hoisin and chili sauce. Stir in sugar. Mash the black beans to a paste. Heat the oil in a wok, and fry the garlic and ginger, add the mashed beans, stir well, then add the meat and the mixture of sauces. Toss the meat well to coat each piece with the sauce. Add stock and extra water if the sauce is too thick. Cook for 5 minutes. Increase the heat, add the bamboo shoot slices, sherry and the sesame seed oil. Serve on a warm platter garnished with the scallion curls.

Steamed Pork Liver and Spare Rib of Pork

INGREDIENTS *serves 4-6*
½lb pork liver
1¼lb spare rib of pork
1 tbsp ground bean paste
1 tbsp shallot, chopped

MARINADE
1 tbsp light soy sauce
1 tsp dark soy sauce
1 tsp sesame seed oil
1 tsp Chinese yellow wine
1 tsp sugar
1 tbsp cornstarch

METHOD
Cut the pork liver into slices ⅛in thick, soak the pieces in water and set aside. Chop the spare rib of pork into bite-sized pieces. Blend together the ingredients for the marinade and add three-quarters of the mixture to the spare rib and the remaining quarter to the liver. Add the bean paste and chopped shallot to the spare rib and mix well. Lay the spare rib in the bottom of small dishes and place two or three pieces of liver on top.

Bring 15 cups water to a boil in a large wok with a bamboo steamer in it. Put the small dishes of spare rib and liver in the steamer, cover and steam over a high heat for 12-15 minutes. Serve.

◀ *Twice-Cooked Pork, bright contrasting colors making a most attractive dish.*

Lion's Head (Pork Meatballs with Cabbage)

The rather alarming name of this dish refers to the pork meatballs, which are supposed to resemble the shape of a lion's head and the cabbage which is supposed to look like its mane.

INGREDIENTS *serves 4*
1lb ground pork, not too lean
½ cup water chestnuts, peeled
2 tbsp dried shrimps, soaked
2 scallions
1 slice ginger root
2 tbsp rice wine or dry sherry
2 tbsp soy sauce
½ tbsp sugar
1 tsp salt
1lb Chinese cabbage
3 tbsp oil
1 cup stock

METHOD
Finely chop the water chestnuts, shrimps, scallions and ginger root. Mix them together well with the pork; add salt, wine or sherry, sugar and soy sauce. Shape the meat mixture into four round balls.

Wash and cut the cabbage into quarters lengthwise. Heat oil until smoking; stir-fry the cabbage until soft, then place the meatballs on top; add stock, bring to a boil and simmer with a lid on for 20-30 minutes.

When serving make sure the meatballs are on top of the cabbage, otherwise it will not look anything like a lion's head.

Explosive-Fried Kidney with Coriander

INGREDIENTS *serves 4*
4 pig's kidneys
2 tbsp salt
2 pieces pork stomach
2 tbsp cornstarch
8 tbsp chicken stock
2 tbsp peanut oil
1 tsp garlic, chopped
2oz coriander stems, cut into 1½in
   lengths
1 tbsp soy sauce
1 tsp Chinese yellow wine
1 tsp sesame oil

METHOD
Split the kidneys in half, remove the membrane and gristle and rub with 1 tbsp salt. Wash them thoroughly and leave them to soak in water for 30 minutes.

Split the stomach, rub it thoroughly with 1 tbsp salt. Wash and rub it vigorously with 2 tbsp cornstarch. Make sure that it is completely clean. Set aside the thick part of the stomach (or you may prefer to cut off the outer skin on both sides). Score it into a diamond pattern and cut it into slices ¾×1½×¼in using a cleaver with the blade held at an angle of 25°.

Cut up the kidney in the same way.

Bring the chicken stock to a boil and set it aside.

Heat the oil in a pan and add the garlic and meat, stirring over a very high heat for 30 seconds. Add the coriander and hot chicken stock and bring to a boil. Drain off the stock and add the light soy sauce, Chinese yellow wine and sesame oil, stir-frying over a very high heat for 20 seconds. Serve.

Explosive frying involves cooking with very intense heat. It's a technique particularly suitable for ingredients with a delicate texture.

Top ◄ Lion's Head – this dish is traditionally served with rice.

▲ Hot and Sour Kidneys, flower-cut and stir-fried in hot oil.

Hot and Sour Kidney

This is a typical Sichuan dish in that you are served several flavors (sweet, salt, sour and hot) all at once.

INGREDIENTS *serves 2-4*
½lb pig's kidney
1 tsp salt
1 tbsp rice wine or dry sherry
½ tbsp cornstarch
1 tbsp dried red chili
1 slice ginger root, peeled
2 scallions
1 clove garlic
oil for deep-frying
1 tsp Sichuan pepper, ground

SAUCE
1 tbsp sugar
1½ tbsp vinegar
1½ tbsp soy sauce
2 tsp cornstarch
water or stock

METHOD
Split the kidneys in half lengthwise and discard the fat and white parts in the middle. Score the surface of the kidneys diagonally in a criss-cross pattern and cut them into oblong stamp-sized pieces. Marinate in salt, rice wine or sherry and cornstarch.

Cut the dried red chili into small bits, discard the seeds; finely chop the ginger root, garlic and onions. Mix the sauce in a bowl or jug.

Heat up the oil and deep-fry the kidney pieces for about 1 minute; scoop them out and drain. Pour off the excess oil leaving about 1 tbsp in the wok; put in the red chili and cook until it turns dark. Add kidney pieces, onions, garlic, ginger and pepper. Stir a few times, then add the sauce mixture; blend well. As soon as the sauce starts to bubble, dish out and serve.

Shredded Kidneys in Wine Sauce

INGREDIENTS *serves 4-6*
1lb pigs' kidneys
5-6 Chinese dried mushrooms
⅓ cup bamboo shoots
½ cup green cabbage heart or broccoli
1½ tbsp rice wine (or sherry)
1 tsp salt
1 tbsp soy sauce
½ tsp monosodium glutamate
1 slice ginger root, peeled
1 scallion
Sichuan peppercorns

METHOD
Peel off the thin white skin covering the kidneys, split them in half lengthwise and discard the white parts in the middle. Shred each half into thin slices and soak them in cold water for an hour or so.

Soak the mushrooms in warm water for 20 minutes, squeeze dry and discard the hard stalks, then cut them into thin shreds. Cut the bamboo shoots and greens into thin shreds, blanch them in boiling water for a few minutes (if using canned bamboo shoots this will be unnecessary as they have already been cooked), then drain and mix them with 1 tsp salt.

Parboil the kidneys in about 4½ cups boiling water for a few minutes, scoop them out, rinse in cold water and drain. Place them in a bowl, add the bamboo shoots, mushrooms, greens, soy sauce, rice wine or sherry and monosodium glutamate; mix well and marinate for 20 minutes or so. Arrange the contents on a serving plate and garnish with finely chopped scallion, ginger root and freshly ground pepper.

This is an ideal starter for a formal meal or dinner party.

▲ ▶ *Shredded Kidneys in Wine Sauce –
an hors d'œuvre dish of contrasting colors,
flavors and textures.*

▶ *Five-Fragrant Kidney Slices, skillfully cut
in the form of a flower.*

Five-Fragrant Kidney Slices

INGREDIENTS *serves 4-6*
½lb pigs' kidneys
1 tsp red coloring
1½ cups chicken stock
1 tbsp soy sauce
1 tbsp rice wine (or sherry)
1 slice ginger root
1 tsp salt
1 tsp five-spice powder
1 scallion

METHOD
Place the kidneys in cold water in a pan; bring to a boil; skim off any impurities floating on the surface; reduce heat and simmer for 30 minutes. Remove and drain.

Place the kidneys in fresh cold water (just enough to cover), add the red coloring (if Chinese red-powder is unobtainable, then use a little cochineal). Bring to a boil, then remove and rinse in cold water and drain.

Put the chicken stock in a pot or pan; add the soy sauce, wine or sherry, ginger root, scallion, salt, five-spice powder and the kidneys. Boil for 5 minutes, then place the kidneys with the stock in a large bowl to cool. This will take 5-6 hours.

Take the kidneys out and cut them into as thin slices as you possibly can – it is possible to cut 80-90 slices from each kidney if your cleaver is really sharp!

Place the unevenly cut slices in the middle of a plate to make a pile, then neatly arrange the rest of the slices all the way around it in two or three layers like the petals of an opened flower, then through a strainer pour a little of the juice in which the kidneys have been cooking over the "flower," but be careful not to disturb the beautiful "petals." Serve cold as an hors d'œuvre. The name "five-fragrant" is, of course, referring to the five-spice powder used.

▲ *Stir-Fried Kidney Flowers.*

Stir-Fried Kidney Flowers

INGREDIENTS *serves 4-6*
½lb pigs' kidneys
5-6 Wood Ears
⅓ cup bamboo shoots
½ cup water chestnuts
1 cup greens in season
1 tbsp cornstarch
3 tbsp clear stock
1 tbsp soy sauce
1 tbsp vinegar
1 tsp salt
2 scallions
1 slice ginger root, peeled
1 clove garlic
oil for deep-frying

METHOD
Peel off the thin white skin covering the kidneys, split them in half lengthwise and discard the white parts.

Score the surface of the kidneys diagonally in a criss-cross pattern and then cut them into small oblong pieces. When cooked they will open up and resemble ears of corn – hence the name "flowers." Mix the kidney pieces with a little salt and ½ tbsp cornstarch.

Soak the Wood Ears in water for about 20 minutes and slice them together with the water chestnuts and bamboo shoots. Cut and blanch the greens and finely chop the scallions, ginger root and garlic. Mix the remaining cornstarch with the soy sauce and stock.

Heat up the oil in a wok until it smokes; deep-fry the kidney "flowers," separate them with chopsticks or a fork, then quickly scoop them out with a perforated spoon. Now pour out the excess oil leaving about 2 tbsp in the wok; toss in the scallions, ginger root and garlic, add the vinegar followed by the bamboo shoots, water chestnuts, Wood Ears and greens and finally the kidneys. Pour in the sauce mixture, blend well and serve.

This dish should have a harmonious balance of aroma, flavor, texture and color and is ideal as an accompaniment to wine.

Stir-Fried Shredded Pork and Chinese White Chives

INGREDIENTS *serves 4-6*
1¼lb fillet of pork
2 medium black mushrooms
8oz Chinese white chives or young leeks
1 cup peanut oil
1½ chopped fresh ginger root
1 tsp garlic, chopped
1 tsp salt
1 tsp Chinese yellow wine or dry sherry

MARINADE
1 tbsp light soy sauce
½ tsp sesame oil
1 egg white
1 tbsp cornstarch
2 tsp Chinese yellow wine or dry sherry

METHOD
Cut the fillet of pork into ⅛in thin slices, then into 2in shreds. Mix the pieces of meat with the marinade and set them aside for 15 minutes.

Soak the black mushrooms in hot water for 30 minutes. Remove and discard the stems and cut the caps into fine shreds. Cut the chives or leeks into shreds 2in long.

Heat the peanut oil in pan. Add the pork, stirring to separate, reduce the heat, and leave to sit in the oil for 2 minutes. Remove, drain and set aside.

Heat 2 tbsp oil in a pan. Add the ginger and garlic, return the pork and add the mushrooms, chives or leeks and salt. Stir and cook over high heat for 2 minutes, add the Chinese yellow wine, stir again and serve.

Steamed Ground Rice-Pork Wrapped in Lotus Leaves

INGREDIENTS *serves 6-7*
3-4 lotus leaves
1½lb belly of pork, thick end
2 tbsp light soy sauce
vegetable oil for deep-frying
2 slices fresh ginger root
2 scallions
1½ tbsp oyster sauce
1½ tsp salt
1½ tsp sugar
2 cloves garlic
3 tbsp ground rice
1½ tsp sesame seed oil

METHOD
Immerse the lotus leaves in warm water for 3-4 minutes to soften. Bring a large pan of water to a boil, add the pork and simmer for 10 minutes. Remove and drain. Rub the pork with the soy sauce. Heat the oil in a wok or deep-fryer. When hot, fry the pork for about 3 minutes. Drain. Cut the pork into ½in slices. Finely chop the ginger and scallions. Mix together the oyster sauce, salt, sugar, ginger, garlic and scallions. Add the ground rice and sesame seed oil. Mix in the pork slices and make sure they are evenly coated. Pile the slices neatly into a stack, then wrap in the softened lotus leaves. Tie securely with string.

Place the parcel in a heatproof dish, put in a steamer and steam for 3 hours. When ready, drain away any excess water and serve straight from the lotus leaves. The pork will be tender and the ground rice will have soaked up any fattiness.

◀ *Stir-Fried Shredded Pork and Chinese White Chives: this may be readily produced in a very short time, either as a hot hors d'œuvre to accompany wine or to be added to rice to increase the savoriness of the whole meal. Chinese chives are not widely available but are worth searching for.*

Mu Hsu Pork

INGREDIENTS *serves 4-6*
¾lb pork
¼lb dried tiger lily stems
5-6 Wood Ears
⅓ cup bamboo shoots
4 tbsp peanut oil
1 tsp chopped fresh ginger root
3 tsp dark soy sauce
2 tsp sugar
6 eggs, lightly beaten
4 tbsp chicken stock
1 tbsp scallion, chopped
20 Chinese pancakes (see page 43)

SEASONINGS
2 tsp light soy sauce
½ tsp sesame oil
1 tsp cornstarch
1 tsp Chinese yellow wine

METHOD
Blend together the seasonings and add the pork, cut into matchstick-sized shreds. Set aside.

Soak the dried tiger lily stems and the Wood Ears in hot water for 30 minutes. Cut away and discard any tough parts and then carefully chop the remainder into 1½in pieces. Next thinly slice the bamboo shoots.

Heat 2 tbsp oil in a pan and add the chopped ginger. When the aroma arises, add the pork and cook, stirring for 1 minute. Add the tiger lily stems, bamboo shoots and Wood Ears. Add 1 tsp dark soy sauce and 1 tsp sugar and cook for 1 minute, continuing to stir. Transfer to a plate and set aside.

Heat 2 tbsp oil in the pan and add the lightly beaten eggs, stirring gently with a spatula over medium heat. Cook until they are set and scrambled. Return the pork and vegetables to the pan and always keep on stirring. Break the egg into pieces.

Add the chicken stock, the remaining soy sauce and then the sugar, stirring rapidly over a very high heat for 1 minute, and the chopped scallion. Serve with Chinese pancakes. To eat, place a pancake flat on the plate and spoon Mu Hsu pork on top. Roll up, fold one end over and eat from the open end.

▲ *These Sichuan dumplings are made by steaming or poaching ground pork wrapped in a thin skin of dough. The sauce is actually red oil made by soaking dried chili peppers in oil overnight.*

▼ *Pearl-Studded Pork Balls, shown here in their bamboo steamer garnished with Chinese mushrooms and parsley.*

Pearl-Studded Pork Balls

INGREDIENTS *serves 4-6*
½lb glutinous rice
2 tbsp dried shrimps
1lb pork, ground
1 tsp salt
1½ tbsp scallion, finely chopped
1 tbsp fresh ginger root, finely chopped
1 tbsp light soy sauce
1 egg
2 tbsp cornstarch

METHOD
Soak the rice in cold water to cover for at least 8 hours. Drain well. Soak the dried shrimps in hot water to cover for 25 minutes. Drain and finely chop. Place the pork in a bowl and add the dried shrimps, salt, scallion, ginger, soy sauce, egg and 1½ tbsp of water. Combine thoroughly. Mix the soaked rice with the cornstarch. Form the pork mixture into even-sized balls and wet each ball lightly with water. Roll the balls in the rice mixture and pat on lightly to get an even covering.

Arrange the balls on a steaming tray in a steamer and steam vigorously for about 25 minutes. Serve on a heated dish and accompany with either soy or tomato sauce.

Sichuan Dumplings in Red Sauce

INGREDIENTS *serves 6-8*
4 medium black mushrooms
½lb fillet of pork
¼lb pork fat
¼lb chives or white of scallions
2 egg whites
2 tbsp cornstarch
1 tsp salt
1 tsp sesame oil
40 *wonton* wrappers

RED SAUCE
2 tbsp sesame oil
1 tbsp chili oil
1 tbsp garlic, chopped
1 tsp Sichuan peppercorn powder
2 tbsp sesame paste
2 tbsp dark soy sauce
1 tbsp young leek or scallion, chopped
2 tsp sugar

METHOD
Soak the black mushrooms in hot water for 30 minutes. Remove and discard the stems. Set aside.

Finely dice the fillet of pork and the pork fat and chop the chives or the white of the scallions into tiny pieces.

Place the pork, mushrooms and chives in a mixing bowl. Add 1 egg white, 1 tbsp cornstarch, 1 tsp salt and 1 tsp sesame oil and mix well.

Put 1 tbsp of the pork mixture in the center of a *wonton* wrapper. Mix the other egg white with 1 tsp cornstarch and wet two of the edges of the wrapper. Fold up the wrapper diagonally to form a triangle and press the edges to seal. Fold two opposite corners over and stick together with more of the egg white and cornstarch mixture.

In a large pan boil 20 cups water and add the dumplings. When they float to the surface, add 1 cup cold water and bring back to a boil again. Remove and drain the dumplings, arranging them in a medium-sized serving bowl (about six dumplings to each bowl). Prepare the red sauce and serve.

Preparing pork spare ribs

Ask the butcher for meaty ribs. If not already divided, take out the large spine section, chop between the rib bones to separate them and then chop each rib across into bite-sized pieces. A heavy Chinese cleaver is the best tool for this operation, especially the last part.

▲ Remove the large bone.

▲ Chop the separated ribs into small pieces.

Capital Spare Ribs

INGREDIENTS *serves 5-6*
1½lb meaty pork spare ribs
1½ tsp salt
pepper to taste
vegetable oil for deep-frying

SAUCE
2 tsp chopped fresh root ginger
2 tsp garlic, chopped
3 tbsp yellow bean paste
2 tsp sugar
2 tbsp good stock
1½ tbsp dark soy sauce
2 tbsp rice wine or dry sherry
1½ tbsp hoisin sauce
1 tbsp cornstarch blended with 2 tbsp
    stock

METHOD
Chop the spare ribs into 1-1½in pieces. Place in a large pan of water and bring to a boil. Simmer for 2 minutes, then drain. Sprinkle with the salt and pepper.

Heat the oil in a wok or deep-fryer. When hot, fry the spare ribs over medium heat for about 8 minutes. Drain thoroughly and pour away the oil to use for other purposes, leaving 2 tbsp. Heat the oil in the wok or pan. When hot, stir in the ginger and garlic for about 15 seconds. Stir in the yellow bean paste and sugar. Add the stock, soy sauce, wine or sherry and hoisin sauce and stir until smooth. Bring to a boil, return the spare ribs to the sauce and simmer for about 1 minute. Pour on the blended cornstarch and stir until the sauce thickens.

▲ Steamed Spare Ribs in Black Bean Sauce, just one of many ways of preparing pork ribs.

Sweet and Sour Spare Ribs

INGREDIENTS *serves 4-6*
1lb pork spare ribs
2 tbsp soy sauce
1 tbsp rice wine or dry sherry
$\frac{1}{2}$ tsp monosodium glutamate (optional)
2 tbsp cornstarch
2 tbsp sugar
1$\frac{1}{2}$ tbsp vinegar
lard for deep-frying
salt and Sichuan pepper for dipping

METHOD
Chop the spare ribs into small bits using a cleaver. Mix $\frac{1}{2}$ tbsp soy sauce with the rice wine or sherry and monosodium glutamate, if using. When they are all well blended together, add 1 tbsp cornstarch. Coat each bit of the spare ribs with this mixture.

In a bowl mix the remaining soy sauce with sugar and vinegar. Warm up the lard in a wok or deep-fryer, put in about half of the spare ribs, fry for 30 seconds, scoop them out. Wait for a while to let the lard heat up again, then fry the rest of the spare ribs for 30 seconds, scoop out. Now wait for the lard to get hot before returning all the spare ribs to the wok to fry for another 50 seconds or so; scoop them out when they turn golden and place them on a serving dish.

Pour off the excess lard, leaving about 1 tbsp in the pan; add the sauce mixture. When it starts to bubble, add the remaining cornstarch mixed in a little cold water; stir to make a smooth sauce, then pour it over the spare ribs.

Serve with salt and pepper mixed as a dip.

Steamed Spare Ribs in Black Bean Sauce

INGREDIENTS *serves 4-6*
$\frac{3}{4}$lb pork spare ribs
1 clove garlic, crushed
1 slice ginger root, peeled
1 tsp oil
1 small red chili pepper

SAUCE
2 tbsp crushed black bean sauce
1 tbsp soy sauce
1 tbsp rice wine or dry sherry
1 tsp cornstarch

GARNISH
2 scallions, cut into short lengths

METHOD
Chop the spare ribs into small pieces, finely chop the garlic, ginger root and red chili. Mix them all together with the sauce and marinate for 15 minutes.

Grease a heatproof plate with oil; place the spare ribs on it. Steam vigorously for 25-30 minutes. Garnish with the scallions and serve.

▲ *Sweet and Sour Spare Ribs, another easy dish, using this cheap cut of meat.*

Spare Rib of Pork, Carp and Salted Plum in a Casserole

INGREDIENTS *serves 4-6*
1$\frac{1}{4}$lb spare rib of pork
2lb carp or any other freshwater fish
2$\frac{1}{2}$ cups chicken stock
2$\frac{1}{2}$ cups water
3-4 salted plums
6 slices fresh ginger root
2 scallions

METHOD
Chop the spare ribs across the bones into bite-sized pieces and blanch them in boiling water for 2 minutes. Remove and set aside.

Clean the carp thoroughly, paying particular attention to a inside of the cavity. Set aside.

Bring the chicken stock and water to the boil in a clay pot. Add all the ingredients and when the mixture boils again, lower the heat to medium. Cook for 5 minutes. Leave the heat further and simmer gently for 15 minutes. Serve.

▲ *Spare Rib of Pork, Carp and Salted Plum in a casserole: this is an unusual but happy combination, the acidity of the pickled plum tempering the richness of the carp and pork. The surface fat should be skimmed off before serving, to leave a highly flavored clear broth.*

Twice-Roasted Pork

The first part of the roasting is ideally done on an open fire or barbecue. The second part is supposed to be done in an oven, but there is no reason why it should not be barbecued as well.

INGREDIENTS *serves 4-6*
3-4lb loin of pork (in one piece)
4 egg whites
1 cup plain flour
3-4 scallions
¼ cup hoisin sauce
½ cup Chinese pickles

METHOD
Pierce the pork with a spit, singe the skin over a high flame then plunge it into a large pot of hot water for 5 minutes. Take the pork out and scrape off any burnt skin. Place it in a large pot, cover with cold water and cook for about 1 hour. Remove.

Make a paste with the egg whites and flour, rub it all over the meat (not the skin), roast in a moderate oven (400°) skin side up for 20 minutes, then turn it over and roast for a further 15-20 minutes.

To serve, carve the crackling, the fat, the meat and spareribs separately and arrange each in a row.

Cut the scallions into shreds, to be eaten with the pork together with the hoisin sauce and the Chinese pickles. Wrap the pork and its accompaniments in "Lotus-leaf" pancakes, or place them inside Greek pita bread which is very similar to a type of bread eaten in northern China.

Shredded Pork in "Fish Sauce"

Despite its name, there is no fish involved in this dish.

INGREDIENTS *serves 4-6*
½lb pork fillet
1 cup soaked Wood Ears
2-3 stalks celery
1 tsp salt
1½ tbsp cornstarch
1 slice ginger root, peeled and finely chopped
1 clove garlic, finely chopped
2 scallions, finely chopped
1½ tbsp soy sauce
1 tbsp chili paste
1 tsp sugar
2 tsp vinegar
3 tbsp oil

METHOD
Cut the pork into thin shreds the size of matches; mix with salt and ½ tsp cornstarch. Shred the soaked Wood Ears and celery.

Heat 1 tbsp oil and stir-fry the pork until the color changes; remove and add the remaining oil to the wok; put in Wood Ears and celery together with ginger root, garlic and scallions; add pork, soy sauce, chili paste, sugar and vinegar. Cook together for 1-2 minutes, then add the remaining cornstarch mixed in a little water; blend well; serve.

▲ *Shredded Pork in "Fish Sauce." The sauce ingredients are added to the meat, ready for final serving.*

▲ *Pork in Hot and Sour Sauce – a spicy and colorful dish.*

▼ *Twice-Roasted Pork. In this picture the skin and meat are shown served together.*

Pork in Hot and Sour Sauce

INGREDIENTS *serves 4-6*
½lb pork fillet
3-4 Chinese dried mushrooms, soaked
1 tbsp Chinese pickled cabbage
2 tbsp bamboo shoots
⅓ cup green hot chili peppers
1 leek
1 egg
2 tbsp cornstarch
1 tsp salt
2 tbsp chili paste
1 tbsp soy sauce
1 tsp sesame seed oil
oil for deep-frying

METHOD
First cut the pork into thick slices, score the surface with a criss-cross pattern, then cut them into small squares; marinate with salt, egg and 1 tbsp cornstarch.

Finely chop the mushrooms, pickled cabbage, bamboo shoots, green chilies and leek.

Warm up the oil, deep-fry the pork until each piece opens up like a flower, scoop out and drain.

Pour off the excess oil leaving about 2 tbsp in the wok; stir-fry all the chopped ingredients, add paste and pork; blend well. Now add soy sauce and the remaining cornstarch mixed with a little cold water. When the sauce thickens, add the sesame seed oil and serve.

Pan-Fried Pork

INGREDIENTS *serves 4-6*
1lb boned picnic shoulder (hand of pork)
1 egg
4 tbsp cornstarch
1½ tbsp soy sauce
1 tsp salt
1½ tbsp rice wine (or sherry)
3 scallions
1 slice ginger root
2 tbsp hoisin sauce
Sichuan peppercorns
5 cups oil for deep-frying

METHOD
Place the pork in a pot of water and boil over a fairly high heat until soft. Remove and rinse in cold water, then cut it into thin slices across the whole joint, keeping the shape of the joint. Place the pork skin side down in a large bowl, add 1 tbsp soy sauce, ginger root, 1 scallion cut into short lengths, 1 tbsp rice wine or sherry; steam for 1 hour; remove and drain off juice.

Mix the cornstarch, egg and salt with the remaining rice wine or sherry and soy sauce, make it into a paste, put half of it on a plate, then place the pork skin side down on it (try to keep the original shape) and spread the remaining paste on top.

Warm up the oil in a deep-fryer, reduce heat and place the plate on the edge of the pan. Gently but firmly push the pork as a whole into the oil; after a while, increase the heat to high, then reduce the heat again when the pork starts to turn golden. Carefully turn it over, continue cooking until the sizzling noises are subdued, then lift it out and drain. Cut it into small pieces, arrange them on a place and garnish with Sichuan pepper.

Cut the remaining 2 scallions into shreds, place them on one side of the plate and put the hoisin sauce on the other side as a dip.

Stir-Fried Pork Slices with Fresh Vegetables

INGREDIENTS *serves 4-6*
½lb pork fillet
1⅓ cup fresh mushrooms
1 small Chinese cabbage
1 tbsp soy sauce
1 tbsp rice wine (or sherry)
1 tsp sugar
½ tbsp cornstarch
1 scallion
1 tsp salt
3 tbsp oil

METHOD
Cut the pork into small slices about the size of an oblong stamp; mix with soy sauce, rice wine or sherry, sugar and cornstarch. Wash the mushrooms and cut them into thin slices. Cut the cabbage into pieces about the same size as the pork. Finely chop the scallion.

Heat up about 1 tbsp oil; before it gets too hot, stir-fry the pork about 1 minute or until the color of the meat changes; then dish out and keep it aside.

Wash and dry the wok; heat up the remaining oil. When it smokes, toss in the finely chopped scallion followed by the mushrooms and cabbage; add salt and stir constantly for about ½ minute, then return the pork to the wok and mix it well with the vegetables; add a little stock or water if necessary. As soon as the gravy starts to bubble it is ready to serve.

Stewed Pork with Bamboo Shoots

This is very much a seasonal dish. Either carrots or white turnips may be substituted for the bamboo shoots.

INGREDIENTS *serves 4-6*
1½lb pork, not too lean
6 cups bamboo shoots (carrots, turnips)
2 tbsp lard or oil
4 tbsp soy sauce
2 tbsp rice wine (or sherry)
1 tbsp sugar
½ cup stock
5 cups water

▲ *Stir-Fried Pork Slices with Fresh Vegetables.*

METHOD

Cut the pork into 1in squares. Cut the bamboo shoots into triangular-shaped chunks of the same size.

Blanch the pork in boiling water, remove as soon as the water starts to boil again. Rinse the pork in cold water and drain.

Warm up the lard or oil, put in the parboiled pork, stir for 30 seconds, add soy sauce, wine or sherry and sugar. When the color starts to darken, add stock, reduce heat, cover with a lid, and cook gently for 1½ hours. Now add the bamboo shoots; blend well and cook for another 30 minutes. This dish can be re-heated and served again.

Steamed Pork with Ground Rice

As a child, this was one of my favorite recipes, perhaps because it was only eaten on special occasions such as the Beginning of Summer festival (usually early in May).

INGREDIENTS *serves 4-6*
1lb belly of pork, boned but with skin on
⅔ cup rice, uncooked
1 star anise
2 tbsp soy sauce
½ tbsp sugar
1 tbsp rice wine (or sherry)
2 tbsp stock

METHOD

Cut the pork into 2×4in thin slices; marinate with soy sauce, sugar, rice wine or sherry and stock for 20 minutes.

Put the rice and star anise in a wok or skillet; stir over a high heat for a while, then reduce heat and continue stirring until golden; remove the rice and crush it with a rolling pin until fine. Coat each piece of pork with the ground rice, pressing it in well.

Place the pork piece by piece into a bowl, skin side down; steam vigorously for at least 2 hours or until the meat is very soft. To serve, turn the meat onto a dish so that the skin side is up.

▲ *Steamed Pork with Ground Rice. This dish is so delicious that children in China eat mounds of it. As a joke, they are weighed before and after the meal to see how much weight they have put on.*

Tung-Po Pork

There are several different recipes for this famous dish. Since Mr Su Tungpo actually lived in Hangzhou for a number of years, this may well be the authentic one. At any rate, my grandmother used to cook it this way, and that is good enough for me.

INGREDIENTS *serves 4-6*
10oz fresh belly of pork
1 tbsp crystal sugar
2 tbsp soy sauce
2 tbsp rice wine (or sherry)
2 scallions
2 slices ginger root, peeled

METHOD

Cut the pork into four equal squares. Put enough cold water in casserole to cover the meat; bring it to a boil, then blanch the meat for 5 minutes. Take it out and rinse in cold water.

Discard the water in which the meat has been blanched; place a bamboo rack at the bottom of the pot, then place the meat skin side down in it; add crystal sugar, soy sauce and rice wine or sherry. Place the scallions and ginger root on top; seal the lid tightly with flour and water paste and cook gently for at least 2 hours or until tender. Discard the ginger root and onions and transfer the meat into a bowl, skin side up this time, with three pieces on the bottom layer and one piece on top. Pour the juice over them, cover and steam vigorously for at least 2 hours before serving.

Fu-Yang Pork

This recipe, dating back over a thousand years, was only recently discovered in Hangzhou.

INGREDIENTS *serves 4-6*
6oz pork fillet
¼ cup pork fat
20 shrimps, peeled, uncooked
1 tsp Sichuan peppercorns
2 tbsp soy sauce
¼ tsp monosodium glutamate
1 tbsp rice wine (or sherry)
¾ cup sesame seed oil for deep-frying

METHOD

Cut the pork into twenty thin pieces of roughly the same size. Cut the pork fat into twenty pieces too; place a piece of pork fat on each piece of pork. Use the flat side of a cleaver to tap the pork and fat together gently, then place a peeled shrimp on top of that and give it a tap.

Bring the sesame seed oil to boiling point; toss in the Sichuan peppercorns and scoop them out after 2-3 seconds when they turn dark. Using a wire basket or a large Chinese perforated spoon, lower the pork into hot oil to deep-fry for 1-2 seconds; take out to let the oil get hot again, then lower once more. Repeat this once or twice more, then pour off the oil and put the pork pieces flat in the pan. Add wine or sherry, soy sauce and monosodium glutamate, cook for 3-4 seconds then arrange them carefully on a plate.

▲ *The partly-cooked Tung-Po Pork is prepared for steaming.*

▲ *Deep-Fried Crispy Fingers of Pork,*
garnished with lemon slices, parsley and a
radish rose.

Sichuan Yu-Hsiang Shredded Pork

INGREDIENTS *serves 4-6*
1½lb pork fillet
2 scallions
2 slices fresh ginger root
2 fresh chilies
1 clove garlic, minced
3-4 dried Chinese mushrooms
⅙ cup drained, canned bamboo shoots
2 egg whites
2 tsp cornstarch
vegetable oil for deep-frying
½ tsp salt
1 tbsp yellow bean paste
1 tbsp good stock
1 tbsp rice wine or dry sherry
1½ tbsp soy sauce
1½ tbsp vinegar
½ tsp white pepper
2 tsp cornstarch blended with 2 tbsp
    cold stock
1 tsp sesame seed oil
2 tsp red chili oil or chili sauce
1 tsp crushed Sichuan peppercorns

METHOD
Shred the pork fillet finely. Chop the
scallions, ginger, chilies, discarding the
seeds, and garlic. Soak the dried
mushrooms in boiling water to cover for 25
minutes. Drain and discard the tough stalks.
Shred the mushroom caps. Shred the
bamboo shoots.

Put the pork in a bowl with the egg
whites, cornstarch and 1 tbsp of oil. Toss
together very well.

Heat the oil in a wok or deep-fryer. When
medium hot, fry the pork for about 1½
minutes. Add the bamboo shoots and
mushrooms and stir for about 1½ minutes.
Drain and pour away the oil.

Reheat the wok or a skillet with about 1
tbsp of oil. When hot, stir-fry the ginger,
garlic, scallions, salt and chilies for 1
minute. Add the bean paste, stock, sherry or
wine, soy sauce, vinegar and white pepper.
Stir and bring to the boil. Add the shredded
pork and vegetables to the wok. Thicken the
sauce with the blended cornstarch. At the
last minute, drizzle over the sesame seed oil
and toss together. Transfer to a heated plate
and sprinkle on the red chili oil and crushed
peppercorns.

Deep-Fried Crispy Fingers of Pork

INGREDIENTS *serves 5-6*
1½lb lean pork
1 tsp salt
¼ tsp pepper
½ tsp ground ginger
1 tbsp rice wine or dry sherry
1 tsp sesame seed oil
vegetable oil for deep-frying

BATTER
1 egg
5 tbsp all-purpose flour
1½ tbsp cornstarch

SAUCE
1½ tbsp vegetable oil
1½ tbsp chopped scallion
2 tsp minced garlic
2 tsp chopped fresh chilies
1½ tbsp chopped fresh ginger root
5 tbsp good stock
2 tbsp vinegar
2 tbsp light soy sauce
1 tsp salt
1 tsp sugar

METHOD
Cut the pork into finger-sized strips. Mix
the salt, pepper, ginger, wine or sherry and
sesame seed oil together. Add the pork and
mix thoroughly. Leave to marinate for 10
minutes.

To make the batter, mix the egg, flour and
cornstarch together.

To make the dip sauce, heat the oil in a
wok or skillet. When hot, add the scallion,
garlic, chili and ginger and stir for a few
seconds. Add the rest of the dip sauce
ingredients. Bring to a boil, then pour into a
small heatproof bowl.

Heat the oil in a wok or deep-fryer. When
very hot, dip the pork fingers in the batter
and put gently into the oil. Fry for about 3
minutes. Drain. Allow the oil to reheat, then
fry the pork again for 30 seconds. Drain.
Arrange the pork fingers on a heated plate
and serve with the dip sauce.

Ground Fried Pork

This fried dish is rather unusual in that it is fried without any oil. In fact, the fat it produces during cooking should be drained, a process known as "dry-frying."

INGREDIENTS *serves 4-6*
1lb pork fillet
½ cup Sichuan preserved vegetable
1 tbsp crushed yellow bean sauce
2 tsp brown sugar
½ tsp salt
½ tbsp soy sauce
1 slice ginger root, peeled
1 scallion
1 tbsp rice wine (or sherry)
1 tsp sesame seed oil

METHOD
Trim off all sinew and gristle from the meat, but keep the fat; now chop the pork coarsely with a cleaver into rice grain-sized pieces. Chop the Sichuan preserved vegetable into small pieces.

Finely chop the ginger root and scallion.

Heat up a wok or skillet over a high heat and stir-fry the pork for 1 or 2 minutes; as soon as it starts to stick on the bottom, reduce the heat to low and scrape the pan well. After about 1 minute, increase the heat to high again until it starts to stick, then reduce heat. Repeat this rather fiddly high-low heat procedure three or four times, when the pork will turn pale in color. Then drain off the fat which the meat will have produced.

Over high heat add the bean sauce, sugar, salt and soy sauce, mixing well; by now the meat should have turned light brown. Now add the chopped Sichuan preserved vegetable, ginger root, scallion and wine or sherry, blend well, and finally add the sesame seed oil and serve.

Sweet and Sour Pork

This is one of the few dishes that people in the West have come to associate with overseas Chinese restaurants. Though it is not Cantonese in origin, it has become one of the most popular dishes in that region.

INGREDIENTS *serves 4-6*
½lb pork, not too lean
⅔ cup fresh bamboo shoots
1 green pepper
1 tsp salt
1½ tbsp Kao Liang spirit
1 egg
½ tbsp cornstarch
2 tbsp flour
1 clove garlic
1 scallion, cut into short lengths
oil for deep-frying

SAUCE
3 tbsp vinegar
2 tbsp sugar
½ tsp salt
1 tbsp tomato paste
1 tbsp soy sauce
½ tbsp cornstarch
1 tsp sesame seed oil

METHOD
Cut the meat into about two dozen small pieces, cut the bamboo shoots and green pepper into pieces of the same size.

Mix the meat pieces with salt and Kao Liang spirit for 15 minutes; add a beaten egg with cornstarch; blend well, then coat each piece of meat with flour.

Deep-fry the meat in slightly hot oil for 3 minutes, then turn off the heat but leave the meat in the oil for 2 minutes; scoop out and drain. Heat up the oil again and re-fry the meat with bamboo shoots for another 2 minutes or until they are golden. Remove and drain.

Pour off the excess oil, put in the garlic and green pepper followed by scallion and the sweet and sour sauce mixture; stir to make it smooth, add the meat and bamboo shoots; blend well. Serve.

▲ *Sweet and Sour Pork – you will find this recipe quite different from the version in some Chinese takeaways.*

"Lychee" Pork

Although lychee is one of the local products it is not used in this dish – the pork is cut in such a way that, when cooked, it resembles the fruit.

INGREDIENTS *serves 4-6*
10oz lean pork
1 tbsp cornstarch
1 tbsp sugar
1½ tsp vinegar
1 tbsp soy sauce
2 scallions, white parts only
1 tsp sesame seed oil
2 tbsp stock
oil for deep-frying

METHOD
First cut the pork into large slices of ¼in thickness; score a criss-cross pattern on each slice, then cut them into diamond-shape pieces; coat each piece with cornstarch. Cut the scallion whites into short lengths.

Heat up the oil, put in the pork piece by piece and deep fry 3 minutes. The pieces should curl up slightly to look like lychee. Scoop them out and drain.

Pour off the excess oil; put in scallions, sugar, vinegar, soy sauce, and stock. When it starts to bubble, add the pork and sesame seed oil; blend well; serve.

FISH AND SHELLFISH

Chrysanthemum Fish Pot

INGREDIENTS *serves 4-6*

¼lb fish maw

¼lb chicken breast meat, boned and
    skinned

2 chicken gizzards

½lb pig's stomach

¼lb bêche-de-mer

¼lb snow peas

½lb spinach leaves

2oz fresh coriander

2 slices fresh ginger root, peeled

2-3 scallions

2 tsp salt

1 tsp freshly ground Sichuan pepper

8 cups stock

1 large dry chrysanthemum (white or
    yellow)

METHOD

Cut the fish maw, chicken gizzard, bêche-de-mer and stomach into slices. Wash the cabbage, snow peas, spinach and coriander; cut them into small pieces.

Finely chop the ginger root and scallions; place them with salt and pepper in a small bowl.

Bring the stock to a rolling boil in the fire pot; arrange the meat and vegetables in the moat. They will only need to be cooked for about 5 minutes. Everybody just helps themselves from the pot with chopsticks, and dips their helping in the "four seasonings" before eating it.

Use the chrysanthemum as a decoration.

▶ *Chrysanthemum Fish Pot, seen from the top. Clockwise from 2 o'clock: bêche-de-mer, with Chinese cabbage heart dividing it from chicken breast meat; egg omelet, sliced chicken gizzards and cabbage; tripe; another omelet, fish maws, and a third omelet. Fish-balls are placed all the way round the "chimney."*

Traditionally the chrysanthemum petals were scattered over the finished dish, but the whole flower may be effectively used.

Steamed Sea Bass with Black Mushrooms and Chinese Ham

INGREDIENTS *serves 4-6*
1½lb fillet of sea bass or any white fish
6 medium black mushrooms
2oz Chinese ham
6 stalks scallions
6 slices fresh ginger root, shredded
½ cup peanut oil
1 clove garlic

MARINADE
1 egg white
1 tsp cornstarch
½ tsp sesame oil
⅛ tsp pepper
1 tsp salt

SAUCE
1 tbsp oyster sauce
1 tbsp light soy sauce
½ tsp sugar
1 tsp sesame oil
1 tsp Chinese yellow wine
1 cup chicken stock

METHOD
Clean the fish and cut it into slices 2×1½×¼in. Mix the marinade, add the fish pieces and set aside.

Soak the black mushrooms in hot water for 30 minutes. Remove and discard the stems and cut each mushroom into three or four slices. Set these aside.

Cut the ham into thin slices, about the same size as the fish pieces, and set aside.

Take four of the scallions, cutting them into 1½in pieces. Use only the white part and the part immediately next to it, discarding the roots and discolored stalks.

Place the remaining two scallions on a large plate. Arrange the fish, ham and mushrooms in layers – one piece of fish, one piece of ham, one piece of black mushroom – on top of the scallions until all the fish, ham and mushrooms are used. Sprinkle the chopped scallions and shredded ginger on top of them.

Bring 4 cups water to a boil in a wok. Put a wire rack in the wok and put the plate on top. Steam vigorously over a high heat for 5-7 minutes only.

Remove the plate of fish from the wok,

drain, and set aside.

Heat the oil in a pan. Add the garlic but remove it when it has browned and discard it. Pour the oil over the fish, draining away any excess from the plate. Add all the sauce ingredients to a pan, stir and bring to a boil. Pour over the fish and serve.

Red-Cooked Shad

INGREDIENTS *serves 3-4*
1½lb shad (bass can be substituted)
3 tbsp lard for frying
3 tbsp soy sauce
1 tbsp sugar
2 tbsp rice wine or dry sherry
⅓ cup bamboo shoots, cut into small slices
2-3 dried Chinese mushrooms, soaked
1 tsp salt
2 scallions
2 slices fresh ginger root, peeled
1 tbsp cornstarch
1¼ cups water

METHOD
Clean the shad or bass, wash and dry it thoroughly. Cut it into slices of uniform thickness.

Warm up the lard, coat the skin of fish with soy sauce and fry for 5 minutes. Turn it over, add the remaining soy sauce, sugar, rice wine or sherry, bamboo shoots,

▲ *Steamed Sea Bass with Black Mushrooms and Chinese Ham: Chinese black mushrooms, ginger and soy sauce are sufficient to give an authentic Chinese flavor to an everyday meal. If sea bass is not available, other fish may be substituted.*

▼ *The first stage in cutting the fish. It has been split in half and the backbone removed.*

mushrooms, salt, scallions, ginger root and water; bring it to a boil and bubble over a high heat for 5 minutes. Reduce heat and simmer for 15 minutes, by then the juice should be reduced somewhat. Remove the fish onto a plate, add the cornstarch to thicken the gravy, then pour it over the fish and serve.

Squirrel Fish

INGREDIENTS *serves 4-6*
1 whole fish, 1½-2lb
3 slices fresh ginger root
1½ tsp salt
pepper to taste
3-4 tbsp cornstarch
vegetable oil for deep-frying

SAUCE
2 tbsp Wood Ears
6 medium dried Chinese mushrooms
2 scallions
2 tbsp lard
⅙ cup canned bamboo shoots, drained
3 tbsp soy sauce
1 tbsp sugar
4 tbsp good stock
2 tbsp wine vinegar
2 tbsp rice wine or dry sherry

METHOD
This dish derives its name from the fact that, when cooked and served, the fish's tail curves up like a squirrel's.

Clean the fish and slit open from head to tail on the underside so that it lays flat. Cut 7-8 deep slashes on one side of the fish and only 2 on the other side. Finely chop the ginger. Rub the fish inside and out with the salt, pepper and ginger, then coat in the cornstarch.

Soak the Wood Ears and mushrooms separately in hot water to cover for 25 minutes. Drain and discard the tough stalks. Cut the mushroom caps into shreds. Finely slice the Wood Ears. Cut the scallions into 2in sections.

Heat the oil in a wok or deep-fryer. When hot, gently fry the fish over medium heat for 4 minutes, then reduce the heat to low. Meanwhile, melt the lard in a smaller wok or pan. When hot, stir-fry the Wood Ears, mushrooms, scallions and bamboo shoots over medium heat for 1½ minutes. Add the soy sauce, sugar, stock, vinegar and wine or sherry.

Stir the ingredients over low heat for 2 minutes. Raise the heat under the wok containing the fish and fry for another 2 minutes. The tail should have curled by now due to an uneven amount of cuts on the fish. Finally, lift out the fish, drain it and place it on a heated dish.

Fried Grouper with Vegetables

INGREDIENTS *serves 3-4*
12oz grouper or other firm white fish steak
¼lb seasonal greens
1 carrot
2-3 Chinese dried mushrooms, soaked
1 slice ginger root, peeled and finely chopped
1 scallion, cut into short lengths
1 tsp salt
1 egg white
2 tbsp soy sauce
2 tbsp rice wine (or sherry)
1 tbsp sugar
½ tbsp cornstarch
1 tsp sesame seed oil
oil for deep-frying

METHOD
Mix the fish steak with a little salt, the egg white and cornstarch.

Wash and cut the greens, cut the carrot into thin slices and cut each mushroom into two or three pieces.

Deep-fry the fish pieces until lightly golden; scoop out and drain.

Pour off the excess oil leaving about 2 tbsp in the wok; stir-fry the ginger root, scallion, greens, mushrooms and carrot; add salt; blend well. Now add the fish pieces with soy sauce, rice wine or sherry and sugar; stir gently for 3-4 minutes, then thicken the gravy with cornstarch mixed with a little water. Finally add sesame seed oil and serve.

▲ *Crispy Squirrel Fish: when the fish is scored on one side and deep fried, the tail curls up to look like a squirrel's tail. Usually served in sweet-and-sour sauce, this dish is popular in north China and along the Yangtze River.*

Fish in Wine-Lee Sauce

INGREDIENTS *serves 4-6*
1½lb fillet of white fish such as sea bass, cod, turbot or halibut
½ egg white
2 tsp cornstarch
3-4 Wood Ears
¾ cup peanut oil

SAUCE
3 tsp rice wine or 2tsp wine-lee paste if available
1 tsp salt
1½ tbsp sugar
1 cup stock
1 tbsp cornstarch dissolved in 2 tbsp water

METHOD
Cut the fish fillet into six pieces and mix it with egg white and 2 tsp cornstarch. Soak the mushrooms in water for 30 minutes and cut them into small pieces.

Heat a pan until it is very hot. Pour in the peanut oil to heat for 20 seconds and add the sliced fish to fry for 15 seconds. Remove and drain away the oil. Add 1tbsp peanut oil, the sauce, the fish and the mushrooms. Finally add the cornstarch to the pan to thicken the sauce. Serve.

Fish Rolls

INGREDIENTS *serves 4-6*
½lb filleted sole
4 medium dried black mushrooms
¼ tsp salt
1 tsp oil
1 small piece ham
1½oz bamboo shoots
2 cups peanut oil (to fry fish rolls)
½ tsp garlic, chopped
½ tsp fresh ginger root, chopped

SEASONINGS
½ tsp salt
1½ tsp cornstarch
½ egg white

SAUCE
2 tbsp stock
1 tbsp oyster sauce
2 tsp soy sauce
1 tsp rice wine or dry sherry
1 tsp cornstarch

METHOD
Cut the fish into pieces approximately
1½×2½in.

Soak the mushrooms in a small bowl of
hot water for 30 minutes. Add ¼ tsp salt and
1 tsp oil to the mushrooms and steam them
for 10 minutes. Shred the mushrooms,
discarding the stems.

Mix the seasoning ingredients and coat
the fish thoroughly with the mixture. Slice
the ham and the bamboo shoots to
matchstick-sized shreds about ¾in long.

Place a combination of the ham, bamboo
shoots and mushrooms in the center of each
fish fillet. Roll the fish up around the
mixture and dust with flour.

Heat the peanut oil until very hot and fry
a few fish rolls for 10-20 seconds until they
become golden. Remove and set aside.
Repeat until all the fish rolls are fried.

Re-heat the pan until it is very hot and
pour in 1tbsp peanut oil. Add the garlic and
ginger to sauté. Return the fish rolls to the
pan. Mix the sauce ingredients and add to
the pan, turning the fish rolls over in the
boiling sauce over a high heat for 10
seconds. Serve as an accompaniment to
soup.

Steamed Whole Fish Wrapped in Lotus Leaves

INGREDIENTS *serves 4-6*
1 whole fish, about 2lb
1½ tbsp dark soy sauce
2 lotus leaves
3 tbsp vegetable oil
1 tsp salt

GARNISH AND SAUCE
3-4oz canned snow pickles
3 slices fresh ginger root
2 scallions
2 fresh chili peppers
2 tbsp light soy sauce

2 tbsp rice wine or dry sherry
6 tbsp good stock
2 tsp sugar

METHOD
Clean the fish and dry well. Rub inside and
out with the soy sauce and salt. Shred the
pickles, ginger, scallions and fresh chilies,
discarding seeds. Soak the lotus leaves in
warm water for 10 minutes to soften. Drain.

Heat the oil in a wok or skillet. When hot,
stir-fry pickles, scallions, ginger and chilies
over medium heat for 1 minute. Add the soy
sauce, rice wine or sherry, stock and sugar,
bring to a boil and stir for 30 seconds. Place
the fish on the lotus leaves. Pour half the
contents of the wok or pan over the length of

◀ *Steamed Whole Fish Wrapped in Lotus Leaves.*

the salt, sugar, monosodium glutamate, wine, lard, scallions and ginger root evenly on top of the fish. Steam vigorously for 20 minutes; discard the scallions and ginger root before serving.

Shredded Fish and Celery

INGREDIENTS *serves 4-6*
½lb fish fillet or steak
2 cups celery heart
2 egg whites
1 tsp salt
½ tbsp rice wine (or sherry)
1 tsp monosodium glutamate
2 tsp sesame seed oil
1½ tbsp soy sauce
½ tbsp cornstarch
½ cup stock
lard for deep-frying

GARNISH
2 tbsp shredded cooked ham

METHOD
Discard all skin and bones from the fish; cut it into match-size shreds; marinate it with rice wine or sherry, salt, egg whites and cornstarch.

Parboil the celery heart for 1-2 minutes; cool it in cold water then cut it into small shreds. Place it on a serving plate; add ½ tsp monosodium glutamate and 1 tsp sesame seed oil, mix well.

Deep-fry the fish shreds in lard over a medium heat for about 4 minutes; separate them with chopsticks or a fork. When all the shreds are floating on the surface of the lard, scoop them out and drain. Gently press them with a spatula, then put them to soak in the stock for a while to cool. Take them out and place on top of the celery. Garnish with ham shreds.

Make a dressing by mixing a tablespoon stock with the soy sauce and the remaining monosodium glutamate and sesame seed oil. Pour it all over the dish and serve.

the fish. Turn the fish over and pour over the remainder. Wrap the fish completely in the lotus leaves. Secure by tying with string. Place in a steamer and steam for 25 minutes.

Steamed Fish

Carp, perch or bream are best, but bass or trout can be substituted.

INGREDIENTS *serves 4-6*
1½lb fish
2 tbsp cooked ham cubes
⅙ cup chopped bamboo shoots
2 large Chinese dried mushrooms soaked
⅛ cup pork fat
1½ tsp salt
1 tsp sugar
½ tsp monosodium glutamate
½ tbsp Shaoxing wine or sherry
2 scallions
2 slices ginger root
2 tbsp lard

METHOD
Scale and gut the fish; clean and dry well. Trim off fins and tail, score the body three or four times half way down, then place it on an oblong dish. Cut the ham, bamboo shoots, mushrooms and pork fat into match-size shreds; arrange them in four different rows according to color in a star shape. Spread

◄ *Sweet and Sour Carp, a specialty of Shandong.*

▲ *Steamed Sea Bass.*

► *Steamed Bass in Salted Black Beans.*

Sweet and Sour Carp

This is the specialty of Jinan (Tsinan), the provincial capital of Shandong. The locally produced vinegar made from Kao Liang (sorghum) and millet, matured in the hot sun, has the same color as the muddy waters of the Yellow River. It tastes much stronger than ordinary vinegar.

INGREDIENTS *serves 4-6*
1½lb Yellow River carp
a little salt
a little all-purpose flour
oil for deep-frying
5-6 Wood Ears, soaked
4-5 water chestnuts, peeled
⅓ cup bamboo shoots
2-3 scallions
2 slices ginger root, peeled
1 clove garlic, finely chopped

SAUCE
3 tbsp wine vinegar
3 tbsp sugar
2 tbsp soy sauce
2 tbsp rice wine (or sherry)
2 tsp cornstarch
½ cup clear stock

METHOD
Scale and gut the carp and clean thoroughly. Score the fish on both sides diagonally in a criss-cross pattern down to the bone. Lift the fish up by the ends so the cuts open up, spread a little salt into them followed by a little flour, then coat the whole fish from head to tail with flour.

Cut the Wood Ears into thin slices together with the bamboo shoots and water chestnuts. Shred the scallions and ginger root into the size of matches, and finely chop the garlic.

Heat up the oil in a wok until it smokes. Holding the fish by the tail, gently lower it into the hot oil, bending the body so that the cuts open up; use a spatula beneath the body to prevent it from sticking to the wok. After 2 minutes turn the fish on its side with its stomach facing up, still holding the tail to make sure the body is kept curved. Cook for 2 more minutes, then turn the fish over so that its stomach is now facing down; after 2 minutes cook the fish on its flat side again, tilting the wok so that the head is in the oil. When the fish has been cooked for 8 minutes in all, take it out (carefully!) and place it on a long dish.

Pour off the excess oil in the wok. Fry the scallions, ginger root and garlic; add the vinegar followed by the rest of the ingredients, together with the sauce mixture; stir and bring to a boil; pour it all over the fish and serve.

96

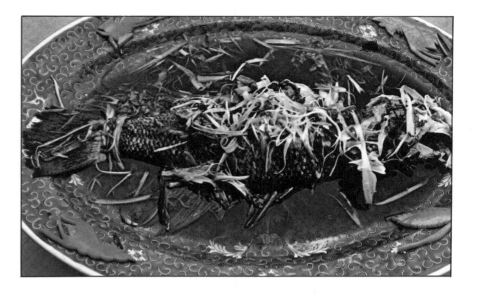

Steamed Bass in Salted Black Beans

INGREDIENTS *serves 4-6*
1½lb bass
⅙ cup pork fat
⅙ cup bamboo shoots
2-3 Chinese dried mushrooms, soaked
2 cloves garlic
2 slices ginger root, peeled
2 scallions
2 tbsp salted black beans
1 tbsp lard or oil
½ tbsp cornstarch

SAUCE
1 tbsp soy sauce
2 tsp sugar
1 tbsp rice wine (or sherry)
2 tbsp stock

GARNISH
shredded scallion
Chinese parsley (fresh coriander)

METHOD
Scale and gut the fish, clean well then plunge it into a pot of boiling water; take it out as soon as the water starts to boil again. Place it on a plate.

Dice the pork fat, bamboo shoots and mushrooms into small cubes.

Crush one clove garlic with the salted black beans, Finely chop the remaining garlic with ginger root and scallions.

Mix the sauce in a jug or bowl.

Heat up the lard or oil; first fry the garlic, ginger root and scallions. When they start to turn golden, add the crushed garlic and black beans followed by the pork, bamboo shoots, mushrooms and the sauce mixture. Bring it to a boil, then add the cornstarch mixed with a little cold water; stir to make into a smooth sauce; pour it all over the fish.

Place the fish in a steamer and steam vigorously for 20 minutes.

Stir-Fried Squid-Flowers and Broccoli

INGREDIENTS *serves 4-6*
1lb squid
2 cups broccoli flowerets
2 scallions
2 slices ginger root, peeled
1 tbsp rice wine (or sherry)
1 tbsp cornstarch
2 tsp salt
1 tsp sugar
4 tbsp oil
1 tsp sesame seed oil

METHOD
Clean the squid; discard the head and transparent backbone as well as the ink bag; make a criss-cross pattern on the outside, then cut into pieces about the size of a matchbox. Mix with 1 slice finely chopped ginger root, 1 tsp salt, rice wine or sherry and cornstarch.

Cut the broccoli into small flowerets, cut the scallions into 1in lengths, shred the remaining slice of ginger root.

Heat up 2 tbsp oil, toss in the scallions and ginger root, followed by the broccoli; add salt and sugar, stir for 2 minutes; remove and put aside.

Heat up the remaining oil, stir-fry the squid for about 1 minute; add the broccoli; blend well. Add the sesame seed oil and serve.

Steamed Sea Bass

INGREDIENTS *serves 4-6*
2lb sea bass
⅙ cup bamboo shoots
2-3 Chinese dried mushrooms, soaked
2 slices ginger root, peeled
2 scallions
1 leek
3 tbsp soy sauce
½ tbsp sugar
1 tbsp oil
1 tbsp rice wine (or sherry)
2 tbsp stock
1 tsp salt

METHOD
Scale and gut the fish, clean thoroughly, then plunge it into a pot of boiling water; take it out as soon as the water starts to boil again. Place it on a long dish.

Shred the bamboo shoots, mushrooms, ginger root, scallions and leek; place them on top of the fish, then pour the soy sauce, oil, sugar, rice wine or sherry, stock and salt over it. Steam vigorously for 20 minutes.

Fish Slices in Sweet and Sour Sauce

INGREDIENTS *serves 4-6*
½lb fish fillet (flounder, or sole)
2 tbsp cornstarch
2½ cups for deep-frying

SAUCE
1 tbsp sugar
1 tbsp soy sauce
1 tbsp vinegar
1 tbsp rice wine (or sherry)
1 tbsp cornstarch
½ tsp monosodium glutamate
1 tbsp lard
1 slice ginger root, finely chopped
1 scallion, finely chopped

METHOD
Cut the fish into small, thin slices about the size of a book of matches and coat them with cornstarch.

Heat up the oil in a wok or deep-fryer over a high heat until smoking. Then reduce the heat and use a pair of chopsticks to put the fish slices into the oil and deep-fry them for about 2 minutes or until golden. Remove and drain.

Heat up the lard in a hot wok or pan; meanwhile, mix the sugar, soy sauce, vinegar, wine or sherry, cornstarch and monosodium glutamate in a bowl. Toss the finely chopped ginger root and scallion into the hot lard, then pour in the sauce mixture and stir until thickened; now add the fish slices, blend well so that each piece is coated with the sauce, then serve.

▲ *Fish Slices in Sweet and Sour Sauce. Most people associate this sauce with Cantonese cooking, but in fact it originated in the north.*

▶ *Squid and Peppers Shrimp Balls.*

▼ *Fried Bass in Sweet and Sour Sauce.*

Fried Bass in Sweet and Sour Sauce

INGREDIENTS *serves 4-6*
1½-2lb sea bass
1 tsp salt
2 tbsp flour
oil for deep-frying

SAUCE
2 tbsp sugar
2 tbsp vinegar
1 tbsp soy sauce
½ tbsp cornstarch
2 tbsp stock or water

GARNISH
2 scallions
2 slices ginger root, peeled
1 small red pepper
Chinese parsley (fresh coriander)

METHOD
Clean and scale the fish, slash both sides diagonally at intervals. Rub salt both inside and out, then coat with flour.

Thinly shred the scallions, ginger root and red pepper.

Deep-fry the fish in hot oil until golden; place it on a long dish.

Pour off the excess oil from the wok, put in the sauce mixture and stir until smooth, then pour it over the fish. Garnish with shredded scallions, ginger root, red pepper and Chinese parsley.

Squid and Peppers with Shrimp Balls

INGREDIENTS *serves 4-6*
1lb squid
2 cups green peppers
1 tsp salt
1 tsp sugar
1 tbsp crushed black bean sauce
2 green chili peppers
1 slice ginger root, peeled
1 scallion
1 tbsp rice wine (or sherry)
1 tbsp soy sauce
oil for deep-frying
20 deep-fried shrimp balls

METHOD
Discard the soft bone, head and ink bag of the squid; peel off the skin and make a criss-cross pattern on the outside, then cut into slices not much bigger than a matchbox.

Cut the green peppers into slices roughly the same size as the squid, finely chop the ginger root, scallion and green chili.

Deep-fry the squid for 1 minute, remove and drain. Pour off the excess oil leaving about 2 tbsp in the wok. Toss in the ginger root, scallion and chilies followed by green peppers; add salt and sugar; stir for a short while then add the squid together with the crushed black bean sauce, rice wine or sherry and soy sauce. Cook for about 1½ minutes and blend everything well. Serve with deep-fried shrimp balls decorating the edge of the plate.

Sautéed Fish Steaks with Garnish

INGREDIENTS *serves 4-6*
1½-2lb fish, cut into 4-6 steaks
2 tsp salt
pepper to taste
6 tbsp vegetable oil
5 slices fresh ginger root

GARNISH AND SAUCE
4 medium dried Chinese mushrooms
2 scallions
2 tbsp lard
2 tbsp onion, coarsely chopped
1½ tbsp fresh ginger root, chopped
4oz ground pork
3 tbsp soy sauce
4 tbsp good stock
2 tbsp rice wine (or sherry)

METHOD
Clean and dry the fish steaks. Rub with salt, pepper and 1 tbsp of the oil. Soak the dried mushrooms in hot water to cover for 25 minutes. Drain and discard the tough stalks. Cut the mushroom caps into matchstick-size shreds. Cut the scallions into 1in sections.

Heat the remaining oil in a wok or skillet. When hot, add the ginger slices and spread out evenly to flavor the oil. Lay the fish steaks in the hot flavored oil and shallow-fry or sauté for 2 minutes on each side. Pour away any excess oil and remove from the heat. Heat the lard in a separate pan. When hot, stir-fry the chopped onion, ginger and mushrooms for 1 minute. Add the ground pork and stir over high heat for 3 minutes. Mix in the soy sauce, stock, wine or sherry and scallions. Bring to the boil and continue to stir-fry for 1 minute. Meanwhile, reheat the first pan and return the fish steaks to it. Heat through, then pour the sauce and garnish over the fish. Transfer contents to a heated serving plate.

Fish in Hot Sauce

INGREDIENTS *serves 4-6*

1½lb freshwater fish
2 tbsp chili paste
1 tbsp tomato paste
1 tbsp soy sauce
2 tbsp rice wine (or sherry)
½ tbsp sugar
1 cup stock
2 slices ginger root, peeled and finely
  chopped
1 clove garlic, finely chopped
1 tbsp vinegar
2 scallions, finely chopped
1 tbsp cornstarch
oil for deep-frying

METHOD

Scale and gut the fish, clean well. Slash each side diagonally four or five times as deep as the bone.

Heat up the oil, deep-fry the fish until golden, turning it over once or twice; remove and drain.

Pour off the excess oil leaving about 1 tbsp in the wok; put in the chili paste, tomato paste, soy sauce, rice wine (or sherry), sugar, stock, finely chopped ginger root and garlic. Bring it to a boil, put the fish back; reduce heat and cook gently for a few minutes turning it over two or three times. Place the fish on a serving dish. Increase the heat, add vinegar and scallions to the sauce, thicken it with the cornstarch then pour it over the fish and serve.

▶ *Fish in Hot Sauce.*

▶▶ *Fish-Head Casserole: this everyday family dish is a Hakka specialty. It is both economical and delicious.*

F*ish*-H*ead Casserole*

Normally the head of a variegated carp (also known as Bighead) is used.

INGREDIENTS *serves 4-6*

1lb fish-head
1 thin slice lean pork
3-4 Chinese dried mushrooms, soaked
2 cakes tofu
2 slices ginger root, peeled
2 scallions
1 tsp salt
2 tbsp rice wine (or sherry)
1 tbsp soy sauce
2 tbsp soy sauce
2 tbsp flour
1¼ cup stock
oil for deep-frying

SAUCE

scallions
red chili peppers
Chinese parsley (fresh coriander)

METHOD

Discard the gills from the fish-head; rub some salt both inside and out; coat the head with flour.

Cut the pork, mushrooms, tofu and ginger root into small slices; cut the scallions into short lengths.

Deep-fry the fish-head over a moderate heat for 10 minutes or until golden. Remove.

Heat a little oil in a sand-pot or casserole. Put in the ginger root and scallions, followed by pork, mushrooms and bean-curd; stir for a while then add rice wine or sherry, sugar, soy sauce, stock and the fish-head; bring it to a boil; add a little salt, reduce heat and simmer for about 7 minutes.

Garnish with scallions, red chili and Chinese parsley (fresh coriander). Serve in a sand-pot or casserole. It is absolutely delicious.

Smoked White Fish French Style

INGREDIENTS *serves 4-6*
1¼lb white fish, such as turbot

SEASONINGS
4 tbsp Western sauce (see below)
¼ tsp white pepper
1 tsp onion powder
1 tsp sugar
1 tsp sherry
1 tbsp butter

GARNISH
½ lettuce
2 tomatoes
4 pieces ham (about 4oz each)
2-3 tbsp mayonnaise

METHOD
Cut the fish into 4 big pieces. Mix the seasonings together and marinate the fish in the mixture for 7-8 hours or overnight.

Drain the fish and bake it in a moderate oven (250°) for 15 minutes. Butter the fish on both sides for a further 10 minutes. Shred the lettuce and slice the tomatoes. Halve each piece of ham. Put the fish on a hot plate and garnish with lettuce, tomatoes, ham and mayonnaise.

To make Western sauce, finely shred 4oz each of celery, carrot and scallion and 2 bay leaves. Add the shredded vegetables to ½pt chicken stock and cook over medium heat until the liquid has reduced by about 50 percent.

▲ ▲ *Smoked White Fish French Style.*

▲ *Tofu Fish in Chili Sauce, garnished with shredded scallions to give a touch of color.*

Braised Fish

In China, only carp from the lower reaches of the Yellow River would be used in this dish; it has golden yellow scales and a delicate flesh. The best season for eating them is the summer months (May to September).

INGREDIENTS *serves 4-6*
1½lb Yellow River carp
2 tbsp soy sauce
½ tbsp sugar
2½ cups clear stock
1½ tbsp rice wine (or sherry)
1 tbsp crushed yellow tofu
2 scallions, finely chopped
1 slice ginger root, peeled and finely chopped
oil for deep-frying

METHOD
Should you find the Yellow River a little too far for you to catch your carp, then by all means use any freshwater fish, only do not expect the same result. No other fish has quite the same taste and I think it is an experience everyone has the right to at least once in their lifetime.

Scale and gut the fish and clean it thoroughly. Score both sides of the fish diagonally down to the bone at intervals of about ¼in. There are two reasons for doing this; since the fish is to be cooked whole, it prevents the skin from bursting; and it allows the heat to penetrate quickly and at the same time helps to diffuse the flavor of the seasoning and sauce.

Heat up about 4⅜ cups oil in a wok or deep-fryer, fry the fish until golden, take it out and drain.

Leave about 1 tbsp oil in the wok, put in the finely chopped scallions, ginger root and sugar; stir to dissolve the sugar, then add the bean sauce, followed by the rice wine or sherry, soy sauce, stock and the fish. Bring to a boil, then reduce the heat and cook until the juice is reduced by half; turn the fish over and continue cooking until the juice is almost evaporated.

Be careful not to break up the fish when lifting it out of the wok; it does not look right unless the fish is served whole with both head and tail intact.

▲ *Braised Fish. The diamond-patterned scoring helps to diffuse the heat, and also makes the finished dish look attractive.*

Tofu Fish in Chili Sauce

The original recipe recommends a carp for this dish but there is no reason why you should not use a sea fish if preferred.

INGREDIENTS *serves 4-6*
1lb mullet or mackerel
2 scallions, white parts only
1 clove garlic
2 slices ginger root, peeled
2 cakes tofu
1 tsp salt
4 tbsp oil
2 tbsp chili paste
1 tbsp soy sauce
2 tbsp rice wine (or sherry)
1 tbsp cornstarch
1½ cups stock

METHOD
Cut the heads off the fish and remove the backbone; crush the garlic, cut it and the ginger root into small pieces; cut the scallion whites into short lengths.

Cut each tofu into about 10 pieces. Blanch them in boiling water; remove and soak them in stock with salt.

Heat up the oil until hot; fry the fish until both sides are golden; put them to one side; tilt the wok, and put in the chili paste. When it starts to bubble, return the wok to its original position, push the fish back, add soy sauce, rice wine or sherry, scallion, ginger root, garlic and a little stock - about ½ cup. At the same time add the tofu taken from the stock and cook with the fish for about 10 minutes.

Now pick out the fish with chop-sticks and place them on a serving dish, then quickly mix the cornstarch with a little cold water. Add to the wok to make a smooth sauce with the tofu; pour it all over the fish and serve.

Braised Whole Fish in Hot Vinegar Sauce

INGREDIENTS *serves 4-6*
2 slices fresh ginger root
1½-2lb whole fish
1 tsp salt
pepper to taste
4 tbsp vegetable oil

SAUCE
3 slices fresh ginger root
⅓ cup canned bamboo shoots, drained
½ red pepper
1 small carrot
1 green chili pepper
2 dried chili peppers
2 scallions
2 tbsp lard
2 tbsp light soy sauce
3 tbsp good stock
6 tbsp vinegar
½ tbsp cornstarch blended with 2 tbsp
    water

METHOD
Finely chop the 2 slices of ginger. Clean the fish and dry well. Rub evenly inside and out with salt, pepper, chopped ginger and 1 tbsp of the oil. Leave to season for 30 minutes. Shred the 3 slices of ginger, bamboo shoots, red pepper, carrot, chilies, discarding seeds, and scallions.

Heat the remaining oil in a wok or skillet. When hot, fry the fish for 2½ minutes on each side. Remove and drain. Add the shredded ginger, bamboo shoots, red pepper, carrot, chilies and scallions to the remaining oil and stir-fry over medium heat for 1 minute. Add the lard, soy sauce, stock and half the vinegar and cook for another minute. Lay the fish back in the wok or pan and cook gently for 2 minutes on both sides, basting. Transfer the fish to a serving dish. Stir the remaining vinegar into the wok, then add the blended cornstarch, stirring over high heat until the sauce thickens.

Pour the sauce from the wok over the length of the fish and garnish with the shredded vegetables.

Stewed Four Treasures

If you have never heard of fish lip, then you do not know what you are missing! It is the lip of a special type of fairly large fish and is preserved like shark's fin but much easier to prepare.

It is bought in a dried state with bones attached and therefore has to be soaked in cold water for two or three days until the lip part becomes soft. After that, simmer it until all the bones can be easily removed. When this is done, clean the lip thoroughly. It is now ready for final preparation.

INGREDIENTS *serves 4-6*
¼lb soaked fish lip
¼lb canned abalone
¼lb broccoli
⅔ cup bamboo shoots
2 slices ginger root
2 cloves garlic
2-3 scallions
3 tbsp chicken fat
2 tbsp rice wine (or dry sherry)
½ cup chicken stock
1½ tbsp soy sauce
2 tsp sugar
1 tbsp cornstarch

METHOD
After the fish lip has been soaked and cleaned, cut it into pieces about the size of a matchbox, wash it once more, then steam over a high flame for about 30 minutes or until soft. Drain the abalone and cut it into pieces roughly the same size as the fish lip.

Wash the broccoli, cut it into small chunks diagonally and parboil for a few minutes only. Drain.

Cut the bamboo shoots also into thin slices the size of a matchbox. Now arrange these "four treasures" in four overlapping rows on a plate.

Slice the ginger root and garlic and cut the scallions into short lengths.

Warm up about 1½ tbsp chicken fat and, before it gets too hot, toss in the garlic, ginger root and scallions. Fry until golden, add rice wine or sherry and stock, bring it to a boil, then scoop out the garlic, ginger root and scallions and discard. Now take a deep breath: with one smooth movement deftly transfer the "four treasures" into the bubbling stock without disarranging them. Add soy sauce and sugar, bring it to a boil again, then pour the cornstarch mixed with a little water to cover the entire surface and add the rest of the chicken fat round the edge. Will you now have the nerve to toss the entire contents out and catch them on a plate without disturbing them? It requires skill as well as nerve. Try it and see: whatever the result, it will make tossing a pancake seem like child's play!

▲ *Braised Whole Fish in Hot Vinegar Sauce, garnished with shredded ginger, bamboo shoots, chilies, carrot and scallions.*

Sweet-Sour Crisp Fish

INGREDIENTS *serves 2-3*
1½lb carp (or freshwater fish)
2 tbsp rice wine (or sherry)
4 tbsp soy sauce
6 tbsp cornstarch
1 clove garlic
2 scallions
2 slices fresh ginger root
2 dried red chili peppers, soaked
⅙ cup bamboo shoots
2-3 dried Chinese mushrooms, soaked
oil for deep-frying
1½ tbsp sugar
1½ tbsp vinegar
½ cup stock

METHOD
Clean the fish; make 6 or 7 diagonal cuts as deep as the bone on each side of the fish. Marinate in rice wine or sherry and 2 tbsp of soy sauce for 15 minutes; remove and wipe dry. Make a paste with 4½ tbsp cornstarch and water and coat the entire fish evenly.

Finely chop the garlic, 1 scallion and 1 slice ginger root. Cut the other scallion and ginger root into thin shreds. Cut the soaked red chilies (discarding the seeds), bamboo shoots and mushrooms all into thin shreds.

Heat up the oil to boiling point, pick up the fish by the tail, lower it head first into the oil, turn it around and deep-fry for about 7 minutes or until golden; remove and drain.

Pour off the excess oil leaving about 2 tbsp in the wok; add finely chopped scallion, ginger root, garlic and red chili, bamboo shoots and mushrooms followed by the remaining soy sauce, sugar, vinegar and stock. Stir a few times, then add the remaining cornstarch mixed with a little water; blend well to make a slightly thick smooth sauce.

Place a cloth over the fish, press gently with your hand to soften the body, then put it on a serving dish and pour the sauce over it; garnish with scallion and ginger root shreds.

Yangtze Fish Salad

INGREDIENTS *serves 5-8*
1lb fish fillets, cod, haddock, sole or turbot
1½ tsp salt
1 egg
2oz cornstarch
3 slices fresh ginger root
3 stalks celery
3 scallions
4oz bean sprouts
vegetable oil for deep-frying
2 tbsp light soy sauce
1½ tbsp wine vinegar
1 tbsp chili sauce
1 tbsp sesame seed oil

METHOD
Cut the fish into thin slices, then cut the slices into matchstick-sized strips. Rub in the salt, coat with the beaten egg and dust with the cornstarch. Cut the ginger into thin shreds. Cut the celery into thick matchstick-sized strips. Blanch the celery in a pan of boiling water for 1½ minutes, then drain.

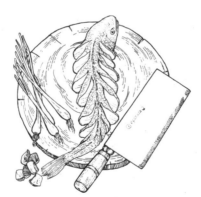

▲ *How to cut the fish for Sweet-Sour Crisp Fish.*

▼ *Fish and Tofu Casserole.*

Cut the scallions into 2in sections. Wash the bean sprouts and drain thoroughly.

Heat the oil in a wok or deep-fryer. When hot, fry the fish in 2 batches for about 2 minutes. Drain.

Place the celery and bean sprouts in the base of a deep-sided dish. Arrange the strips of fish, like French fries, in one layer on top. Sprinkle with the ginger, scallions, soy sauce, vinegar, chili sauce and sesame seed oil. Toss the salad before eating.

Fish and Tofu Casserole

The original recipe calls for a species of fish only to be found hidden under rocks in the waters off the two Guangs. Its nearest Western equivalent is called the grouper and belongs to the family *Serranidae*. The flesh is firm, delicately flavored and free of bone. Bass or sea perch can be substituted.

INGREDIENTS *serves 2-4*
¼lb fish steak
2 cakes tofu
⅓ cup chopped cooked ham
2 egg whites
1 tsp salt
½ tsp monosodium glutamate (optional)
1 slice ginger root, peeled
1 scallion
1 tsp sesame seed oil
1 tbsp cornstarch
2½ cups stock
freshly ground Sichuan pepper
2 tbsp oil
Chinese parsley as garnish

METHOD
Cut the fish into thin strips. Coarsely chop the tofu and finely chop the ham. Shred the ginger root and scallion.

Heat up the oil; toss in the ginger root followed by the fish; stir gently for a while; add stock, salt, and tofu; bring it to a boil. Thicken with cornstarch mixed with a little water, then add egg whites, sesame seed oil and the scallion; blend well. Transfer to a dish or serve in a casserole garnished with chopped ham and Chinese parsley.

Steamed Eel

INGREDIENTS *serves 4-6*
2lb white eel
6 slices fresh ginger root
2 scallions
8 tbsp peanut oil
1 tsp Chinese yellow wine
$\frac{1}{2}$pt chicken stock
1 tsp salt
1 tsp sugar
$\frac{1}{2}$ tsp pepper
1 tbsp cornstarch

METHOD

Put the eel in a basin and pour over it $2\frac{1}{4}$pts boiling water with 2 tbsp salt added. Wash the fish thoroughly. Slit the eel open, remove the intestines and clean the inside carefully. Pat it dry with absorbent paper towels.

Make deep cuts (about three-quarters of the way through the flesh) at 1in intervals along the eel and place it on a plate, bending it into a ring form. Arrange the ginger and scallion on top.

Steam the eel over a medium heat for 20 minutes. Remove the ginger and scallions and discard them and drain away the liquid from the plate. Heat the oil and pour it over the eel, again draining any excess from the plate.

Add the remaining ingredients to the pan, stir and bring to a boil. Pour the sauce over the eel and serve.

Sizzling Eel

INGREDIENTS *serves 4-6*
2lb yellow eels
10 cups boiling water
2 tbsp salt
4 tbsp peanut oil
2 tsp fresh ginger root, chopped
$\frac{1}{2}$ tsp pepper
2 tsp Chinese yellow wine
1 tbsp sugar
2 tbsp dark soy sauce
8 tbsp chicken stock
$1\frac{1}{2}$ tbsp cornstarch dissolved in $1\frac{1}{2}$ tbsp water
2 tsp scallion, chopped
2 tbsp sesame seed oil
2 tsp ham, ground
$1\frac{1}{2}$ tsp fresh coriander, chopped

METHOD

Place the eels in a basin. Pour over them the boiling water (to which has been added 2 tbsp salt) and let them stand for 3 minutes. Take the eels out of the water and rinse them in cold water from the tap.

Separate the meat from the bone with the handle of a teaspoon, then cut the eel meat into $\frac{1}{2} \times 2$in strips. Set aside. Heat the oil until very hot. Add the eel, stirring, and add the chopped ginger, pepper, yellow wine, sugar, soy sauce and chicken stock. Cook for 5 minutes. Stir in the cornstarch and transfer to a plate. Make a small well in the center of the eels and put into it the chopped scallion.

Heat 2 tbsp sesame seed oil until very hot and pour it into the "well." Add the ham, garnish with coriander and serve.

Steamed Eel with Pickled Plum and Soy Bean Paste

INGREDIENTS *serves 4-6*

2lb freshwater eel

2 tbsp salt

4-6 pickled plums (remove and discard the pits)

1 tbsp sugar

2 tbsp soya bean paste

2 tsp dark soy sauce

2 tsp garlic, chopped

1-2 tsp red chili pepper, finely shredded

2 tbsp peanut oil

1 tbsp chopped coriander

METHOD

Rub the eel with 2 tbsp salt. Put it in a basin and pour over it approximately 1½pts boiling water. Clean and pat dry. Cut off the back fin, slit it open from the back and remove the bones. Cut the eel into sections 2in long and place them on a large plate.

Mix together the pickled plums, sugar, soy bean paste, dark soy sauce, chopped garlic and finely shredded red chili and spread evenly over the eel. Steam over medium heat for 35 minutes. Pour 2 tbsp very hot (boiling) peanut oil over the fish, sprinkle with the chopped coriander and serve.

◀ *Steamed Eel.*

◀ *Sizzling Eel: eel is a favorite dish all along the Yangtze River. The eel is first fried, then cut into strips to be given a turn in a highly spiced sauce; and is best served with quantities of rice.*

▲ *Shark's Fin with Crab Meat in Brown Sauce: in this treatment of a traditional delicacy, the sweetness of the crab meat, with its color, provides a visual and full-flavored contrast with the shark's fin.*

◀ *Aromatic Chiu Chow Rich Fish Soup: the Chinese seldom use rice for soup. But this is a thick soup, the consistency of thin porridge, which is eaten for supper or perhaps for breakfast rather than as an accompaniment to other dishes.*

Aromatic Chiu Chow Rich Fish Soup

INGREDIENTS *serves 4-6*
5oz fillet of sea bream or other white
    fish
¼lb squid
1 tsp sesame seed oil
1 tsp salt
1 fillet dried sole
2-3 tbsp peanut oil
2 medium black mushrooms
1 Chinese celery
2½ cups chicken stock
1 cup plain cooked rice

METHOD

Cut the fillet of sea bream or whichever white fish you are using into thick slices and cut the squid into bite-sized pieces. Mix the fish and squid with 1 tsp sesame seed oil and 1 tsp salt.

Break or chop the fillet of dried sole into tiny pieces and deep-fry with 2-3 tbsp oil over low heat until crisp. Drain and set aside.

Soak the black mushrooms in hot water for 30 minutes. Remove and discard the stems and cut the caps into fine shreds. Chop the celery coarsely. Bring the chicken stock to a boil and add the celery, black mushrooms and rice. When the soup boils again, add the sliced fish and squid and when it boils again, sprinkle with chopped dried fish.

Shark's Fin with Crab Meat in Brown Sauce

INGREDIENTS *serves 4-6*
1½lb dried shark's fin, skin and bone
    removed
8 tbsp peanut oil
4 slices ginger root
1 scallion
4 cups chicken stock
½lb crab meat
1½ tbsp Chinese yellow wine
1 tbsp oyster sauce
1 tsp sugar
1 tbsp light soy sauce
½ tsp pepper
1 tsp sesame oil
2 tbsp cornstarch softened in 2 tbsp
    water
1 tsp dark soy sauce

METHOD

Prepare the shark's fin, following the method given in the recipe for Shark's Fin Consommé (page 202). Set it aside.

Heat the peanut oil in a pan. Add the ginger and scallion, but remove and discard them when they turn brown.

Add the shark's fin and the chicken stock to the pan and bring the mixture to a boil over medium heat. Add the crab meat and reduce the temperature to low.

When the mixture boils again add 1 tsp Chinese yellow wine and the oyster sauce, sugar, light soy sauce, pepper and sesame oil. Stir in the softened cornstarch, add the dark soy sauce and 1 tbsp Chinese yellow wine and serve.

West Lake Fish

INGREDIENTS *serves 4-6*
2lb carp
2 tbsp ginger, shredded
3 tbsp scallion, shredded
generous ½ cup peanut oil

SAUCE
1 cup chicken stock
1 tbsp sugar
1 tbsp brown vinegar
1 tsp salt
¼ tsp pepper
1½ tbsp cornstarch
2 tsp Chinese yellow wine

METHOD

Put the fish in a basin. Pour over it 5 cups boiling water and leave it to stand for 1 minute.

Scrape off the scales and place the fish on a chopping board. Slicing horizontally, cut the fish in two, one side with the backbone, the other without. On the side with the backbone, make five deep slits, approximately 1½in apart.

On the meat side of the other half make a long lengthwise slit, but do not cut through the skin.

Place the whole fish, including the head, on a plate. Spread the ginger and half the scallion over it and steam over a high heat for 10 minutes. Remove and discard the scallions and arrange the remaining fresh scallions on top of the fish. Heat ¼ cup peanut oil in a pan and pour it over the fish, draining away any excess from the plate.

Heat 2 tbsp oil in a pan and add the sauce ingredients. Bring the sauce to a boil, pour it over the fish and serve.

Fu Yung Crab Meat

Ideally you should use freshwater crabs as their meat is much more delicate, but they are almost impossible to obtain in the West.

INGREDIENTS *serves 4*
10oz crab meat
3 tbsp lard
2 tbsp rice wine or dry sherry
1 tbsp soy sauce
1 tbsp wine vinegar
1 tbsp sugar
6 egg whites
1 tsp cornstarch
2 cloves garlic, finely chopped
1 slice ginger root, peeled and finely
   chopped
2 scallions, finely chopped
2 large crab shells (or 4 small ones)
3 tbsp stock

METHOD
Warm up about 2 tbsp lard; fry about half of the finely chopped ginger root and scallions followed by the crab meat. Add rice wine or sherry, continue stirring until all the liquid has evaporated, then put the crab meat into the empty shells.

Beat the egg whites with salt and a little water until foamy; pour on top of the crab meat and steam the stuffed shells vigorously for 6 minutes. By then the egg whites will have become solid. Remove and place them on a long serving dish.

Heat the last tbsp lard, add the finely chopped garlic together with the remaining scallion and ginger root, followed by soy sauce, vinegar, sugar and stock. When it starts to bubble, add the cornstarch mixed with a little cold water. When it is smooth and thickened pour it over the crab meat and serve.

▶ *Fu Yung Crab Meat: the crab meat and egg-white mixture in the bamboo steamer.*

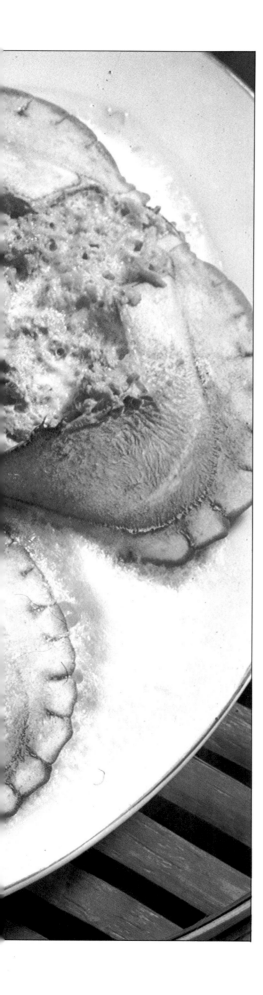

Sliced Abalone in Oyster Sauce with Lettuce

INGREDIENTS *serves 4-6*
1¼lb can abalone
⅔ cups peanut oil
1 tbsp salt
1¼lb lettuce
2-3 slices fresh ginger root
1-2 cloves garlic
1 tbsp Chinese yellow wine
2 tbsp oyster sauce
1 tsp dark soy sauce
1 tsp sesame oil
1 tsp sugar
4 tbsp chicken stock
4 tbsp abalone stock (from can)
1 tsp Chinese yellow wine
1 tbsp cornstarch

METHOD
Stand the unopened can of abalone in plenty of water and boil for 3 hours. Remove the abalone from the can, saving 4 tbsp juice to make the sauce. Trim the abalone into thin slices and set aside.

Heat 4 tbsp oil and the salt with 4 cups water in a pan. Bring to a boil and blanch the lettuce leaves for 1 minute. Remove, drain thoroughly and place on a serving dish.

Heat 6 tbsp oil in the pan and add the ginger and garlic. Remove and discard the garlic when it has turned brown. Add the abalone slices and 1 tbsp Chinese yellow wine and sauté them lightly.

Add the remaining ingredients, stir and cook for 30 seconds over medium heat. Transfer to the serving dish with the lettuce.

You can make this dish more saucy by using all the abalone stock from the can and doubling the portions of the other sauce ingredients.

▶ *Sliced Abalone in Oyster Sauce with Lettuce: properly prepared, abalone is a great delicacy and is deservedly one of the highlights of the Chinese banquet menu.*

Fukien Clam Soup

INGREDIENTS *serves 4-5*
3lb clams
2 tbsp salt
1½ tbsp dried shrimps
2 slices fresh ginger root
3 scallions
2 cloves garlic
2 tsp salt
pepper to taste
1½ chicken bouillon cubes
4 cups light soy sauce
1 tbsp vinegar
½ tsp sesame seed oil

METHOD
Wash and clean the clams well with a stiff brush under running water. Bring 5 cups water to a boil in a saucepan and add the salt. Simmer the clams for 2 minutes then leave to stand in the water, off the heat, for a further minute. Drain. Discard any clams which are unopened. Soak the dried shrimps in hot water for 5 minutes, then drain. Finely shred the ginger and scallions. Crush the garlic.

Place the poached clams in a saucepan. Add the dried shrimps, ginger, garlic, salt, pepper and crumbled bouillon cubes. Pour in the bouillon and bring to a boil. Reduce the heat and simmer for 10 minutes. Add the scallions, soy sauce and vinegar, and continue to simmer for another 5 minutes.

Place the clams and soup in a large heated serving bowl and sprinkle over the sesame seed oil. Serve in individual bowls and eat like moules marinière, or the dish can be eaten from a large central bowl.

Stir-Fried Crab in Curry Sauce

INGREDIENTS *serves 5-6*

2lb crab
2 tbsp cornstarch
2 cups peanut oil
6 slices fresh ginger root
2 tsp garlic, chopped
¼lb scallions cut into 2-in pieces
1 tbsp curry paste
1⅓ cups chicken stock
2 tsp sugar
1 tsp salt
1 tsp Chinese yellow wine

METHOD

Place the crab on a chopping board, belly side up, and cut through the middle with a cleaver, but avoid cutting into the top shell. Chop off the claws, lightly crush the shell and set them aside. Lift off the top shell and clean the crab, discarding the "dead men's fingers." Chop the body into 4 or 6 pieces, depending on the size, and lightly coat the crab meat with cornstarch.

Heat the oil in a pan and fry the crab for 2 minutes over a very high heat. Remove, drain and set aside.

Heat 2 tbsp oil in the pan. Add the ginger, garlic, scallion and curry paste, stir and cook for 1½ minutes.

Return the crab to the pan, stirring, and add the chicken stock, sugar and salt. Cover the pan and cook over medium heat for 10 minutes, turning the contents once or twice to ensure that they are evenly cooked. Sprinkle with Chinese yellow wine and serve.

▲ *Stir-Fried Crab in Curry Sauce.*

▶ *Crab Casserole.*

Deep-Fried Crab Meat Balls

INGREDIENTS

2 pieces dried tofu sheet
$\frac{1}{2}$lb shrimp, shelled and deveined
$\frac{1}{3}$ cup pork fat
$\frac{2}{3}$ cup water chestnuts
1 egg white
2 tbsp cornstarch
1 tbsp chopped leek (white part only)
1 tbsp chopped scallion
1 tsp salt
$\frac{1}{2}$ tsp pepper
$\frac{1}{4}$lb crab meat
3 cups peanut oil

METHOD

Soak the dried tofu sheets in water until they have softened. Remove and pat dry. Set aside. Grind or finely chop the shrimps and dice the pork fat and water chestnuts into small pieces.

Place the ground shrimps, the egg white and cornstarch in a mixing bowl and, using a fork, stir in one direction until the mixture becomes sticky and firm. Add the pork and continue stirring until the mixture is thick and firm.

Add the water chestnuts, stirring and mixing well, and then the chopped leek, the chopped scallion, the salt and pepper, and the crab meat, mixing each ingredient in thoroughly.

Place the tofu sheet on a board. Put the shrimp and crab meat mixture on it, making it into the shape of a thick sausage about 1in in diameter. Roll the tofu sheet firmly around the mixture, trimming off any excess at the ends.

Place the "sausage" on a heat-proof platter, and steam it over a high heat for 7 minutes. Remove, set aside and when it has cooled, cut it into $1\frac{1}{2}$in slices.

Heat the oil in a pan. When it is hot, add the crab meat slices. Reduce the heat to low and fry until the tofu wrapper is nicely golden in color. Serve with Chiu Chow tangerine jam.

Deep-fried shrimp balls and crab balls are often served together, so it is advisable to double the quantity given in the shrimp ball recipes and use half of the shrimp mixture in conjunction with the crab meat dish.

Crab Casserole

INGREDIENTS

2 crabs (approximately $1\frac{1}{4}$lb each)
1 tbsp cornstarch
3 cups peanut oil
2 tsp chopped garlic
3-4 slices fresh ginger root
2 stalks scallions

SEASONINGS

8 tbsp good stock
1 tbsp oyster sauce
1 tsp oil
few drops sesame oil
1 tsp sugar
1 tsp rice wine

METHOD

Clean the crabs and crush the pincers. Chop each crab into six pieces. Dry and dust with cornstarch.

Heat the peanut oil and fry the crabs for 1 minute. Remove the crab from the pan and drain the oil.

Heat the large pan or wok. Add the garlic, ginger and scallions and sauté for 15 seconds to release their aromatic flavors. Mix and turn them quickly with the crab before transferring the mixture to a casserole.

Add the seasonings. Cover the pot and cook for 2 minutes over a high heat, turning the contents from time to time.

Serve in the casserole.

Asparagus Topped with Crab Meat Sauce

INGREDIENTS *serves 4-6*

1 medium-sized crab
1¼lb fresh asparagus
4 tbsp peanut oil
8 tbsp chicken stock
4 slices fresh ginger root
1 clove garlic

SAUCE

1 egg white
8 tbsp chicken stock
1 tsp sesame seed oil
2 tsp Chinese yellow wine
½ tsp sugar
¼ tsp pepper
1½ tsp cornstarch

METHOD

Steam a medium-sized crab for 20 minutes. Scoop out the crab meat from the shells and set aside.

Clean the asparagus and cut the stalks into 1½in sections, discarding the part close to the roots.

Heat 1 tbsp oil and add the chicken stock to the pan. Cook the asparagus until the stock is almost absorbed. Transfer to a plate and set aside to keep warm. Heat 3 tbsp oil in the pan, add the ginger and garlic and when browned, remove and discard.

Add the crab meat to the pan and sauté for 30 seconds. Mix the sauce ingredients, stir into the pan and bring to a boil. Pour the mixture over the asparagus and serve.

◄ ▲ *Asparagus Topped with Crab Meat Sauce: Chinese chefs are famous for preparing vegetables in such a way as to maintain freshness and flavor. Here, the combination of asparagus and crab meat offers a particularly successful harmony of flavors.*

▲ *Crab Balls served cold, garnished with flower-cut cucumber and Chinese parsley (fresh coriander).*

▼ *Crab with Scallions and Ginger – fragrant and aromatic.*

Crab Balls

INGREDIENTS *serves 6-8*
½lb crab meat
⅓ cup pork fat
½ cup water chestnuts, peeled
2 eggs
2 tbsp rice wine or dry sherry
1 tsp monosodium glutamate (optional)
1 tsp salt
2 tbsp cornstarch
1 slice fresh ginger root, finely chopped
1 scallion, finely chopped
½ cup chicken stock
1lb lard for deep-frying
1oz cooked ham, finely chopped

METHOD
Finely chop the crab meat, pork fat and
water chestnuts and add 2 eggs, 1 tbsp wine
or sherry, ½ tsp monosodium glutamate (if
using), ½ tsp salt, and 1 tbsp cornstarch
together with the finely chopped ginger root
and scallion. Blend well, then make into
small balls about the size of walnuts.

Heat up the lard over high heat for about
3-4 minutes, then reduce the heat to
moderate and deep-fry the crab balls for
about 5 minutes until pale golden. Scoop
them out with a perforated spoon and serve
them hot or cold. Alternatively, place them
in a bowl with a little chicken stock – not
quite enough to cover them – then place the

bowl in a steamer and steam for 15 minutes.
Now mix the remaining wine or sherry,
monosodium glutamate (if using), salt and
cornstarch with the chicken stock and make
a white sauce over a moderate heat, then
pour it over the crab balls. Garnish with
finely chopped ham and serve.

Crab with Scallions and Ginger

INGREDIENTS *serves 4*
1 crab (about 1lb)
4-5 scallions, finely chopped
4-6 slices ginger root, peeled and finely
    chopped
2 tbsp rice wine or dry sherry
1 tbsp cornstarch
2 tbsp soy sauce
1 tbsp sugar
1 tbsp vinegar
4 tbsp oil
greens to garnish

METHOD
Separate the legs and claws of the crabs. If
the crabs are large, break the body into two
or three pieces. Heat up the oil and fry the
crab pieces until golden. Remove and drain.

Toss in the finely chopped scallions and
ginger root in what is left of the oil in the

wok; add soy sauce, sugar, rice wine or
sherry and vinegar. Thicken with cornstarch
mixed with a little cold water, then return
the crab pieces to be coated by this sauce.
Blend well and serve.

Crab with Fermented Beans and Peppers

INGREDIENTS *serves 4-6*
2 crabs (approximately 1lb each)
2 red chili peppers
1 green bell pepper
4 pieces ginger root
3 scallions
2 cloves garlic
2 cups peanut oil (for frying crab)
3 tsp salted, fermented soy beans
8 tbsp stock or chicken soup

SEASONING
1 tsp sugar
1 tsp salt
2 tsp oyster sauce
½ tsp monosodium glutamate (optional)
2 tsp rice wine or dry sherry

METHOD
Clean the crabs and chop the flesh of each
into 6 pieces. Finely chop the chili and the
green pepper. Slice the ginger and cut the
scallions into ¾in pieces. Crush and chop
the garlic.

Heat the oil in a pan and add the crab,
ginger and scallions. Fry for 2 minutes and
remove from the pan to drain. Re-heat the
pan to smoking point and add 1 tbsp oil. Fry
the garlic and beans for 10 seconds, then
return the crab to the pan.

Mix the seasoning ingredients with the
stock or chicken soup and add the mixture
to the pan. Turn and stir contents for 30
seconds. Serve.

◄ *Crab with Fermented Beans and*
Peppers: fermented beans, more
commonly known as black beans, are
widely used in Cantonese cooking, usually
with red chili and garlic. Together they
make a unique spicy sauce that is
unmistakably Cantonese.

Steamed Lobster

INGREDIENTS *serves 2-4*
1½-2lb lobster

SAUCE
2 scallions, finely chopped
2 slices fresh ginger root, finely chopped
1 tsp salt
1 tsp sugar
½ tbsp cornstarch
1 tsp sesame seed oil
4 tbsp stock
freshly ground Sichuan pepper
1 tbsp oil

METHOD
Steam the lobster for 20 minutes. Leave to cool, then split in two lengthwise, and cut each half into four pieces.

Crack the shell of the claws so that the flesh can be taken out easily.

Make the sauce by heating up the oil in a wok or saucepan; toss in the finely chopped scallions and ginger root; add salt, sugar, stock and ground pepper. Thicken with the cornstarch mixed with a little water. Finally add the sesame seed oil; pour it all over the lobster and serve.

Steamed Lobster (a second method)

INGREDIENTS *serves 2-4*
2lb fresh or frozen lobster (cooked red lobster is *not* suitable)
6 slices fresh ginger root
⅓ cup chicken fat, finely chopped
2 tbsp peanut oil
1 tbsp shrimp sauce
1 tsp Chinese yellow wine
1 tbsp light soy sauce

METHOD
Chop the lobster flesh, including the shell, into large bite-sized pieces and spread them out on a plate. (Do not pile the pieces in the center of the plate.) Sprinkle the ginger and chopped chicken fat on top of the lobster pieces.

Bring 5 cups water to a boil in a wok. Place a rack in the wok and put the plate on top of the rack. Steam the lobster over a very high heat for 5-7 minutes. Remove, drain any liquid from the lobster into a bowl and set aside.

Heat 2 tbsp peanut oil in a pan. Add the liquid from the steamed lobster and the shrimp sauce, yellow wine and light soy sauce to make a sauce. Pour over the lobster and serve.

Braised Mussels with Tofu and Mushrooms

INGREDIENTS *serves 5-6*
2½pts mussels
4 slices fresh ginger root
6 medium dried Chinese mushrooms
2 cakes fresh tofu
3 cloves garlic
3 scallions
2 cups good stock
4-5 tbsp rice wine or dry sherry
½ tsp salt
pepper to taste
1 chicken bouillon cube
1 tbsp cornstarch blended with 2 tbsp water
1 tsp sesame seed oil

METHOD
Scrub the mussels thoroughly. Poach in a large saucepan of simmering water with the ginger for 1½ minutes, then drain. Discard any unopened ones. Transfer the mussels to a large pan or flameproof casserole. Soak the dried mushrooms in hot water to cover for 25 minutes. Drain and discard the tough stalks. Cut the mushroom caps into quarters. Cut the tofu into cubes or rectangles. Finely chop the garlic. Shred the scallions.

Place the pan of mussels over medium-high heat. Pour in the stock and wine or sherry, then add the tofu, mushrooms, garlic, half the scallions, salt and pepper. Bring to a boil and sprinkle in the crumbled bouillon cube. Stir, then simmer gently for 10 minutes. Stir in the blended cornstarch. Sprinkle with the remaining scallions and the sesame seed oil.

▲ *Steaming lobster produces a purer taste than frying, and if ginger and scallion are used, the flavor is more delicate than with other methods of cooking.*

▶ *Lobster can be prepared in a number of ways, but steaming it like this preserves all the delicate flavor of the flesh. It can be served hot or cold and the recipes above show just two of the accompanying sauces which can be made to complement the fresh-tasting lobster.*

Deep-Fried Oysters

INGREDIENTS *serves 4-6*
20-25 medium oysters
1 tsp salt
pepper to taste
2 tsp finely chopped fresh ginger root
vegetable oil for deep-frying
1½ tbsp scallions, finely chopped

BATTER
1 egg
5 tbsp all-purpose flour
1 tbsp cornstarch
5 tbsp water
½ tsp baking powder

METHOD
Shell and drain the oysters. Sprinkle with salt, pepper and ginger. Combine the ingredients for the batter until smooth. Heat the oil in a wok or deep-fryer. When very hot, dip the oysters individually into the batter. Fry in batches for 3 minutes until golden brown. Drain. Transfer to a heated serving dish and sprinkle with scallion.

Rice in Lotus Leaves

INGREDIENTS *serves 4*
3 cups long-grain rice
5oz dried scallops (if dried scallops are too expensive, use dried shrimp)
10 cups water
5oz roast duck
¼lb fresh shrimp
3½oz crab meat
2 tbsp chopped ham
1 tsp sesame oil
¼ tsp pepper
1 tbsp soy sauce
1 tsp salt
1 large dried lotus leaf

METHOD
Wash and drain the rice. Put the scallops into the water and boil them over a low heat until only about half the water is left.

Put the rice in a large bowl or basin together with the scallop soup and steam the mixture for 15-20 minutes.

Mix the steamed rice and scallops with all the other ingredients and wrap the rice mixture in a large lotus leaf, which has been cleaned by rinsing under boiling water and steamed for another 30 minutes. Secure the lotus package with string and place it in a steamer to steam for another 10 minutes.

Serve by bringing the "package" to the table, to be unwrapped on serving.

Oyster Omelet

INGREDIENTS *serves 2*
4 medium oysters
1 tbsp cornstarch
4 eggs
2 stems scallions
1 stem fresh coriander
½ tsp sesame oil
1 tsp pepper
1 tsp salt
2 tbsp peanut oil

METHOD
Clean the oysters, cut them into small pieces (¼in) and mix them with 1 tbsp cornstarch. Set aside.

Beat the eggs together lightly until well mixed. Chop the scallions and coriander into fine shavings and add to the egg.

Blanch the diced oyster in boiling water for 30 seconds. Drain and add the sesame oil, pepper and salt. Mix well.

Heat a pan over medium heat and add 2 tbsp peanut oil. Pour half the egg mixture into the pan and half of the diced oyster. When the edge of the omelet browns slightly turn it over to complete cooking. Repeat with the rest of the egg and diced oyster. Serve on well-heated dish.

Steamed Scallops with Black Bean Sauce

INGREDIENTS *serves 6*
12 fresh scallops, with shells

SAUCE
1½ tbsp salted black beans
4 tbsp vegetable oil
1 tbsp fresh ginger root, finely chopped
½ tbsp red chili, finely chopped
½ tbsp garlic, crushed
1 tsp pounded Sichuan peppercorns
1 tbsp scallion, finely chopped
2 tbsp soy sauce
1 tbsp rice wine or dry sherry
2 tbsp good stock
1 tsp sesame seed oil

METHOD
Scrub the scallops under running cold water, then remove the flat shell. Soak black beans in hot water for 5 minutes. Drain and crush.

Put the scallops on a large heatproof dish, place in a steamer and steam for 8-9 minutes. Meanwhile, heat the vegetable oil in a small wok or saucepan. When hot, stir-fry the ginger, chili, garlic, peppercorns, scallions and black beans for 30 seconds. Add the soy sauce, sherry and stock and continue to stir-fry for another 15 seconds. Sprinkle on the sesame seed oil.

Drip about 2 tsp of the sauce over each scallop and serve them in the shells. The diners should be able to remove the scallops from their shells, then drink the remaining sauce from the shells.

▲ *Deep-Fried Oysters in a light-crisp batter.*

◀ *Steamed Scallops, beautifully presented in their own shells, accompanied by a highly flavored Black Bean Sauce.*

Scallops and Roast Duck with Garlic

INGREDIENTS *serves 3-4*
5-6 dried scallops
3oz garlic
good ¹/₂lb roast duck breast
5oz spinach
¹/₂ tsp salt
2 tbsp oil

SEASONINGS
1 tbsp soy sauce
¹/₄ tsp sugar
1 tbsp oyster sauce
few drops sesame oil
1 tsp cornstarch
2 tsp rice wine

METHOD
Soak the scallops for 3-4 hours and steam for 30 minutes. Fry the garlic until brown.

Cut the duck breast into 12 slices (each slice with skin attached) and arrange the meat in a big bowl (the skin to the bottom of the bowl), add a layer of scallops and finally the garlic. Steam for 45 minutes.

Fry the spinach with a little salt and oil and spread it out on a plate. Put the roast duck, scallops and garlic on top of the spinach and reserve the gravy.

Boil the gravy from the bottom of the bowl in a pan. Add the seasonings and stir into a sauce. Pour the sauce over the dish and serve.

Cantonese Fresh Poached Shrimp with Two Dips

INGREDIENTS *serves 4-5*
1¹/₄lb fresh unshelled shrimp
1¹/₂ tsp salt

DIP 1
2 scallions
3 slices fresh ginger root
2 green chili peppers
3 tbsp vegetable oil
3 tbsp light soy sauce
1 tbsp wine vinegar
¹/₂ tbsp sesame seed oil

DIP 2
1 tbsp shredded fresh root ginger
3 tbsp vinegar

METHOD
Wash the shrimp thoroughly under running water. Finely chop the scallions, ginger and chilies, discarding the seeds, together. Place them in a small heatproof bowl.

Bring 5 cups water to a boil in a saucepan and add the salt. Simmer the shrimp for 2 minutes, then leave to stand in the water, off the heat, for a further minute. Drain.

Place the shrimp in a medium bowl. Heat the vegetable oil in a pan. When smoking hot, pour over the ginger, scallions and chilies. Leave for 30 seconds, then add the soy sauce, vinegar and sesame oil; stir well. For the other dip, place the shredded ginger in a small bowl and spoon over the vinegar. To eat, peel each shrimp up to the tail and then, holding the tail, dip into the dip sauces.

Braised Shrimp in their Shells

INGREDIENTS *serves 4-6*
1lb large shrimp in their shells
2 tbsp soy sauce
2 tbsp rice wine or dry sherry
1 tsp salt
¹/₂ tbsp sugar
4 tbsp stock
5oz lard

METHOD
Trim off the legs and heads of the shrimp but keep the shells and tails on.

Heat up the lard, fry the shrimp for about 5 minutes or until golden. Using a slotted spoon, remove the shrimp from the wok and then drain off the excess lard from the wok. Return the shrimp; add rice wine or sherry, soy sauce, stock, sugar and salt. Cook until all the juice is absorbed. Serve either hot or cold.

Stir-Fried Scallops with Snow Peas, Celery, Water Chestnuts and Black Fungus

INGREDIENTS *serves 4-6*
1lb scallops (fresh or frozen)
1oz dried black fungus (cloud ear)
½lb snow peas
½lb celery
1 cup water chestnut
2 cups peanut oil
1 tsp salt
2 tbsp stock
2 tsp ground ginger
2 tsp ground garlic

MARINADE
1 tsp salt
½ tsp pepper
1 tsp sesame oil
1¼ tbsp ginger juice
1 tbsp cornstarch

SAUCE
1 tbsp oyster sauce
1 tsp dark soy sauce
1 tbsp light soy sauce
2 tbsp stock
1 tsp sugar
½ tsp sesame oil
1 tbsp cornstarch
2 tsp Chinese yellow wine

METHOD
Cut the scallops horizontally in half. Mix the marinade ingredients and add the scallops. Set aside.

Soak the black fungus in hot water for about 10 minutes.

Trim the snow peas, cutting them slantwise into 2×¾in pieces. Cut the celery into pieces the same size. Slice the water chestnuts into ¼in pieces.

Heat the oil in a pan until very hot: test by putting in a thin slice of ginger; if it curls up and browns immediately the temperature is right. Add the scallops, stirring to separate and prevent them from sticking. Turn off the heat and allow to stand for 30 seconds. Drain thoroughly and set aside.

Heat 2 tbsp oil in the pan. Add the snow peas, celery, water chestnuts and black fungus, sauté and stir for 1 minute. Add 1 tsp salt and 2 tbsp stock and cook for another minute. Remove from the pan and set aside. Heat 1 tbsp oil in the pan. Add the ginger and garlic and, when the aroma rises, add the scallops and other ingredients. Stir rapidly over a high heat for 15 seconds.

Mix the sauce ingredients and add to the pan. Stir rapidly for another 15 seconds and serve.

▲ *Scallops and Roast Duck with Garlic: a good way to deal with left-over roast duck is to steam it until it is very tender, adding conpoy (dried scallops) and garlic for flavor.*

◄ *Stir-Fried Scallops with Snow Peas, Celery, Water Chestnuts and Black Fungus: the combination of vegetables used here appeals to both eye and palate, providing a skillful contrast of colors, textures and tastes to offset seafood, meat or poultry.*

121

Fried Shrimp-Balls

INGREDIENTS *serves 4-6*
1lb uncooked shrimp
$\frac{1}{2}$ cup water chestnuts, peeled
$2\frac{1}{2}$ tbsp glutinous rice powder
1 egg
1 tsp salt
1 tbsp rice wine (or sherry)
$\frac{1}{2}$ tsp monosodium glutamate
oil for deep-frying

DIP
2 tbsp tomato sauce
salt and Sichuan pepper

METHOD
Shell the shrimp; dry them well and marinate with salt for 5 minutes, then chop them into rice-grain-sized pieces.

Finely chop the water chestnuts; mix them with the shrimp, egg, glutinous rice powder, rice wine or sherry and monosodium glutamate; blend well.

Heat the oil in a deep-fryer; before it gets too hot, take a handful of the shrimp mixture and squeeze it through your fist between the thumb and forefinger to form a ball about the size of a walnut. Scoop it off with a wet spoon and dip it into the oil (you should be able to make about 20 balls); fry for about 2 minutes. Stir to separate them and when they start to turn golden, scoop them out and drain.

Serve with the tomato sauce, and salt and pepper mixed as a dip.

"Dragon and Phoenix" Legs

INGREDIENTS *serves 4-6*
6oz lean pork
$\frac{1}{4}$lb chicken breast meat
6oz shelled shrimp, uncooked
$\frac{1}{4}$ cup onions
1 tbsp rice wine (or sherry)
2 tsp salt
5 tbsp cornstarch
freshly ground Sichuan pepper
2 eggs
A large sheet of edible Chinese
   cellophane paper
1 tbsp sesame seed oil
oil for deep-frying

METHOD
Coarsely chop the lean pork, chicken, shrimp and onions; mix with salt, rice wine or sherry and pepper and divide into 10 portions.

Beat the eggs and mix with 2 tbsp cornstarch.

Cut the cellophane paper into 10 pieces roughly 2×4in. On the middle of each piece place a portion of the filling, rub some egg and cornstarch mixture all around it, then wrap the sheet round the filling to make the shape of a chicken leg, making 10 "legs" in all. Put them on a plate and steam for about 10 minutes, then take them out and place on a cold plate.

Mix the remaining 3 tbsp cornstarch with 3 tbsp water to make a batter; heat the oil in a wok or deep-fryer, dip each of the "legs" in the batter and deep-fry until golden and serve hot.

Phoenix Tail Shrimp

This recipe originated from a Moslem restaurant in Nanjing. Oil can be used instead of the duck fat it calls for.

INGREDIENTS *serves 4-6*
½lb unshelled large shrimp
½ cup green peas
2 scallions, white parts only
1 egg white
1½ tbsp cornstarch
½ tbsp rice wine (or sherry)
1 tsp salt
½ tsp monosodium glutamate
6 tbsp chicken stock
duck fat or oil for deep-frying

METHOD
Parboil the peas for 3 minutes, drain and rinse in cold water in order to keep the bright green color. Finely chop the onion whites. Pull off the heads and shell the shrimp, but leave the tail pieces firmly attached. Marinate them with ½ tsp salt, egg white and ½ tbsp cornstarch.

Heat the duck fat (or oil); deep-fry the shrimp for about 1 minute; stir to separate them; remove and drain.

Pour off the excess fat; add the stock, salt, rice wine or sherry, cornstarch, monosodium glutamate and onions. Bring it to a boil; stir to make a thickish smooth gravy; add the shrimp and peas; blend well and serve.

▲ *This dish of "Dragon and Phoenix" Legs is served with deep-fried seaweed as garnish. "Dragon" refers to the shrimp, and "phoenix," of course, is the chicken. Traditionally you are supposed to place a piece of chicken bone on the edge of the "legs" to be used as a handle when eating.*

▶ *Phoenix Tail Shrimps.*

◀ *Fried Shrimp-Balls.*

Wine-Marinated Shrimp

INGREDIENTS *serves 4-6*
½lb fresh large shrimp
3 tbsp rice wine (or sherry)
2 scallions, white parts only
⅓ cup celery
⅓ cup carrots
1 tbsp peas

SAUCE
2 tbsp soy sauce
1 tsp sesame seed oil

METHOD
Wash the shrimp well, and place in a dish. Pour the wine or sherry over them, add the scallion whites cut to 1in lengths; and then cover and marinate for 5 minutes.

Slice the celery and carrot; parboil with the peas for 5 minutes. Drain and add to the shrimp. Mix together both the sauce ingredients and then pour it over the shrimp and serve.

▲ *Wine-Marinated Shrimp: the fresher the shellfish the better.*

◄ *Rapidly-Fried Shrimp served in their shells with a strong Chinese spirit.*

Sweet and Sour Shrimp

INGREDIENTS *serves 4-6*

1lb unshelled, uncooked large Pacific
    shrimp
1 egg white
2 tbsp sugar
2 slices ginger root, peeled
1¹/₂ tbsp cornstarch
1¹/₂ tbsp vinegar
1 scallion
2 tbsp chicken stock
oil for deep-frying

METHOD

Shell the shrimp, make a shallow incision
down the back of each shrimp and remove
the black intestinal parts. Wash and clean,
then cut each shrimp in half lengthwise.
Make a criss-cross pattern on each half and
marinate them with the egg white and ¹/₂
tbsp cornstarch.

    Finely chop the scallion and ginger root.
Heat up about 4 cups oil in a wok and,
before the oil gets too hot, put in the shrimp
piece by piece; fry until golden, take them
out and drain.

    Leave about 1 tbsp oil on the wok; stir-fry
the finely chopped scallion and ginger root
until their color changes, then put in the
shrimp; stir and add sugar and continue
stirring until all the sugar has dissolved.
Add the remaining cornstarch mixed with
the chicken stock, blend well, then serve.

    You will find this dish quite different from
the ones you have tasted in ordinary
Chinese restaurants; the secret is in the
method of cooking.

Rapidly-Fried Shrimp

Shrimp from the West Lake are succulent
and tender; substitute freshwater shrimp
where available rather than sea varieties for
a more authentic result.

INGREDIENTS *serves 4-6*

¹/₂lb uncooked, unshelled large shrimp
1¹/₂ tbsp soy sauce
1 tbsp Shaoxing wine or sherry
¹/₂ tbsp sugar
¹/₂ tbsp vinegar
1 stick ginger root, peeled and finely
    chopped
1 scallion, finely chopped
2¹/₂ cups lard for deep-frying

METHOD

Trim the shrimp, but keep the shell on. Dry
well.

    Heat the lard in a wok and when it is
bubbling deep-fry the shrimp twice (3-4
seconds only each time); scoop out and
drain.

    Pour out all the lard, then return the
shrimp to the same wok. Add soy sauce,
wine sugar, scallions and ginger root; stir a
few times; add vinegar and serve.

Salt and Pepper Prawns

INGREDIENTS *serves 6-7*

1lb king prawns
8 tbsp vegetable oil
2 scallions
2 cloves garlic
2 dried chili peppers
1¹/₂ tsp Sichuan peppercorns
1¹/₂ tsp salt

METHOD

Wash and shell the prawns. Sprinkle on 1¹/₂
tsp of the oil. Cut the scallions into 1in
sections. Thinly slice the garlic. Shred the
chilies. Lightly pound the peppercorns and
mix with the salt.

    Heat the remaining oil in a wok or skillet.
When hot, stir-fry the prawns over a high
heat for 1 minute. Remove the prawns and
pour away the oil to use for other purposes,
except for 1 tbsp. Reheat the oil in the wok
or pan. When hot, quickly stir-fry the chili,
garlic and scallions. Spread out the scallions
and chili and return the prawns. Sprinkle on
the salt and pepper mixture and stir-fry for
another 45 seconds.

▲ *Sweet and Sour Shrimp.*

"Dragon-Well" Shrimp

The original recipe called for the shrimp to be cooked with tea-leaves. The exquisite flavor of "Dragon-Well" tea has to be tasted to be believed, and the fresh shrimp from the West Lake also have a truly superlative flavor; but to mix these two together is something I personally find difficult to approve, so I have omitted the tea-leaves from this recipe.

INGREDIENTS *serves 4-6*
1lb large freshwater shrimp
1 egg white
1 tbsp Shaoxing wine or sherry
$\frac{1}{4}$ tsp monosodium glutamate
1 tsp salt
1 tbsp cornstarch
1 scallion, cut into 1in lengths
lard for deep-frying

METHOD
Shell the shrimp, put them in cold water and stir with chopsticks for 2-3 minutes. Change the water two or three times, then drain. Mix them with the salt, monosodium glutamate, egg white and the cornstarch; marinate for 3 hours.

Heat the lard and deep-fry the shrimp, separate them with chopsticks after 15 seconds or so, scoop them out and drain. Pour off the excess lard, return the shrimp to the wok, add the wine, and stir a few times. It is then ready to serve.

▲ *"Dragon-Well" Shrimp. Be careful not to overcook the shrimp during the last stage, otherwise they will toughen and lose their tender texture.*

Fried Shrimp Balls with Baby Corn

INGREDIENTS *serves 4-6*
$\frac{1}{2}$lb large Pacific shrimp
1 small can of baby corn cobs
3-4 Chinese dried mushrooms, soaked
1 slice ginger root, peeled
2 scallions
$\frac{1}{2}$ tbsp salt
1 egg white
1 tbsp cornstarch
1 tbsp rice wine (or sherry)
1 tsp sugar
1 tsp sesame seed oil
oil for deep-frying
Chinese parsley (fresh coriander) for garnish

METHOD
Shell the shrimp; use a sharp knife to make a deep incision down the back of each one, and pull out the black intestinal "vein". Cut each shrimp into two or three pieces. Mix with a little salt, egg white and cornstarch.

Finely chop the ginger root and scallions, cut large mushrooms into two or three pieces; smaller ones can be left whole. Drain the baby corn cobs. Deep-fry the shrimp in warm oil for 30 seconds; remove and drain.

Pour off the excess oil, leaving about 2 tbsp oil in the wok; wait until it smokes, toss in the finely chopped ginger root and scallions followed by mushrooms, baby corn cobs and shrimp; add salt, rice wine or sherry and sugar. Stir until well blended; add sesame seed oil just before serving. Garnish with Chinese parsley (fresh coriander).

Jadeite Shrimp

The white and green of jadeite are provided by the shrimp and the peas. The red of the tomato and ham is used to give a contrast in color. Here we garnished the dish with a few cocktail cherries.

INGREDIENTS *serves 4-6*
1lb uncooked shrimp, peeled
1 egg white
$\frac{1}{2}$ tsp salt
$\frac{1}{2}$ tbsp cornstarch
$\frac{1}{2}$ cup green peas
$\frac{1}{6}$ cup cooked ham or 1 small red tomato
1 scallion
oil for deep-frying

SAUCE
$\frac{1}{2}$ tsp salt
$\frac{1}{2}$ tsp pepper
1 tbsp rice wine (or sherry)
$\frac{1}{2}$ tbsp cornstarch
3 tbsp stock or water

METHOD
Marinate the peeled shrimp with the egg white, salt and cornstarch. Dice the ham or tomato into small cubes; cut the scallion into short lengths. Mix the sauce in a bowl or jug.

Heat up the oil; deep-fry the shrimp for about 15 seconds; stir to separate them; scoop them out and drain. Pour off the excess oil; return the shrimp to the wok together with the green peas, ham or tomato. Stir for a little while; add the sauce mixture. When the sauce thickens, the dish is ready to serve.

Braised Shrimp

INGREDIENTS *serves 4-6*
$\frac{1}{2}$lb shrimp, unshelled
1 tbsp rice wine (or sherry)
4 tbsp stock
4 dried red chilies, soaked and finely chopped
1 tbsp chili paste
$\frac{1}{2}$ tbsp Kao Liang spirit
1 slice ginger root, peeled and finely chopped
1 scallion, finely chopped
1 tsp salt
$\frac{1}{2}$ tsp Sichuan pepper
2 tbsp tomato paste
1 tbsp cornstarch
oil for deep-frying
$\frac{1}{2}$ tsp sesame seed oil

METHOD
Clean the shrimp, cut them into two or three pieces but keep the shells on.

Heat up the oil and deep-fry the shrimp until they turn bright pink. Scoop them out and pour off the excess oil. Put the shrimp back in the pan, together with the rice wine or sherry and a little stock; cook for about 1 minute; remove.

Heat about 1 tbsp oil in the wok; add the red chilies, chili paste, Kao Liang spirit, ginger root, scallions, salt and pepper, the remaining stock and the shrimp. Reduce heat and braise for 2 minutes, then add the tomato paste and the cornstarch mixed with a little water. Blend well; add sesame seed oil and serve.

▲ *Braised Shrimp cooked in their shells with a piquant sauce.*

Stir-Fried Shrimp in Garlic and Tomato Sauce

INGREDIENTS *serves 5-6*
$\frac{3}{4}$lb peeled shrimp, fresh or frozen
1 tsp salt
$\frac{3}{4}$ tbsp cornstarch
1 egg white
2 cloves garlic
2 scallions
2 small firm tomatoes
6 tbsp vegetable oil

SAUCE
2 tbsp tomato paste
$\frac{1}{4}$ tsp salt
1 tbsp sugar
pinch or monosodium glutamate (optional)
6 tbsp good stock
$1\frac{1}{2}$ tbsp cornstarch blended with 3 tbsp water
1 tsp sesame seed oil

METHOD
Toss the shrimp in the salt, dust with the cornstarch and coat in the egg white. Crush the garlic. Cut the scallions into shreds. Skin the tomatoes and cut into eighths.

Heat the oil in a wok or skillet. When hot, stir-fry the shrimp over high heat for $1\frac{1}{2}$ minutes. Remove from the wok or pan. Pour away the excess oil and reheat the wok or pan. When hot, stir-fry the garlic, half the scallions and tomatoes over high heat for 30 seconds. Add the tomato paste, salt, sugar, monosodium glutamate, if using, and stock and continue stir-frying for another 30 seconds. Stir in the blended cornstarch until the sauce thickens. Sprinkle on the sesame seed oil and remaining scallions. Return the shrimp to the wok or pan, stir once more and serve.

Three Delicacies Stuffed with Shrimp

INGREDIENTS *serves 4*
1 eggplant
4 green peppers
4 tomatoes
¼ lb pork fat
¾ lb fresh shelled shrimp
few drops sesame oil
2 tbsp cornstarch
2 tbsp peanut oil

SEASONING
1 egg white
1 tsp cornstarch
½ tsp salt
¼ tsp peppers

SAUCE
1 tbsp tomato juice
2 tsp catsup
2 tsp soy sauce
5 tbsp chicken stock
1 tsp sugar

METHOD
Cut the eggplant into slices ½ in thick and cut a slit in each piece.

Cut the green peppers in half and remove the seeds, and cut the tomatoes in half and remove the pulp.

Dice the pork fat finely. Chop and mash the shrimp into a paste, continuing to stir and beat the paste until it becomes sticky. Add the diced pork fat and continue to stir, and then mix the seasonings with the shrimp paste. Refrigerate for 2 hours.

Coat the inside of the eggplant, green peppers and tomatoes with cornstarch and stuff them with the shrimp mixture.

Heat the pan over a high heat. Add 2 tbsp oil and fry the vegetables, open side down, over a medium heat for 1½ minutes.

Mix and blend the sauce ingredients in a bowl and pour the mixture evenly over the stuffed vegetables. Cover the pan and cook for 2 more minutes, then serve piping hot.

Shrimp and Seasonal Greens

INGREDIENTS *serves 4-6*
½ lb uncooked large shrimp
½ lb Chinese cabbage or broccoli
1 egg white
½ tbsp salt
1 tsp cornstarch
1 tsp sugar
3 tbsp oil

METHOD
Shell the shrimp and cut each one into 2-3 pieces; mix in salt, egg white and cornstarch.

Wash and cut the vegetable. Heat the oil; fry the shrimp in oil for 1-2 minutes; scoop out with a perforated spoon, then stir-fry the greens in hot oil until soft. Add salt and sugar, return the shrimp to the wok; blend well. Serve hot.

Quick-Fried Crystal Shrimp

INGREDIENTS *serves 4-5*
¾lb king shrimp, fresh or frozen,
    unshelled
1 tsp salt
1½ tbsp cornstarch
1 egg white
½ tsp sugar
pepper to taste
⅔ cup vegetable oil
2 scallions
2 slices fresh ginger root
3-4 tbsp peas (optional)
2½ tbsp good stock
1½ tbsp dry sherry or white wine

METHOD
Shell the shrimp. Wash in salted water, then rinse under running cold water. Drain well. Place in a bowl. Add salt, cornstarch, egg white, sugar, pepper and ½ tsp vegetable oil. Mix well. Finely chop the onions and ginger.

Heat the oil in a wok or deep skillet. When hot, add the shrimp, stir around and fry over medium heat for 1¾ minutes. Remove and drain. Pour away the oil to use for other purposes, leaving only 1-1½ tbsp. Re-heat the wok or pan. When hot, stir-fry the ginger, scallion and peas over high heat for 15 seconds. Add the stock and sherry or wine. As the sauce boils, return the shrimp and adjust the seasoning. Fry for 1 minute.

Squid Stuffed with Shrimp

INGREDIENTS *serves 4-6*
¼lb dried squid
¼lb pork fat
14oz shrimp, shelled and deveined
2 tbsp cornstarch
½ tsp pepper
¼ tsp salt
1 egg white

METHOD
Soak the dried squid in hot water for 1 hour before cutting it into pieces 1½× 2½in.

Cut the pork fat into ⅛in cubes and blanch in boiling water for 2 minutes. Remove and drain.

Pound the shrimp with the flat side of a cleaver and place them in a mixing bowl. Add 1 tbsp cornstarch, the salt and pepper and the egg white to the shrimp and, using a fork, stir in one direction only until the mixture becomes sticky. Add the pork fat and stir until sticky again. Set aside.

Take a piece of squid and dust one side with some of the remaining cornstarch. Place 1 tbsp of the shrimp and pork fat mixture on the floured side of the squid and press gently. Continue until all the squid pieces and shrimp mixture are used.

Arrange the stuffed squid on a plate and steam for 10 minutes over a high heat.

Fried Squid with Peppers

INGREDIENTS *serves 4-6*
¾lb squid
1 red pepper
2 slices ginger root, peeled
1 tsp salt
1 tbsp rice wine or dry sherry
1 tbsp soy sauce
½ tsp fresh ground black pepper
1 tsp vinegar
1 tsp sesame seed oil
oil for deep-frying
Chinese parsley (fresh coriander) for
    garnish

METHOD
Discard the head, transparent backbone and ink bag of the squid. Peel off the thin skin and score a criss-cross pattern on the outside, then cut into small pieces the size of a matchbox.

Thinly shred the red pepper and ginger root.

Deep-fry the squid in oil over a moderate heat for 30 seconds; scoop out and drain. Pour off the excess oil, leaving about 1 tbsp in the wok; toss in the ginger root and red pepper followed by the squid; add salt, rice wine or sherry, soy sauce, black pepper and vinegar. Stir-fry for about 1 minute, add sesame seed oil and serve. Garnish with Chinese parsley.

◄ *Three Delicacies Stuffed with Shrimp: In this dish the elements of contrast are present to a marked degree in flavors that are both rich and delicate. The bitter melon, when used as an alternative vegetable, provides a counterpoint to the stuffing.*

► *Fried Squid with Peppers: when cooking squid it is important not to overcook, or the flesh will turn rubbery.*

VEGETABLES

Eggplant with Sichuan "Fish Sauce"

INGREDIENTS *serves 4-6*
1lb eggplant
4-5 dried red chili peppers
oil for deep-frying
3-4 scallions, finely chopped
1 slice ginger root, finely chopped
1 clove garlic, finely chopped
1 tsp sugar
1 tbsp soy sauce
1 tbsp vinegar
1 tbsp chili bean paste
2 tsp cornstarch, with 2 tbsp water
1 tsp sesame seed oil

METHOD
Soak the dried red chilies for 5-10 minutes, cut into small pieces. Peel the eggplant, and cut into diamond-shaped chunks.

Heat the oil in a wok and deep-fry the eggplant for 3½-4 minutes or until soft. Remove with a slotted spoon and drain.

Pour off the oil and return the eggplant to the wok with the red chilies, scallions, root ginger and garlic. Stir a few times and add the sugar, soy sauce, vinegar and chili bean paste. Stir for 1 minute. Add the cornstarch and water mixture, blend well and garnish with sesame seed oil. Serve hot or cold.

Braised Eggplant

INGREDIENTS *serves 4-6*
10oz eggplant
2½ cups oil for deep-frying
2 tbsp soy sauce
1 tbsp sugar
2 tbsp water
1 tsp sesame seed oil

METHOD
Choose the long, purple variety of eggplant, rather than the large round kind, if possible. Discard the stalks and cut the eggplant into diamond-shaped chunks.

Heat oil in a wok until hot. Deep-fry the eggplant chunks in batches until golden. Remove with a slotted spoon and drain.

Pour off excess oil leaving about 1 tbsp in the wok. Return the eggplant to the wok and add the soy sauce, sugar and water. Cook over a fairly high heat for about 2 minutes, adding more water if necessary. Stir occasionally. When the juice is reduced to almost nothing, add the sesame seed oil, blend well and serve.

▲ *The eggplant is peeled, cut into thick chunks, and deep-fried in oil like potato chips.*

◄ *Braised Eggplant makes a rich vegetable dish which goes well with a vinegary fish dish and rice.*

► *The "Two Winters" of the title are Chinese mushrooms, dried to provide a tasty additive to many dishes throughout the winter months, and the tender young shoots of bamboo.*

The Two Winters

INGREDIENTS *serves 4-6*
4-5 cups dried Chinese mushrooms
$\frac{2}{3}$ cup winter bamboo shoots
2 tbsp soy sauce
$\frac{1}{2}$ tbsp sugar
1 tsp monosodium glutamate (optional)
3 tbsp vegetable oil
$\frac{1}{2}$ tbsp cornstarch
$\frac{1}{2}$ tbsp sesame seed oil

METHOD
Try to select mushrooms of a uniformly small size. Soak them in warm water; squeeze dry and keep the water as mushroom stock.

Cut the shoots into thin slices not much bigger than the mushrooms.

Heat up the oil until it smokes; stir-fry the mushrooms and bamboo shoots for about 1 minute; add soy sauce and sugar, stir, add 4 tbsp mushroom stock (soaking water).

Bring it to a boil and cook for about 2 minutes; add monosodium glutamate, if using, and cornstarch. Blend together very well, then add sesame seed oil and serve.

Braised Bamboo Shoots

INGREDIENTS *serves 4-6*
4 cups fresh bamboo shoots
$\frac{1}{4}$ cup green seaweed, or 4oz green cabbage
1 slice fresh ginger root, peeled and finely chopped
1lb lard for deep-frying
2 tbsp oyster sauce
$1\frac{1}{2}$ tbsp sugar
1 tsp monosodium glutamate (optional)
1 tbsp rice wine or dry sherry
4 tbsp chicken stock
1 tbsp sesame seed oil

METHOD
Peel off the skin of the bamboo shoots and discard the tough parts of the root. Cut them into small slices about $\frac{1}{4}$in thick, then into strips about $1\frac{1}{2}$in long. Finely chop the seaweed or cabbage and ginger root.

Warm up the lard, deep-fry the bamboo shoots for 1-2 minutes, then reduce heat and continue cooking for 2-3 minutes. When their color turns golden, scoop them out and drain.

Keep about 2 tbsp lard in the wok or pan, increase the heat and put in the seaweed or cabbage and ginger root, followed by the bamboo shoots; add the oyster sauce, sugar, monosodium glutamate, if using, and rice wine or sherry; blend well. Add the chicken stock, bring it to a boil, then reduce the heat and let it simmer until almost all the juice is evaporated. Now increase the heat again, add the sesame seed oil, stir a few times and serve.

Stir-Fried "Four Treasures"

Like stir-fried mixed vegetables, the ingredients are specially selected to achieve a harmonious balance of colors, textures and flavors.

INGREDIENTS *serves 4-6*
3-4 tbsp Wood Ears, dried
½lb broccoli
1 cup bamboo shoots
¼lb oyster mushrooms
3-4 tbsp oil
1½ tsp salt
1 tsp sugar
1 tsp sesame seed oil

METHOD
Soak the Wood Ears in water for 15-20 minutes. Rinse until clean. Discard the hard roots if any and cut the extra large ones into smaller pieces.

Wash the broccoli and cut into whole flowerets. Do not discard the stalks; peel off the tough outer skin and cut them into small pieces.

Cut the bamboo shoots into slices, or, if using winter bamboo shoots, cut them into roughly the same size pieces as the broccoli stalks.

Wash and trim the mushrooms. Do not peel if using fresh ones. Canned oyster mushrooms are ready to cook; just drain off the water.

Heat a wok or large skillet over high heat until really hot. Add the oil and wait for it to smoke. Then stir the oil with a spatula so that most of the surface of the wok is well greased.

Add the broccoli first, and stir until well coated with oil. Then add the bamboo shoots and mushrooms and continue stirring for about 1 minute. Add the Wood Ears, salt and sugar and stir for another minute or so. The vegetables should produce enough natural juices to form a thick gravy; if the contents in the wok are too dry, add a little water and bring to a boil before serving. The sesame seed oil should not be added until the very last minute.

▲ *Stir-fried "Four Treasures."*   ▶ *Casserole of vegetables.*

▼ *Vegetarian Chop Suey.*

132

Vegetarian Chop Suey

Many of you know that chop suey is a creation of the West, but in China there is a dish called tsa-sui, which literally means "miscellaneous fragments," or "mixed bits and pieces." The genuine article should have all the ingredients specially selected in order to achieve the desired harmonious balance of colors, textures and flavors. It should never be the soggy mass one often finds in a cheap take-out.

INGREDIENTS *serves 4-6*
2 cakes of tofu
2 tbsp Wood Ears, dried
6oz broccoli or snow peas
1 cup bamboo shoots
¼lb mushrooms
4-5 tbsp oil
1½ tsp salt
1 tsp sugar
1-2 scallions, finely chopped
1 tbsp light soy sauce
2 tbsp rice wine or dry sherry
1 tsp cornstarch mixed with 1 tbsp cold
    water

METHOD
Cut the tofu into about 24 small pieces. Soak the Wood Ears in water for about 20-25 minutes, rinse them clean and discard any hard roots.

Cut the broccoli and bamboo shoots into uniformly small pieces.

Heat a wok over a high heat, add about half of the oil and wait for it to smoke. Swirl the pan so that its surface is well greased. Add the tofu pieces and shallow-fry them on both sides until golden, then scoop them out with a slotted spoon and set them aside.

Heat the remaining oil and add the broccoli. Stir for about 30 seconds and then add the Wood Ears, bamboo shoots and the partly cooked bean curd. Continue stirring for 1 minute and then add the salt, sugar, scallions, soy sauce and wine. Blend well and when the gravy starts to boil, thicken it with the cornstarch and water mixture. Serve hot.

Casserole of Vegetables

INGREDIENTS *serves 4-6*
2 tbsp Wood Ears, dried
1 cake tofu
4oz green beans or snow peas
¼lb cabbage or broccoli
¼lb baby corn cobs or bamboo shoots
¼lb carrots
3-4 tbsp oil
1 tsp salt
1 tsp sugar
1 tbsp light soy sauce
1 tsp cornstarch mixed with 1 tbsp cold
    water

METHOD
Soak the Wood Ears in water for 20-25 minutes, rinse them and discard the hard roots, if any.

Cut the tofu into about 12 small pieces and harden the pieces in a pot of lightly salted boiling water for 2-3 minutes. Remove and drain.

Trim the green beans or snow peas. Leave whole if small; cut in half if large.

Cut the vegetables into thin slices or chunks.

Heat about half of the oil in a flameproof casserole or saucepan. When hot, lightly brown the tofu on both sides. Remove with a slotted spoon and set aside.

Heat the remaining oil and stir-fry the rest of the vegetables for about 1½ minutes. Add the tofu pieces, salt, sugar and soy sauce and continue stirring to blend everything well. Cover, reduce the heat and simmer for 2-3 minutes.

Mix the cornstarch with water to make a smooth paste, pour it over the vegetables and stir. Increase the heat to high just long enough to thicken the gravy. Serve hot.

Stir-Fried Lima Beans, Shrimp, Ham and Button Mushrooms

INGREDIENTS *serves 4-6*
1½lb lima beans
½lb shrimp, shelled and deveined
¼lb ham
¼lb button mushrooms
1 cup peanut oil
3-4 slices fresh ginger root
2 cloves garlic, crushed
1 cup chicken stock
1 tsp Chinese yellow wine
2 tbsp cornstarch
1 tsp sugar
1 tsp salt

MARINADE
½ egg white
1 tsp cornstarch
1 tsp salt
¼ tsp sesame oil

METHOD
Skin the beans and trim them. Set aside.

Prepare the marinade. Clean the shrimp, pat them dry and set them aside to marinate.

Cut the ham into ⅛in slices, then cut it into ½in squares. Set aside.

Cut the mushrooms horizontally in halves. Set aside.

Heat the oil. When it is hot add the shrimp, stirring to separate. After 30 seconds remove and drain. Set aside.

Fry the beans and button mushrooms in the oil for 1½ minutes over a high heat. Remove, drain and set aside.

Heat 3 tbsp oil in the pan. Sauté for 30 seconds, stir and add the lima beans, ham and mushrooms. Add the remaining ingredients, stir and bring to a boil quickly. Continue to stir-fry over high heat for 1½ minutes and serve.

Bean Sprout Salad

INGREDIENTS *serves 6-8*
1lb fresh bean sprouts
1 tsp salt
10 cups water
2 tbsp light soy sauce
1 tbsp vinegar
2 scallions, finely shredded

METHOD
Wash and rinse the bean sprouts in cold water discarding the husks and other bits and pieces that float to the surface. It is not necessary to trim each sprout.

Blanch the sprouts in a pan of salted, boiling water. Pour them into a colander and rinse in cold water until cool. Drain.

Place the sprouts in a bowl or a deep dish and add the soy sauce, vinegar and sesame seed oil. Toss well and garnish with thinly shredded scallions just before serving.

▲ ▲ *Bean Sprout Salad: bean sprouts have a pleasing crunchy texture, but need a flavorsome dressing to overcome their blandness.*

▲ *Stir-fried Lima Beans, Shrimp, Ham and Button Mushrooms. In this semi-soup dish the flavor of the beans is set off against the savoriness of the shellfish and the richly flavored sauce.*

Colorful Bean Sprouts

INGREDIENTS *serves 4-6*
3 pieces dried, spiced tofu
2 green peppers
2 fresh red chili peppers
1½oz salted sour cabbage
2oz leeks
1 tsp sugar
4 tbsp peanut oil
1½ tsp chopped garlic
1½ tsp chopped ginger root
12oz bean sprouts
2 tsp rice wine

SEASONINGS
2 tsp oyster sauce
1 tsp monosodium glutamate (optional)
2 tsp soy sauce
½ tsp salt
1 tsp sugar
¼ tsp pepper
1 tbsp cornstarch
4 tbsp stock
few drops sesame oil

METHOD
Cut the tofu, peppers, chilies and salted sour cabbage into matchstick-sized shreds, and cut the leeks slantwise into 2in slices. Mix the cabbage with 1 tsp sugar.

Heat the pan until it is very hot and pour 1 tsp peanut oil into it. Add ½ tsp garlic and ½ tsp ginger. Stir-fry the bean sprouts for 30 seconds and put them on one side.

Reheat the pan until it is very hot and pour in 3 tbsp peanut oil. Add 1 tsp garlic and 1 tsp ginger and sauté until fragrant. Add the shredded tofu, chilies and peppers and stir-fry over a high heat for 30 seconds. Add the seasonings and continue to stir-fry for 10 seconds. Sprinkle with rice wine and serve.

Dry-Braised Bamboo Shoots with Preserved Snow Cabbage

INGREDIENTS *serves 4-6*
1⅓ cups bamboo shoots
6oz preserved snow cabbage
4-6 scallions, white part only
4 tbsp peanut oil
3-4 slices fresh ginger root
1 tsp salt
1 tbsp sugar
2 tbsp Chinese yellow wine
4 tbsp chicken stock

METHOD
Cut the bamboo shoots into wedges ¾in long.

Soak the preserved snow cabbage in 5 cups cold water for 30 minutes. Change the water and soak for a further 15 minutes. Chop into sections 1½in long. Cut the scallions into sections the same length.

Heat 2 tbsp oil in a pan and add the scallions and ginger. When the aroma arises, add the bamboo shoots and snow cabbage and stir-fry over a high heat for 2 minutes.

Add the remaining ingredients and continue to stir-fry and cook over a very high heat for 3 minutes. Remove from the heat and drain away any remaining liquid.

Heat 2 tbsp oil in the pan until very hot. Return the drained bamboo shoots and snow cabbage and fry for a further 2 minutes. Remove and drain again on a paper towel before transferring to the serving dish.

▲ *Dry Braised Bamboo Shoots with preserved Snow Cabbage: This is a dish for the connnoisseur because the flavor of the fresh bamboo shoot is extremely subtle. Here it is set off by a typical east Chinese pickle which is extremely salty. The dish is often served as a hot as hors d'œuvre for diners to nibble at while they sip their wine.*

Stir-Fried Green Beans and Bean Sprouts

INGREDIENTS *serves 4-6*
225g/8oz green beans — haricots verts, runner beans or mange-toute (snow peas)
225g/8oz fresh bean sprouts
3-4 tbsp oil
1½ tsp salt
1 tsp sugar

METHOD
Wash and trim the beans. Shred if necessary.

Wash and rinse the bean sprouts in a bowl of cold water and discard the husks and other bits and pieces that float to the surface.

Heat the oil in a hot wok or large frying-pan and when it starts to smoke, swirl the wok so that its surface is well greased. Add the green beans first, stirring to make sure that each piece is well covered with oil, then the bean sprouts and stir-fry for about 30 seconds. Add the salt and sugar.

Continue stirring for about 1 minute at the most. Overcooking will turn both the green beans and bean sprouts into a soggy mass.

Quick-Fried French Beans with Dried Shrimps and Pork

INGREDIENTS *serves 4-6*
700g/1½lb French beans
2 tbsp dried shrimps
1 tbsp chopped Sichuan Ja Chai hot pickle
vegetable oil for deep-frying
20g/¾oz lard
3 tsp garlic, chopped
75g/3oz pork, minced (ground)
3 tbsp good stock
1 tbsp soy sauce
½ tbsp sugar
2 tsp salt
3 tbsp water
1 tsp sesame seed oil
2 tsp vinegar
2 tbsp spring onions (scallions) (optional)

METHOD
Trim the French beans. Soak the dried shrimp in hot water to cover for 20 minutes. Drain and chop. Finely chop the pickle.

Heat the oil in a wok or deep-fryer. When hot, fry the beans for 2 minutes. Remove and put aside. Pour away the oil to use for other purposes. Heat the lard in the wok or frying pan. When hot, add the garlic and stir a few times. Add the pork, shrimps, stock and pickle and stir-fry for 2 minutes. Stir in the soy sauce, sugar, salt and water. Add the French beans and turn and toss until the liquid in the pan has nearly all evaporated. Sprinkle with the sesame seed oil, vinegar and finely chopped onions. Turn and stir once more, then serve.

▲ *Stir-fried green beans and bean sprouts: Dwarf French beans are best for this recipe, but if they are not available, use thinly shredded runner beans or mange-tout (snow peas).*

String Beans in Garlic

INGREDIENTS *serves 4-6*
400g/14oz string beans
1 large or 2 small cloves garlic
3 tbsp oil
1 tsp salt
1 tsp sugar
1 tbsp light soy sauce

METHOD
Trim the beans. Leave them whole if they are young and tender; otherwise, cut them in half. Crush and finely chop the garlic.

Blanch the beans in a pan of lightly salted boiling water, drain and plunge in cold water to stop the cooking and to preserve the beans' bright colour.

Heat the oil in a wok or frying pan. When it starts to smoke, add the crushed garlic to flavour the oil. Before the colour of the garlic turns dark brown, add the beans and stir-fry for about 1 minute. Add the salt, sugar and soy sauce and continue stirring for another minute at most. Serve hot or cold.

Dry-Fried French Beans

INGREDIENTS *serves 4-6*
350g/12oz French (or other thin, green) beans
1 dried red chilli
1 cup/250ml/8fl oz peanut oil
1 tbsp garlic, chopped
1 tsp fresh ginger, chopped
1 tbsp dried shrimp, chopped
2 tsp dark soy sauce
¼ cup/60ml/2fl oz water
½ tsp sesame oil
1 tsp vinegar

SEASONINGS
2 tsp rice wine
1 tsp monosodium glutamate (optional)
½ tsp salt
1 tsp sugar

METHOD
Trim the beans and cut each one in half. Chop the chilli into small pieces.

Heat the pan until it is very hot. Add the peanut oil. Fry the French beans and remove after 30 seconds. Drain the oil away.

Heat 1 tbsp oil in pan, add the chopped garlic, ginger and dried shrimp and stir-fry until fragrant (about 30 seconds). Add the seasonings and French beans to the pan and sauté for a further 30 seconds.

Add soy sauce and water and simmer over low heat until the sauce has almost evaporated.

Add the sesame oil and vinegar and sauté for a short while longer over high heat. Serve.

▼ *Dry fried French beans: Highly savoury pure vegetable dishes — such as this Sichuan speciality — are often used as a contrast to a pure meat dish in the composition of a well-balanced meal.*

Braised Chinese Broccoli

INGREDIENTS *serves 4-6*
1lb Chinese broccoli
3 tbsp oil
1 tsp salt
1 tsp sugar
1 tbsp soy sauce

METHOD
Trim off the tough leaves and blanch the rest in slightly salted boiling water until soft. Remove and strain.

Heat a wok until hot. Add the oil and wait until it starts to smoke. Stir-fry the broccoli with the salt and sugar for 1½-2 minutes. Remove and arrange neatly on a long serving dish. Pour on the soy sauce and serve.

Chinese Cabbage and Mushrooms

INGREDIENTS *serves 4-6*
6-8 dried Chinese mushrooms
1lb Chinese cabbage leaves
3 tbsp oil
1 tsp salt
1 tsp sugar
1 tbsp soy sauce
1 tsp sesame seed oil

METHOD
Soak the mushrooms in warm water for about 20 minutes. Squeeze them dry and discard the hard stalks. Keep the water. Cut each mushroom in half or into quarters depending on the size. Cut the cabbage leaves into pieces about the size of a large postage stamp.

Heat the oil in a wok, add the cabbage and the mushrooms and stir-fry until soft. Add the salt, sugar and soy sauce and cook for a further 1½ minutes. Mix in some of the water in which the mushrooms were cooked and the sesame seed oil.

▲ *Braised Chinese Broccoli.*

▶ *Chinese Cabbage and Mushrooms.*

▶ *Braised "Three Precious Jewels."*

Stir-Fried Broccoli

INGREDIENTS *serves 4-6*
9oz broccoli
3 tbsp oil
1 tsp salt
1 tsp sugar
2 tbsp water

METHOD

Cut the broccoli into small pieces and remove the rough skin from the stalks.

Heat the oil in a wok until hot and stir-fry the broccoli for about 1-1½ minutes. Add the salt, sugar and water and cook for a further 2 minutes. Serve hot.

Braised "Three Precious Jewels"

INGREDIENTS *serves 4-6*
2 cakes of tofu
½lb broccoli or snow peas
½lb carrots
4 tbsp oil
1 tsp salt
1 tsp sugar
1 tbsp light soy sauce
1 tbsp rice wine or dry sherry

METHOD

Cut the tofu into small pieces.

Cut the broccoli into flowerets. Peel the stems and cut diagonally into small pieces.

Peel the carrots and cut diagonally into small chunks.

Heat about half of the oil in a hot wok or skillet. Add the tofu pieces and shallow-fry on both sides until golden. Remove and keep aside.

Heat the rest of the oil. When very hot, stir-fry the broccoli and carrots for about 1-1½ minutes. Add the tofu, salt, sugar, wine and soy sauce and continue stirring, adding a little water if necessary. Cook for 2-3 minutes if you like the broccoli and carrots to be crunchy. If not, cook another minute or two. This dish is best served hot.

139

"Coral" Cabbage

Chinese white cabbage, also known as Chinese leaves or celery cabbage, is now widely available in the West.

Discard the outer tough leaves and use the tender heart only.

INGREDIENTS *serves 4-6*
1lb Chinese white cabbage
4-5 Chinese dried mushrooms
1/2 cup bamboo shoots
4-5 dried red chilies
2 tbsp sugar
1 tbsp soy sauce
1/2 tbsp rice wine or dry sherry
1 1/2 tbsp vinegar
1 tsp salt
1 scallion
1 slice ginger root, peeled
2 tbsp sesame seed oil

METHOD
Parboil the cabbage; remove and drain, marinate with 1/2 tsp salt for 5 minutes, then squeeze dry and cut into matchbox-sized pieces: arrange on a serving dish.

Soak the mushrooms in warm water for 20 minutes, then squeeze dry and discard the stalks. Cut the mushrooms, bamboo shoots, red chilies, scallion and ginger root into thin shreds the size of matches.

Heat up the sesame seed oil in a wok, stir-fry all the vegetables (except the cabbage) for 2 minutes. Add the sugar, soy sauce, rice wine or sherry, vinegar and salt with about 2 tbsp water or stock; stir-fry for 1-2 minutes more and pour over the cabbage.

This is a multi-colored dish and is especially delicious when served cold.

Hot and Sour Cabbage

INGREDIENTS *serves 4-6*
1 1/2lb white cabbage
10 Sichuan peppercorns
5 small dried red chili peppers
3 tbsp oil
2 tbsp soy sauce
1 1/2 tbsp vinegar
1 1/2 tbsp sugar
1 1/2 tsp salt
1 tsp sesame seed oil

METHOD
Choose a round, pale green cabbage with a firm heart – never use loose-leafed cabbage. Wash in cold water and cut the leaves into small pieces the size of a matchbox. Cut the chilies into small bits. Mix the soy sauce, vinegar, sugar and salt to make the sauce.

Heat the oil in a preheated wok until it starts to smoke. Add the peppercorns and the red chilies and a few seconds later the cabbage. Stir for about 1 1/2 minutes until it starts to go limp. Pour in the prepared sauce and continue stirring for a short while to allow the sauce to blend in. Add the sesame seed oil just before serving. This dish is delicious both hot and cold.

Chinese Cabbage Casserole

INGREDIENTS *serves 4-6*
1lb Chinese cabbage
2oz deep-fried tofu or 2 cakes fresh tofu
4oz carrots
3 tbsp oil
1 tsp salt
1 tsp sugar
2 tbsp light soy sauce
2 tbsp rice wine or dry sherry
1 tsp sesame seed oil

METHOD
Separate the Chinese cabbage leaves, wash and cut them into small pieces. If using fresh tofu, cut each cake into about 12 pieces and fry them in a little oil until golden.

Peel the carrots and cut them into diamond-shaped chunks.

Heat the oil in a hot wok and stir-fry the cabbage with the salt and sugar for a minute or so. Transfer it to a casserole and cover it with the tofu, carrots, soy sauce and sherry. Put a lid on the pot and when it comes to a boil reduce the heat and simmer for 15 minutes.

Stir in the sesame oil. Add a little water if necessary and cook for a few more minutes. Serve hot.

▶ *Hot and sour cabbage.*

▶▶ *In Northern China, cabbage is still the principle winter vegetable, and this recipe can be adapted for any of the more robust kinds of Chinese leaves which are available.*

Chinese Cabbage Salad

INGREDIENTS *serves 4-6*
1 small Chinese cabbage
2 tbsp light soy sauce
1 tsp salt
1 tsp sugar
1 tbsp sesame seed oil

METHOD
Wash the cabbage thoroughly, cut into thick slices and place in a bowl.

Add the soy sauce, salt, sugar and sesame seed oil to the cabbage. Toss well and serve.

NOTE
Green or or red peppers (or both) can be added to the cabbage.

Stir-Fried Chinese Greens

This variety of Chinese cabbage has bright green leaves with pale green stems and sometimes a sprig of yellow flowers in the center. Its other name is rape and rape seed oil is widely used for cooking in China.

INGREDIENTS *serves 4-6*
1lb Chinese green cabbage
1-2 slices ginger root, peeled
3 tbsp oil
1 tsp salt
1 tsp sugar
1 tbsp light soy sauce

METHOD
Wash the green cabbage and trim off any tough roots. Discard any outer, discolored leaves.

Cut the peeled ginger root into small pieces.

Heat the oil in a hot wok until it smokes and swirl it to cover most of the surface. Add the ginger root pieces to flavor the oil. Add the greens, stir for about 1 minute and then the salt and sugar. Continue stirring for another minute so. Pour in the soy sauce and cook for a little longer. Serve hot. This dish is often used to add color to a meal.

▲ *Chinese Cabbage Salad.*

◀ *Stir-Fried Chinese Greens.*

Stir-Fried Mixed Vegetables

INGREDIENTS *serves 4-6*
¼lb Chinese cabbage
¼lb carrots
¼lb snow peas
5-6 dried Chinese mushrooms
3 tbsp oil
1 tsp salt
1 tsp sugar
1 tsp water

METHOD

Soak the dried mushrooms in warm water for 25-30 minutes. Squeeze them dry, discard the hard stalks and cut into thin slices. Trim the snow peas and cut the Chinese cabbage and carrots into slices.

Heat the oil in a preheated wok. Add the Chinese cabbage, carrots, mange-tout peas and dried mushroom and stir-fry for about 1 minute. Add the salt and sugar and stir for another minute or so with a little more water if necessary. Do not overcook or the vegetables will lose their crunchiness. Serve hot.

Stir-Fried Green Cabbage

INGREDIENTS *serves 4-6*
1lb green cabbage
3 tbsp oil
1½ tsp salt
1 tsp sugar

METHOD

Choose a small, fresh cabbage and discard any outer tough leaves. Wash it under the cold water tap before cutting it into small pieces. In order to preserve its vitamin content, cook it as soon as you have cut it to limit exposure to the air.

Heat the oil in a hot wok until smoking, swirling it to cover most of the surface. Add the cabbage and stir-fry for about 1 minute. Add the salt and sugar and continue stirring for a further minute or so. Do not overcook because the cabbage will lose its crispness and its bright color. No water is necessary since the high heat will bring out the natural juice from the cabbage, particularly if it is fresh. This dish can be served hot or cold.

▲ *Stir-Fried Mixed Vegetables.*　　　▼ *Stir-Fried Green Cabbage.*

Shredded Cabbage with Red and Green Peppers

INGREDIENTS *serves 4-6*
1lb white cabbage
1 green pepper
1 red pepper
3 tbsp oil
1 tsp salt
1 tsp sesame seed oil

METHOD
Thinly shred the cabbage. Core and seed the green and red peppers and thinly shred them.

Heat the oil in a wok until hot. Add the cabbage and the peppers and stir-fry for 1-1½ minutes. Add the salt and stir a few more times. Add the sesame seed oil to garnish and serve either hot or cold.

▲ *Shredded Cabbage with Red and Green Peppers.*

▼ *Spicy Cabbage – Sichuan Style.*

Spicy Cabbage — Sichuan Style

INGREDIENTS *serves 4-6*
1lb white cabbage
2 tsp salt
3-4 dried hot chili peppers, soaked and finely chopped
3 scallions, finely chopped
2 tsp finely chopped fresh ginger root
2 tbsp sesame seed oil
2 tbsp sugar
¼ cup water
2 tbsp vinegar

METHOD
Discard the outer tough leaves of the cabbage and cut the tender heart into thin slices. Sprinkle with salt and let stand for 3-4 hours. Pour off the excess water and dry the cabbage thoroughly. Place it in a bowl or a deep dish.

Heat the sesame seed oil in a pan until very hot. Add the finely chopped chilies, scallions and ginger root. Stir for a few seconds and then add the sugar and water. Continue stirring to dissolve the sugar. Add the vinegar and bring the mixture to a boil. Remove the pan from the heat and allow the sauce to cool; then pour it over the cabbage. Cover the bowl or plate and leave to stand for 3-4 hours before serving.

Poached Vegetables with Oyster Sauce

INGREDIENTS *serves 6-8*
2lb Chinese greens (flowering cabbage, Chinese spinach or lettuce)
3-4 tbsp peanut oil
3-4 tbsp oyster sauce

METHOD
Clean the vegetables. If you are using Chinese greens or Chinese kale, remove and discard the flowers and tough woody stem.

Put the vegetables into boiling water and cook for 3-5 minutes (if you are using lettuce, cook for only 1 minute). Remove and cut into 2in pieces.

Place the vegetables on a plate, add boiling peanut oil and oyster sauce and serve.

Instead of oyster sauce, 1 tbsp of light and 1 tbsp of dark soy sauce is an equally tasty alternative.

Chinese Cabbage and Straw Mushrooms in Cream Sauce

INGREDIENTS *serves 4-6*
14oz Chinese cabbage
$\frac{3}{4}$lb canned straw mushrooms or $\frac{1}{2}$lb fresh straw mushrooms
4 tbsp oil
1$\frac{1}{2}$ tsp salt
1 tsp sugar
1 tbsp cornstarch mixed with 3 tbsp cold water
$\frac{1}{2}$ cup milk

METHOD
Separate the cabbage leaves and cut each leaf in half lengthwise.

Drain the straw mushrooms. If using fresh ones, do not peel them but just wash and trim off the roots.

Heat 3 tbsp oil in a hot wok and stir-fry the cabbage leaves for about 1 minute. Add the salt and sugar and continue stirring for another minute or so. Remove the cabbage leaves and arrange them neatly on one side of a serving dish.

Heat the remaining oil until hot, then reduce the heat and add the cornstarch and water mixture and the milk and stir until thickened. Pour about half of the sauce into a pitcher and keep warm.

Add the mushrooms to the remaining sauce in the wok and heat them thoroughly over high heat. Remove the mushrooms and place them next to the cabbage leaves on the plate. Pour the sauce from the jug evenly over the cabbage and mushrooms and serve.

▼ *Chinese Cabbage and Straw Mushrooms in Cream Sauce.*

Vegetarian "Lion's Head" Casserole

Vegetarian cuisine has a long history in China, and many interesting and imaginative dishes have been created. This is a non-meat version of the lion's head casserole on page 76.

INGREDIENTS *serves 4-6*
4 cakes fresh tofu
¼lb fried gluten
½ cup sliced cooked carrots
4-5 dried Chinese mushrooms, soaked
⅓ cup bamboo shoots
6 cabbage or lettuce hearts
5 large cabbage leaves
1 tsp finely chopped fresh ginger root
2 tbsp rice wine or dry sherry
1 tbsp salt
1 tbsp sugar
1 tsp ground white pepper
2 tsp sesame seed oil
1 tbsp cornstarch
½ cup ground rice or breadcrumbs
oil for deep-frying
all-purpose flour for dusting

METHOD

Squeeze as much liquid as possible from the tofu, using cheesecloth, and then mash. Finely chop the gluten, carrots, mushrooms and bamboo shoots. Place them with the mashed tofu in a large mixing bowl. Add 1 tsp salt, the finely chopped ginger root, ground rice, cornstarch and sesame seed oil and blend everything together until smooth. Make 10 meatballs from this mixture and place them on a plate lightly dusted with flour. Trim off any hard or tough roots from the cabbage or lettuce hearts.

Heat the oil in a wok or deep-fryer. When hot, deep-fry the 'meatballs' for about 3 minutes, stirring very gently to make sure that they are not stuck together. Scoop out with a slotted spoon or strainer and drain.

Pour off the excess oil leaving about 2 tbsp in the wok. Stir-fry the cabbage hearts with a little salt and sugar. Add about 2½ cups water and bring to a boil. Reduce the heat and let the mixture simmer.

Meanwhile, line the bottom of a casserole with the cabbage leaves and place the "meatballs" on top. Pour the cabbage

hearts with the soup into the casserole and add the remaining salt, ground pepper and wine or sherry. Cover, bring to a boil, reduce the heat and simmer for 10 minutes.

To serve, take off the lid and rearrange the cabbage hearts so that they appear between the "meatballs" in a star-shaped pattern.

Chinese Cabbage, Noodles, Dried Shrimps and Shredded Pork

INGREDIENTS *serves 6-8*
1¼lb Chinese cabbage
¼lb cellophane noodles
5oz dried shrimps
2oz fillet of pork
3-4 tbsp peanut oil
3-4 slices fresh ginger root
4 cups chicken stock
1 tsp salt
2 tsp Chinese yellow wine

SEASONING
1 tsp salt
2 tsp cornstarch
½ tsp sesame oil
½ tsp sugar

METHOD
Cut the Chinese cabbage into ½×2in pieces.

Soak the mung bean noodles and the dried shrimp in water for about 15 minutes until they are softened.

Shred the fillet of pork and mix the meat with the seasoning ingredients.

Heat 3-4 tbsp oil in a clay pot or a wok and add the ginger slices and shredded fillet of pork, stirring to separate. Then add the dried shrimps.

Add the Chinese cabbage, stir and mix well. Pour in the chicken stock and bring the contents to a boil. Reduce the heat and simmer for 15 minutes. Add the mung bean noodles and simmer for a further 2-3 minutes. Finally add salt and Chinese yellow wine and serve.

This simple recipe nevertheless has marvellous flavor. If you increase the quantities of chicken stock and wine, the dish becomes more soup-like in consistency. Either way, it should be served with a bowl of rice.

▲ *Chinese Cabbage, Noodles, Dried Shrimp and Shredded Pork: an inexpensive, homly dish with a semi-soup consistency. Dried shrimp – stronger in flavor than fresh – are used in China like boullion cubes in the west, to provide a savory base. More than half the liquid is absorbed by the transparent noodles.*

Chinese White Cabbage with Chilies

INGREDIENTS *serves 5-6*
1 3lb Chinese white cabbage
3 small fresh red chili peppers
2 dried red chili peppers
1½ tsp Sichuan peppercorns
2 tsp salt
½ tsp sesame seed oil
1 tbsp vegetable oil

METHOD
Chop the cabbage coarsely, discarding the tougher parts. Coarsely chop the chilies, discarding the seeds. Pound the peppercorns lightly. Place the cabbage in a large bowl, sprinkle evenly with the salt, chilies and peppercorns. Toss to mix. Refrigerate for 2-3 days before serving. Sprinkle the cabbage with the oils; toss well and serve.

Three Whites in Cream Sauce

INGREDIENTS *serves 6-8*
10oz Chinese cabbage hearts
10oz canned white asparagus spears
1-2 celery hearts
1 tbsp oil
1 scallion, cut into short lengths
2-3 slices ginger root, peeled
1½ tsp salt
1 tsp sugar
½ cup milk
1 tbsp cornstarch mixed with 3 tbsp cold
   water

METHOD
Cut the cabbage hearts lengthwise into thin strips. Blanch them in boiling water until they are soft and remove and arrange them neatly in the middle of a long serving dish.

Drain and place the asparagus spears on one side of the cabbage hearts.

Cut the celery hearts lengthwise into strips, blanch until soft and place them on the other side of the cabbage.

Heat the oil over low heat and add the scallion and ginger root to flavor the oil. Discard as soon as they start turning brown. Add the milk, salt and sugar and bring to the boil. Add the cornstarch and water mixture

to thicken, stir to make it smooth and pour evenly over the vegetables. Serve hot or cold.

▲ ▲ *Three Whites in Cream Sauce – unusually, a dish with a milk-based sauce.*

▲ *Chinese cabbage is here prepared as a sort of "instant pickle."*

▲ *Sweet and Sour Cucumber*   ▼ *Stir-Fried Cauliflower.*

Sweet and Sour Cucumber Salad

INGREDIENTS *serves 4-6*
1 cucumber
2 tsp finely chopped fresh ginger root
1 tsp sesame seed oil
2 tbsp sugar
2 tbsp rice vinegar

METHOD
Select a dark green and slender cucumber; the fat pale green ones contain too much water and have far less flavor. Cut it in half lengthwise, then cut each piece into slices. Marinate with the ginger and sesame seed oil for about 10-15 minutes.

Make the dressing with the sugar and vinegar in a bowl, stirring well to dissolve the sugar.

Place the cucumber slices on a plate. Just before serving, pour the sugar and vinegar dressing evenly over them and toss well.

Celery Salad with Scallion and Oil Dressing

INGREDIENTS *serves 4-6*
10oz celery
1 tsp salt
1 tsp sugar
3-4 scallions, finely chopped
3 tbsp salad oil

METHOD
Wash and dry the celery. Cut into thick slices. Sprinkle with salt and sugar. Leave to marinate for 10-15 minutes.

Place the finely chopped scallions in a heat-resistant bowl. In a pan, heat the oil until quite hot and pour over the scallions. Add the tomatoes, toss well and serve.

NOTE
Other vegetables such as cucumber, tomatoes and green peppers can be served in the same way.

Stir-Fried Cauliflower

INGREDIENTS *serves 4-6*
1 cauliflower
3 tbsp oil
2 tsp salt
1 tsp sugar
4 tbsp water

METHOD
Wash the cauliflower in cold water and discard the tough outer leaves. Cut into flowerets.

Heat the oil in a wok and stir-fry the cauliflower for about 1 minute. Add the salt, sugar and water and cook for a further 2 minutes or, if you prefer your vegetables well done, for 5 minutes, adding a little water if necessary. Serve hot.

Steamed Cauliflower

INGREDIENTS *serves 4-6*
1 medium-sized cauliflower
1 tsp salt
1 tbsp rice wine or dry sherry
1 tbsp sesame seed oil
1 cube fermented red bean curd

METHOD
When choosing cauliflower, make sure the leaves that curl round the flower are bright green and not withered. Bright leaves show that the cauliflower is fresh. Wash the cauliflower well under the cold water tap, trim off the hard root and discard the tough outer leaves. Keep a few of the tender leaves on as they add to the color and flavor.

Place the cauliflower in a snugly fitting bowl. Mix salt, wine and sesame seed oil and pour them evenly over the cauliflower, covering its entire surface. Place the bowl in a steamer and cook over high heat for 10-15 minutes.

To serve, remove bowl from the steamer. Crush the fermented red bean curd with a little sauce and pour it over the cauliflower. You should be able to break the cauliflower into flowerets either with a spoon or a pair of chopsticks. Serve hot.

Celery Salad

INGREDIENTS *serves 4-6*
1 celery
1 tsp salt
7½ cups water
2 tbsp light soy sauce
1 tbsp vinegar
1 tbsp sesame seed oil
2 slices fresh ginger root, finely shredded

METHOD
Remove the leaves and outer tough stalks of the celery. Thinly slice the tender parts diagonally. Blanch them in a pan of boiling, salted water. Then pour them into a colander and rinse in cold water until cool. Drain.

Mix together the soy sauce, vinegar and sesame seed oil. Add to the celery and toss well.

Garnish the salad with finely shredded ginger root and serve.

▲ *Steamed Cauliflower.*   ▼ *Celery Salad.*

149

Crispy "Seaweed"

You might be surprised or even shocked to learn that the very popular "seaweed" served in Chinese restaurants is, in fact, green cabbage! Choose fresh, young collard greens with pointed heads. Even the deep green outer leaves are quite tender. This recipe also makes an ideal garnish for a number of dishes, particularly cold appetizers and buffet dishes.

INGREDIENTS *serves 6-8*
1½lb collard greens
2½ cups oil for deep-frying
1 tsp salt
1 tsp sugar

METHOD
Wash and dry the green leaves and shred them with a sharp knife into the thinnest possible shavings. Spread them out on paper towels or put in a large colander to dry thoroughly.

Heat the oil in a wok or deep-fryer. Before the oil gets too hot, turn off the heat for 30 seconds. Add the collard green shavings in several batches and turn the heat up to medium high. Stir with a pair of cooking chopsticks. When the shavings start to float to the surface, scoop them out gently with a slotted spoon and drain on paper towels to remove as much of the oil as possible. Sprinkle the salt and sugar evenly on top and mix gently. Serve cold.

Stir-Fried Leeks with Wood Ears

INGREDIENTS *serves 4-6*
½oz Wood Ears
1lb leeks
3 tbsp oil
1 tsp salt
1 tsp sugar
1 tsp sesame seed oil

METHOD
Soak the Wood Ears in water for 20-25 minutes, rinse well and discard the hard roots if any. Drain.

Wash the leeks and cut them diagonally into chunks.

Heat the oil in a hot wok or skillet. Use a scooper or spatula to spread the oil so that most of the surface is well greased. When the oil starts to smoke, add the leeks and Wood Ears, and stir-fry for about 1 minute. Add the salt and sugar and continue stirring. Wet with a little water if necessary. Add the sesame seed oil to garnish and serve hot.

Stir-Fried Lettuce

INGREDIENTS *serves 4-6*
1 large Romaine lettuce
3 tbsp oil
1 tsp salt
1 tsp sugar

METHOD
Discard the tough outer leaves. Wash the remaining leaves well and shake off the excess water. Tear the larger leaves into 2 or 3 pieces.

Heat the oil in a wok or large saucepan. Add the salt followed by the lettuce leaves and stir vigorously as though tossing a salad. Add the sugar and continue stirring. As soon as the leaves become slightly limp, transfer them to a serving dish and serve.

▲ *Crispy "Seaweed" garnished with dried scallops. Toasted split almonds make another interesting topping.*

◄ *Leeks are here combined with the charmingly and appropriately named Wood Ear fungus in a quick and easy stir-fried dish.*

▲ *Pan-Fried Chive and Dried Shrimp Cakes: this is a luxury version of the more standard onion cakes. The cakes are* *actually thickish pancakes containing chives or onion and garnished with shrimp. The dough is shallow-fried.*

Pan-Fried Chive and Dried Shrimp Cakes

INGREDIENTS *serves 8-10*
1 cup all-purpose flour
6 tbsp cold water
2oz dried shrimps
1¼lb Chinese chives
4 tbsp peanut oil
1 tsp Chinese yellow wine
1 tbsp light soy sauce
2 tbsp fresh ginger root, shredded
6 tbsp brown sugar

METHOD
Mix the flour and water in a bowl, first stirring with a fork, then kneading with your hands. Transfer the dough to a clean bowl, cover and leave to stand for 45 minutes.

Soak the dried shrimps in 4 tbsp hot water for 30 minutes before grinding them.

Chop the chives and set them aside.

Heat 3 tbsp oil in a pan. Add the shrimps and sauté for 30 seconds, then add the Chinese yellow wine, soy sauce and the chopped chives, stir and cook for 30 seconds. Remove from the pan and set aside.

Knead the dough for about 5 minutes until it is smooth. Roll it into a sausage shape and divide it into approximately 30 portions. Roll each piece into a ball. Flatten the dough with your hands and roll each one into a disc about 2in across.

Put 1 tbsp chives and shrimps in the center of each piece of dough and cover it with another piece. Seal the edges and place it on a lightly floured surface. Cover with a damp cloth. Repeat until all the dough is used up.

Place the cakes on lightly greased plates and steam over a high heat for 15 minutes. Remove and set aside.

Heat the pan and add 1 tbsp oil. Place the cakes in the pan and fry over low heat until golden in color; turn over and fry the other side until golden. Serve with shredded ginger and brown vinegar.

◄ *Stir-Fried Lettuce only needs the briefest of cooking – too long over the flames and the leaves will lose all "bite."*

Fresh Mushrooms and Bamboo Shoots in Shrimp Roe Sauce

INGREDIENTS *serves 6-8*
14oz fresh or canned straw mushrooms
2¹⁄₃ cups bamboo shoots
1 cup peanut oil
1 clove garlic
4 slices fresh ginger root
1 tbsp dried shrimp roe (if not available use bottled shrimp sauce)
1 tsp salt
1 tsp sugar

SAUCE
1 tbsp oyster sauce
1 tbsp light soy sauce
1 tsp dark soy sauce
¹⁄₂ tsp sugar
1 tsp sesame oil
1 tsp Chinese yellow wine
1¹⁄₂ tbsp cornstarch
¹⁄₂ cup chicken stock

METHOD
Cut the mushrooms in half, and cut the bamboo shoots into slices 1×2×¹⁄₈in.

Blanch the bamboo shoots in boiling water for 5 minutes. Remove and set aside. (If you are using canned bamboo shoots this is not necessary.)

Blanch the mushrooms in boiling water for 1 minute. (Again, this is not necessary if you are using canned mushrooms.) Remove and set aside.

Heat the oil in a pan. Add the bamboo shoots and fry for 1 minute, then add the mushrooms and fry for 1 minute. Remove, drain and set aside.

Heat 3-4 tbsp oil in a pan and add the ginger and garlic. When they have browned, remove them with a perforated spoon and discard.

Add the dried shrimp roe (or 2¹⁄₂ tsp shrimp sauce) and return the bamboo shoots and mushrooms to the pan. Add 1 tsp salt and 1 tsp sugar, stirring quickly, and cook for 1 minute.

One by one, add the sauce ingredients to the pan, stirring continually over a high heat until the liquid is reduced to half. Serve hot.

Stir-Fried Snow Peas with Chinese Mushrooms

INGREDIENTS *serves 4-6*
6-8 dried Chinese mushrooms
8oz snow peas
3 tbsp oil
1 tsp salt
1 tsp sugar

METHOD
Soak the dried mushrooms in warm water for 25-30 minutes. Squeeze dry and discard the hard stalks. Keep the water. Cut each mushroom into small pieces.

Wash and trim the snow peas. If large, they should be snapped in half. Smaller ones can be left whole.

Heat the oil in a very hot wok or large skillet until smoking. Cook the snow peas by stir-frying for a few seconds. Then add the mushrooms, the salt and sugar and continue stirring for about 30 seconds. Add a little of the water in which the mushrooms were soaked. Serve as soon as the liquid starts to boil.

NOTE
A little cornstarch mixed with cold water can be added to thicken the liquid at the last minute.

San Shian — "The Three Delicacies"

INGREDIENTS *serves 4-6*
1¹⁄₃ cups winter bamboo shoots
¹⁄₄lb oyster or straw mushrooms
10oz fried gluten or deep-fried tofu
4 tbsp oil
1¹⁄₂ tsp salt
1 tsp sugar
1 tbsp light soy sauce
1 tsp sesame seed oil
fresh coriander leaves to garnish (optional)

METHOD
Cut the bamboo shoots into thin slices. The oyster mushrooms can be left whole if small; otherwise halve or quarter them. Straw mushrooms can be left whole.

Heat the oil in a hot wok or skillet, swirling it so that most of the surface is well greased. When the oil starts to smoke, add the bamboo shoots and mushrooms and stir-fry for about 1 minute. Add the gluten or tofu together with salt, sugar and soy sauce. Continue stirring for 1-1¹⁄₂ minutes longer, adding a little water if necessary. Finally add the sesame seed oil, blend well and serve hot.

▲ *Fresh Mushrooms and Bamboo Shoots in Shrimp Roe Sauce: mushrooms have a fairly distinctive flavor in themselves, particularly if the dried kind are used, but the taste of this dish is made even stronger by the addition of shrimp roe.*

▶ *San Shian: the "Three Delicacies" are bamboo shoots, mushrooms and fried gluten.*

▲ *Stewed Ham and Mustard Green in a casserole. The mustard greens are slightly vinegary and salty, which counteracts the richness of the ham. But care must be taken during long cooking that the dish does not become too salty.*

◀ *Braised Collard Hearts: select only the furled inner heart leaves for this recipe – the tougher outer leaves can be used to make crispy "seaweed."*

▲ *Stuffed Green Peppers, garnished with shredded ham.*

Stewed Ham and Mustard Greens in a Casserole

INGREDIENTS *serves 4-6*
½lb mustard greens
½lb cabbage
6 medium black mushrooms
⅓ cup Chinese ham
1 cup peanut oil
4 slices fresh ginger root
1 cup chicken stock

SAUCE
1 tbsp oyster sauce
1 tbsp light soy sauce
1 tsp dark soy sauce
1 tsp sugar
1 tsp sesame oil
2 tsp Chinese yellow wine

METHOD
Cut the mustard greens into pieces 1×2in and cut the cabbage into strips the same size.

Soak the mushrooms in hot water for 30 minutes. Remove and discard the stems and cut each cap into half.

Heat the oil and fry the cabbage for 1 minute. Drain well and set aside. Fry the mustard greens for 1 minute. Drain and set aside.

Heat 2 tbsp oil in a clay pot or casserole and add the mushrooms, cabbage and mustard greens. Place the ham on top but do not mix. Add the chicken stock and bring to a boil, reduce the heat and simmer for 30-45 minutes. Add the sauce ingredients and simmer for 2 minutes. Serve in a casserole or Chinese clay pot.

Stuffed Green Peppers

INGREDIENTS *serves 4-6*
½lb pork
¼lb fish fillet
1lb small round green peppers
1 tsp salt
1 tbsp rice wine or dry sherry
1 tbsp soy sauce
1 tbsp cornstarch
2 tsp sugar
1 clove garlic, crushed
½ tbsp crushed black bean sauce
2 tbsp oil

METHOD
Finely chop the pork and fish; mix with a little salt and cornstarch.

Wash the green peppers; cut them in half and remove the seeds and stalks. Stuff them with the meat and fish mixture; sprinkle with a little cornstarch.

Heat up 1 tbsp oil in a flat frying pan; put in the stuffed peppers, meat side down; fry gently for 4 minutes, adding a little more oil from time to time. When the meat side turns golden, add the crushed garlic, bean sauce, rice wine or sherry, sugar and a little stock or water. Simmer for 2-3 minutes, then add soy sauce and a little cornstarch mixed with cold water. Serve as soon as the gravy thickens.

Braised Collard Hearts

INGREDIENTS *serves 4-6*
1lb collard hearts
3-4 tbsp oil
1 tsp salt
1 tsp sugar
1 tbsp light soy sauce

METHOD
There is very little preparation. Just trim off the hard and tough roots if any.

Parboil the greens in a pot of boiling water for about 1 minute and then rinse them in cold water to preserve their bright green color.

Heat the oil in a hot wok or skillet and stir-fry the greens with salt and sugar. Cook for about 1-1½ minutes. Add the soy sauce and a little water and braise for another minute at the most. Serve hot.

Pickled Radishes

INGREDIENTS
24 radishes
2 tsp sugar
1 tsp salt

METHOD
Choose fairly large radishes that are roughly equal in size, if possible, and cut off and discard the stalks and tails. Wash the radishes in cold water and dry them thoroughly. Using a sharp knife, make several cuts from the top about two-thirds of the way down the sides of each radish.

Put the radishes in a large jar. Add the sugar and salt. Cover the jar and shake well so that each radish is coated with the sugar and salt mixture. Leave to marinate for several hours or overnight.

Just before serving, pour off the liquid and spread out each radish like a fan. Serve them on a plate on their own or as a garnish with other cold dishes.

Stir-Fried Green and Red Peppers

INGREDIENTS *serves 3-4*
1 large or 2 small green peppers, cored and seeded
1 large or 2 small red peppers, cored and seeded
3 tbsp oil
1 tsp salt
1 tsp sugar

METHOD
Cut the peppers into small diamond-shaped pieces; if you use one or two orange peppers, the dish will be even more colorful.

Heat the oil in a hot wok or skillet until it smokes. Spread the oil with a scooper or spatula so that the cooking surface is well greased. Add the peppers and stir-fry until each piece is coated with oil. Add salt and sugar. Continue stirring for about 1 minute and serve if you like your vegetables crunchy and crisp. If not, you can cook them for another minute or so until the skin of the peppers becomes slightly wrinkled. Add a little water if necessary during the last stage of cooking.

▲ *Green Beans and Red Pepper Salad.*

Green Bean and Red Pepper Salad

INGREDIENTS *serves 4-6*

½lb green beans

1 medium or 2 small red peppers, cored
   and seeded

2 slices fresh ginger root, thinly
   shredded

1½ tsp salt

1 tsp sugar

1 tbsp sesame seed oil

METHOD

Wash the green beans, snip off the ends and
cut into 2in lengths. Cut the red peppers
into thin shreds. Blanch them both in
boiling water and drain.

Put the green beans, red peppers and
ginger into a bowl. Add the salt, sugar and
sesame seed oil. Toss well and serve.

▲ *Stir-Fried Green Peppers, Tomatoes
and Onions.*

Stir-Fried Celery with Mushrooms

INGREDIENTS *serves 4-6*
1 small head of celery
4oz white mushrooms
3 tbsp oil
1½ tbsp oil
1 tsp sugar

METHOD
Wash the celery and thinly slice the stalks diagonally.

Wash the mushrooms and cut them into thin slices. Do not peel.

Heat the oil in a wok or skillet until it smokes, swirling it so that it covers most of the surface.

Add the celery and mushrooms and stir-fry for about 1 minute or until each piece is coated with oil. Add the salt and sugar and continue stirring. Add a little water if the contents get too dry. Do not overcook because the celery will lose its crunchy texture. This dish can be served either hot or cold.

Stir-Fried Green Peppers, Tomatoes and Onions

INGREDIENTS *serves 4-6*
1 large or 2 small green peppers
1 large or 2 small firm tomatoes
1 large or 2 small onions
3 tbsp oil
1 tsp salt
1 tsp sugar

METHOD
Core and seed the green peppers and peel the onions. Cut all the vegetables into uniform slices.

Heat the oil in a wok and wait for it to smoke. Add the onions and stir-fry for 30 seconds. Add the green peppers and continue cooking for 1 minute. Add the tomatoes, salt and sugar and cook for 1 minute more. Serve hot or cold.

◄ *Stir-Fried Celery with Mushrooms.*

Buddha's Fry

INGREDIENTS *serves 6-8*

1 tbsp dried Chinese mushrooms

1 tbsp golden needles (dried tiger lily
  buds)

2-3 Wood Ears

2 tbsp dried tofu skin

4 tbsp fresh straw mushrooms

$\frac{1}{3}$ cup bamboo shoots

$\frac{1}{2}$ cup Chinese cabbage or celery

$\frac{1}{2}$ cup snow peas, or green beans

$\frac{1}{2}$ cup broccoli or cauliflower

$\frac{1}{2}$ cup carrots

4 tbsp vegetable oil

2 tbsp soy sauce

$\frac{1}{2}$ tbsp sugar

1 tsp monosodium glutamate (optional)

1 tbsp cornstarch

$\frac{2}{3}$ cup mushroom stock

METHOD

Soak all the dried ingredients in separate
bowls; cut the larger dried mushrooms into
4 pieces, smaller ones can be left
ncut. Cut the golden needles in half; tear the
tofu skin into pieces roughly the same size as
the Wood Ears. Cut all the fresh vegetables
into a roughly uniform size.

Heat up about 2 tbsp oil; stir-fry the dried
mushrooms, golden needles, bamboo
shoots, snow peas and carrots for about 1
minute, add about half the soy sauce and
sugar; stir a few times more, then add about
half of the monosodium glutamate (if using)
and stock. Cover and cook for about 1
minute; mix in $\frac{1}{2}$ tbsp cornstarch to thicken
the gravy, then dish it out and keep warm.

Meanwhile heat up the remaining oil and
stir-fry the other ingredients (the Wood Ears
and tofu skin, fresh mushrooms, Chinese
cabbage and broccoli), add the remaining
soy sauce, sugar, monosodium glutamate
and stock. Cover and cook for about 1
minute, then add $\frac{1}{2}$ tbsp cornstarch, blend
well and put it on top of the first group of
vegetables. Garnish with sesame seed oil
and serve.

Ideally these two groups of vegetables
should be cooked simultaneously, for there
will be a loss of the fine quality if the gap
between the finishing cooking time of each
is too long.

Precious Things Casserole

INGREDIENTS *serves 4-6*

4-6 medium black mushrooms
4 tbsp peanut oil
3-4 slices fresh ginger root
4 tbsp dried shrimp
9oz Chinese cabbage
4 cups chicken stock
1/3 cup sliced bamboo shoots
1/3 cup chopped ham
1/3 cup sliced cooked chicken
1/3 cup cooked shrimps
1/3 cup sliced abalone
2 tsp salt
1 tsp sesame seed oil

METHOD

Soak the mushrooms in hot water for 30 minutes. Remove and discard the stems and set the caps to one side.

Heat the oil in a clay pot. Add the ginger slices, dried shrimp and Chinese cabbage cut into strips 1/2×3in and cook for 2 minutes.

Add the chicken stock, bring to a boil and cook over a medium heat for 10 minutes. Add the sliced bamboo shoots, mushrooms and ham and continue to cook over a medium heat for 15 minutes. Add the cooked chicken, fresh shrimp, abalone, salt and sesame seed oil. Serve.

The Four Seasons

INGREDIENTS *serves 4-6*

1 small can baby corn cobs (spring) – (bamboo shoots or young carrots can be used instead)
1 celery heart (summer)
1/2lb fillet of pork (autumn)
4-5 Chinese dried mushrooms (winter)
3 tbsp oil
1 tsp salt
1 tsp sugar
1 tbsp soy sauce
2 tbsp rice wine or dry sherry

METHOD

Soak the mushrooms in warm water for 20 minutes and discard the hard stalks. Cut the celery into small pieces. Drain the baby corn cobs. (If you are using carrots or bamboo shoots, cut into thin slices.)

Heat up 1 tbsp oil in a wok or skillet. Stir-fry the pork until the color changes. Remove the pork from the wok, add the remaining oil, and allow it to get hot. Put in the whole mushrooms and the other vegetables, and add the salt, sugar and pork. Stir a few times and add the soy sauce and rice wine or sherry. As soon as the juice starts to bubble, it is ready.

◄ *Buddha's Fry was traditionally made from eighteen ingredients, representing the eighteen buddhas. Nowadays it is more*

▲ *Precious Things Casserole.*

Pickled Vegetables

INGREDIENTS
Use four to six of the following vegetables, or more:

cucumber
carrot
radish or turnip
cauliflower
broccoli
green cabbage
white cabbage
celery
onion
fresh ginger root
leek
scallion
red pepper
green pepper
green beans
garlic

20 cups boiled water, cooled
6oz salt
2oz chili peppers
3 tsp Sichuan peppercorns
$\frac{1}{4}$ cup Chinese distilled spirit (or white rum, gin or vodka)
4oz fresh ginger root
4oz brown sugar

METHOD
Put the cold boiled water into a large, clean earthenware or glass jar. Add the salt, chilies, peppercorns, spirit, ginger and sugar.

Wash and trim the vegetables, peel if necessary and drain well. Put them into the jar and seal it, making sure it is airtight. Place the jar in a cool place and leave the vegetables to pickle for at least five days before serving.

Use a pair of clean chopsticks or tongs to pick the vegetables out of the jar. Do not allow any grease to enter the jar. You can replenish the vegetables, adding a little salt each time. If any white scum appears on the surface of the brine, add a little sugar and spirit. The longer the pickling lasts, the better.

Vegetarian Spring Rolls

INGREDIENTS *makes 20 rolls*
1 pack of 20 frozen spring roll skins
$\frac{1}{2}$lb fresh bean sprouts
$\frac{1}{2}$lb young tender leeks or scallions
$\frac{1}{4}$lb carrots
$\frac{1}{4}$lb white mushrooms
oil for deep-frying
$1\frac{1}{2}$ tsp salt
1 tsp sugar
1 tbsp light soy sauce

METHOD
Take the spring roll skins out of the packet and leave them to defrost thoroughly under a damp cloth. Wash and rinse the bean sprouts in a bowl of cold water and discard the husks and other bits and pieces that float to the surface. Drain. Cut the leeks or onions, carrots and mushrooms into thin shreds

To cook the filling, heat 3-4 tbsp oil in a preheated wok or skillet and stir-fry all the vegetables for a few seconds. Add the salt, sugar and soy sauce and continue stirring for about 1-1$\frac{1}{2}$ minutes. Remove and leave to cool a little.

To cook the spring rolls, heat about 6 cups oil in a wok or deep-fryer until it smokes. Reduce the heat or even turn it off for a few minutes to cool the oil a little before adding the spring rolls. Deep-fry 6-8 at a time for 3-4 minutes or until golden and crispy. Increase the heat to high again before frying each batch. As each batch is cooked, remove and drain it on paper towels. Serve hot with a dip sauce such as soy sauce, vinegar, chili sauce or mustard.

◀ *A firm favorite in Chinese restaurants, Vegetarian Spring Rolls are ideal for a buffet-style meal or for a snack.*

▼ *A selection of pickled vegetables, bottled when they are in season, provides extra dimension to a Chinese menu.*

Vegetarian Casserole

INGREDIENTS *serves 4-6*

9oz eggplant
¼lb green beans
9oz Chinese cabbage
6 medium black mushrooms
2oz transparent (cellophane) noodles
1¼ cups peanut oil
4 pieces sweet dried tofu
4 slices fresh ginger root
1 tsp garlic, chopped
2 tbsp fermented red tofu
2 cups chicken stock or water
2 pieces fried tofu
1 tsp salt
1½ tbsp cornstarch blended with 1½ tbsp water
1 tsp Chinese yellow wine
1 tsp sesame seed oil

METHOD

Cut the eggplant into long, thick strips, the green beans in half and the cabbage lengthwise into quarters. Soak the black mushrooms in hot water for 30 minutes. Remove and discard the stems and cut the caps in half. Soak the noodles in hot water for 10 minutes.

Heat the oil in a pan and fry all the vegetables for 1 minute over a high heat. Remove, drain and set aside. Sauté the sweet dried tofu over a low heat until it is slightly browned and then remove and set aside.

▲ *Vegetarian Casserole: any number of vegetables can be combined in this casserole, including root vegetables, leafy vegetables, bean sprouts, bamboo shoots or eggplant. They are cooked in meat stock or orange stock, and noodles, and perhaps tofu, may be added. The resulting semi-soup is a light accompaniment to heavier dishes.*

Heat 2 tbsp oil in a clay pot or casserole and add the ginger and garlic. Break the fermented red tofu into pieces and add 2 tbsp to the pot, stirring over a high heat to release the aroma.

Place all the vegetables in the clay pot and cook, stirring continuously, for 2 minutes. Add the chicken stock or water, place the fried tofu and sweet dried tofu sheets on top of the vegetables and bring to a boil. Cover the pot, lower the heat and simmer for 10 minutes.

Add the noodles and salt, recover the pot and cook for another 2 minutes over high heat. Stir in the softened cornstarch, add the Chinese yellow wine and sesame seed oil and serve immediately while still hot.

TOFU AND EGG DISHES

Eight Treasure Stuffed Tofu

This is a well-known Hakka dish. It may appear to be rather complicated, but it is worth the extra effort.

INGREDIENTS *serves 8-10*
6 cakes tofu
¼lb pork
¼lb fish fillet
¼lb shrimp, shelled
2 Chinese dried mushrooms, soaked
½ tsp salt
1 tbsp rice wine or dry sherry
½ tbsp cornstarch
1 tbsp soy sauce
2 tbsp oyster sauce
2 scallions
3 tbsp oil

METHOD
Parboil the tofu in salted water – 1 tsp salt in 8 cups water – for 2 minutes in order to harden them; remove and drain. Then cut each cake into four triangular pieces.

Coarsely chop the pork, fish, shrimp, mushrooms and 1 scallion; mix with salt, rice wine or sherry, soy sauce and cornstarch. Cut a slit on each tofu triangle and stuff with meat/fish mixture.

Fry the stuffed tofu, with the meat side down first, in hot oil for about 2 minutes, turning it over until both sides are golden. Add oyster sauce and a little water or stock and simmer for 3-4 minutes.

Garnish with scallion cut into short lengths; serve.

"Pock Marked Woman" Tofu

This is a nationally popular dish that originated from Sichuan. The "pock marked woman" was the wife of a well-known chef who worked in Chengdu about a hundred years ago; it was she who created this dish.

INGREDIENTS *serves 4-6*
3 cakes tofu
¼lb ground beef (or pork)
¼ tsp salt
1 tsp salted black beans
1 tbsp chili paste
3 tbsp stock
1 leek or 3 scallions
½ tbsp soy sauce
1 tbsp cornstarch
Sichuan pepper, freshly ground

METHOD
Cut the tofu into ½in cubes; blanch for 2-3 minutes to get rid of its plaster odor; remove and drain. Cut the leek or scallions into short lengths.

Heat up the oil until smoking; stir-fry the beef or pork until it turns dark in color; add salt, stir a few times, then add salted black beans. Crush them with the cooking ladle to blend well with the meat, then add chili paste; continue stirring. When you can smell the chili, add stock followed by the tofu and leek or scallion. Reduce heat; cook gently for 3-4 minutes; add soy sauce and the cornstarch mixed in a little water; stir gently to blend well and serve with freshly ground Sichuan pepper as a garnish.

▲ *Braised Tofu in Shrimp Roe Sauce with Chinese Flowering Cabbage: tofu tastes very bland unless cooked with strongly flavored foods. Here shrimp roe provides the savory taste.*

▶ *Fu-yung tofu should be light and creamy.*

Braised Tofu in Shrimp Roe Sauce with Chinese Flowering Cabbage

INGREDIENTS *serves 8-10*
6 cakes tofu
2lb Chinese green flowering cabbage
2 cups plus 2 tbsp peanut oil
1 tsp chopped fresh ginger root
1 tsp chopped garlic
1 tbsp shrimp roe
1 tbsp oyster sauce
1 tbsp light soy sauce
2 tsp Chinese yellow wine
1 tbsp cornstarch
4 tbsp chicken stock
1 tsp salt
1 tsp dark soy sauce
1 tsp sesame oil

METHOD
Cut each tofu cake into four pieces.

Remove the outer leaves of the Chinese flowering cabbage and blanch the heart for 3 minutes in boiling, salted water with 2 tbsp oil added. Remove the cabbage and set it aside keeping it warm.

Heat 2 cups oil in a pan. Add the pieces of tofu and cook until they are nicely golden in color. Remove them from the pan, drain and set them aside.

Heat 2 tbsp oil in the pan and add the ginger and garlic. When the aroma rises, add the shrimp roe, oyster sauce, light soy sauce, Chinese yellow wine, cornstarch and stock, stir and cook for 30 seconds. Return the tofu pieces to the pan and mix them thoroughly in the sauce.

Sprinkle the salt, dark soy sauce and sesame oil over the pan, stir and serve with the cabbage.

Fu-Yung Tofu

In most Chinese restaurants, fu yung means 'omelet', but strictly speaking, it should mean scrambled egg whites with a creamy texture.

INGREDIENTS *serves 4-6*
1 cake tofu
4 egg whites
1 romaine lettuce heart
$\frac{1}{2}$ cup green peas
1 scallion, finely chopped
$\frac{1}{2}$ tsp finely chopped ginger root
1 tsp salt
1 tbsp cornstarch mixed with 2 tbsp water
$\frac{1}{4}$ cup milk
oil for deep-frying
1 tsp sesame seed oil

METHOD
Cut the tofu into long, thin strips and blanch in a pan of salted boiling water to harden. Remove and drain.

Lightly beat the egg whites. Add the cornstarch mixture and milk.

Wash and separate the lettuce heart. If you use frozen peas, make sure they are thoroughly defrosted.

Wait for the tofu to cool and then coat with the egg white mixture.

Heat the oil in a wok or deep-fryer until it is very hot. Turn off the heat and let the oil cook a bit before adding the coated tofu. Cook for about 1-1$\frac{1}{2}$ minutes and then scoop out with a slotted spoon and drain.

Pour off the excess oil leaving about one tbsp in the wok. Increase the heat and stir-fry the lettuce heart with a pinch of salt. When lightly done, remove and set aside on a serving dish.

Heat another tbsp oil in the wok and add the finely chopped scallion and ginger root followed by the peas, salt and a little water. When the mixture starts to boil, add the tofu strips. Blend well, add the sesame seed oil, and serve on the bed of lettuce heart.

Crispy-Coated Coral Tofu

INGREDIENTS *serves 4-6*
14oz fresh shrimp
¼ cup pork fat
1 tsp salt
½ tsp pepper
1 tsp sesame oil
2 egg whites
2 tsp cornstarch
7oz tofu, crushed
3 cups peanut oil

PANCAKES
2 egg whites
3 tbsp cornstarch

SWEET AND SOUR SAUCE
4 tsp vinegar
3½ tsp sugar
2 tsp tomato catsup
1 tsp Worcestershire sauce
2 tsp ground red chili
salt to taste

METHOD
Shell and devein the shrimp. Wash them in salt water, drain and pat them dry with a paper towel. Crush with the flat side of chopper.

Dice the pork fat into small cubes and put the shrimp, pork fat, salt, pepper, sesame oil, 2 egg whites and the cornstarch into a bowl. Stir the ingredients in one direction until they are sticky, then add the crushed tofu and continue to stir until well mixed.

To make the pancakes beat the egg whites and add the cornstarch, stirring and mixing thoroughly. Heat a skillet, rub it with peanut oil and add sufficient egg white mixture to make a wafer-thin pancake. Peel and set aside. Continue until all the pancake mixture is used.

Flatten 1 tsp of the shrimp mixture on the palm of your hand and coat it with a little dry cornstarch. Wrap the mixture in one of the pancakes to form a roll about 1½×3in. Repeat until the mixture is used up.

Heat the peanut oil and deep-fry the rolls at a moderate heat until they are brown.

Serve with sweet and sour sauce spiced with the chili.

Steamed Stuffed Tofu

INGREDIENTS *serves 6-8*
3 cakes fresh tofu
1 tbsp dried shrimp
1 clove garlic
¼lb ground pork
¼ tsp salt
pepper to taste
½ tbsp vegetable oil
1 egg white
12 medium fresh or frozen shrimp

SAUCE
1½ tbsp vegetable oil
1½ tsp finely chopped fresh root ginger
2 tbsp coarsely chopped scallions
3 tbsp good stock
1 tbsp oyster sauce
½ tbsp light soy sauce
1 tsp sesame seed oil

METHOD
Cut each cake of tofu into 4 pieces. Scoop out a deep hollow in the center of each piece, about halfway through. Soak the dried shrimp in hot water to cover for 5 minutes, then drain and finely chop. Crush the garlic. Mix the pork, garlic, shrimp, salt, pepper, half of the oil and the egg white together in a bowl. Spoon this mixture into the tofu and place a whole fresh shrimp firmly on top.

Arrange the 12 pieces of stuffed tofu on a heatproof dish, place in a steamer and cook for 20 minutes. Meanwhile, heat the oil for the sauce in a small pan. When hot, add the ginger, scallion, stock, oyster sauce and soy sauce. Bring to a boil and stir well. When the tofu is ready, add the sesame seed oil to the sauce and pour it evenly over the tofu.

Five-Spice Tofu

INGREDIENTS *serves 3-4*
4 cakes tofu
3 tbsp light soy sauce
2 tbsp dark soy sauce
1 tsp salt
1 tbsp white or brown sugar
3 tbsp rice wine or dry sherry
2-3 scallions
2-3 slices ginger root
2 tsp five-spice powder

METHOD
Place the tofu in a saucepan and cover with cold water. Bring to a boil, cover and cook over a high heat for 10 minutes. By then the tofu will resemble a beehive in texture.

Reduce the heat and add the soy sauces, salt, sugar, wine, scallions, ginger root and five-spice powder. Bring to a boil gently under a cover and simmer for 30 minutes. Turn off the heat and leave to cool.

Remove the tofu and cut it into small slices or strips. Serve them either on their own or as part of an hors d'œuvre.

Tofu with Mushrooms

INGREDIENTS *serves 3-4*

4 cakes tofu
3-4 medium-sized dried Chinese
   mushrooms
1 tbsp sherry
4 tbsp oil
1 tbsp soy sauce
1 tsp cornstarch
½ tsp salt
½ tsp sugar
1 tsp sesame seed oil

METHOD

Soak the dried mushrooms in warm water for about 30 minutes. Squeeze them dry and discard the stalks. Keep the water for use as stock.

Slice each square of tofu into ¼ in thick slices and then cut each slice into 6 or 8 pieces.

Heat the oil in a wok and stir-fry the mushrooms for a short time. Add about ⅔ cup of the water in which the mushrooms have been soaking. Bring to a boil and add the tofu with the salt and sugar. Let it bubble for a while and then add the sherry and the sesame seed oil. Mix the cornstarch with the soy sauce and a little water in a bowl and pour it over the tofu in the wok so that it forms a clear, light glaze. Serve immediately.

▲ *Tofu with Mushrooms: the creamy taste and texture of the tofu in this recipe provides a good foil for the smokiness of the Chinese mushrooms.*

◄ *Five-Spice Tofu: an interesting addition to a platter of hors d'œuvres.*

► *Crispy-Coated Coral Tofu: the tofu is deep-fried briefly so that it is firm enough to pick up with chopsticks and is dipped into the sauce.*

Stir-Fried Spinach and Tofu

INGREDIENTS *serves 3-4*

½ lb spinach
2 cakes tofu
4 tbsp oil
1 tsp salt
1 tsp sugar
1 tbsp soy sauce
1 tsp sesame seed oil

METHOD

Wash the spinach well, shaking off the excess water. Cut up each cake of tofu into about 8 pieces.

Heat the oil in a wok. Fry the tofu pieces until they are golden, turning them over once or twice gently. Remove them with a slotted spoon and set aside.

Stir-fry the spinach in the remaining oil for about 30 seconds or until the leaves are limp. Add the tofu pieces, salt, sugar and soy sauce, blend well and cook for another 1-1½ minutes. Add the sesame seed oil and serve hot.

Sichuan Tofu

INGREDIENTS *serves 4-6*

2 tbsp dried Wood Ears or dried Chinese
   mushrooms
3 cakes tofu
1-2 leeks or 2-3 scallions
3 tbsp oil
1 tsp salted black beans
1 tbsp chili bean paste
2 tbsp rice wine or dry sherry
1 tbsp light soy sauce
1 tsp cornstarch mixed with 1 tbsp cold
   water
Sichuan pepper, freshly ground to
   garnish

METHOD

Soak the Wood Ears in water for 20-25
minutes, rinse them clean, discard any hard
roots and then drain. If you use dried
mushrooms, they should be soaked in hot or
warm water for at least 30-35 minutes.
Squeeze them dry, throw out the hard stalks
and cut into small pieces, retaining the
water for later use.

Cut the tofu into ½in square cubes.
Blanch them in a pan of boiling water for 2-
3 minutes, remove and drain.

Cut the leeks or scallions into short
lengths.

Heat the oil in a hot wok until it smokes
and stir-fry the leeks or scallions and the
Wood Ears or mushrooms for about 1
minute. Add the salted black beans, crush
them with the scooper or spatula and blend
well. Now add the tofu, the chili bean paste,
rice wine or sherry and soy sauce and
continue stirring to blend. Add a little water
and cook for 3-4 minutes more. Finally add
the cornstarch and water mixture to thicken
the gravy. Serve hot with freshly ground
Sichuan pepper as a garnish.

Tofu à la Maison

INGREDIENTS *serves 4-6*

4 cakes tofu
¼lb pork
⅓ cup leeks
5-6 red chilies
1 tbsp rice wine (or sherry)
1 tbsp soy sauce
2 tbsp crushed yellow bean sauce
½ tsp salt
½ tsp sesame seed oil
oil for deep-frying

METHOD

Split each cake of tofu into three or four thin
slices crossways, then cut each slice
diagonally into two triangles.

Cut the pork into small, thin slices;
diagonally cut the leek into chunks; cut the
dried red chilies into small pieces.

Heat up the oil; deep-fry the tofu pieces
for about 2 minutes; remove and drain.

Pour out the excess oil, leaving about 1
tbsp in the wok. Put in the pork and red
chilies, stir; add rice wine or sherry, soy
sauce, tofu, leek and crushed bean sauce;
cook for about 3 minutes. Add sesame seed
oil and serve.

Fried Tofu

INGREDIENTS *serves 4-6*

2-3 cakes tofu
1 slice peeled ginger root
1 scallion
2 tbsp oil
1 tsp salt
1 tbsp rice wine (or sherry)
½ tsp monosodium glutamate
2 tsp cornstarch
2 tbsp chicken stock
1 tsp sesame seed oil

METHOD

Coarsely cut the tofu and finely chop the
ginger root and scallion.

Heat up a wok or skillet over high heat
before putting in the oil. Fry the ginger root
and scallion, followed almost immediately
by the tofu; stir-fry for about 2-3 minutes,
breaking up the tofu into even smaller bits.
Then add salt, sherry and monosodium
glutamate together with cornstarch mixed
in chicken stock. Blend well.

Finally add sesame seed oil and serve.

◄ *Sichuan tofu.*

► *Tofu à la maison – I have given the dish
this name because it is such a typical
everyday Chinese dish.*

Basic Steamed Egg and Fancy Steamed Eggs

INGREDIENTS *serves 4-6*
2 eggs
1¼ cups good stock, or water
salt and pepper to taste
1 tbsp soy sauce
1 tbsp finely chopped scallion

OPTIONAL EXTRAS
2-3 tbsp shredded crab meat or shrimp
1-2 tbsp ham, chopped
1-2 tbsp peas

METHOD
The most basic Chinese steamed egg dish consists of no more than 2 eggs mixed with 1¼ cups stock or water in a dish with seasoning added and cooked in a steamer for about 15 minutes, or until the custard has set. It is then topped with a spoonful of soy sauce and a scattering of chopped scallion.

A more elaborate version consists of using the best grade stock, perhaps with a little shredded crab meat or other shellfish added. After steaming, the top of the custard should be set and firm enough so that more seafood can be arranged on top, together with some chopped ham and peas. The dish is then returned to the steamer for a further 3-4 minutes. After the second steaming, a large pinch of chopped scallion is sprinkled over the top. When cooking this dish, never use too many eggs, as this will cause the custard to become too firm and hard after steaming.

"Gold-Coin" Eggs

INGREDIENTS *serves 6-8*
6 eggs
1½ tbsp cornstarch
oil for shallow-frying

SAUCE
1 slice ginger root, peeled and finely chopped
1 scallion, finely chopped
2 green hot chilies, finely chopped
2 tbsp soy sauce
1 tbsp vinegar
1 tsp sugar
1 tbsp rice wine or dry sherry
½ tsp monosodium glutamate (optional)
½ tsp sesame seed oil
1 tbsp cornstarch

METHOD
Hard boil the eggs for 5-6 minutes, shell and cut each egg into five coin-shaped slices. Coat each slice with a little cornstarch; shallow-fry both sides in a little hot oil until golden. Mix the sauce and pour it over the egg slices; stir gently to blend them very carefully. Arrange the "gold coins" on a serving dish.

Scrambled Eggs with Roast Duck Fat

INGREDIENTS *serves 2-3*
5-6 tbsp roast duck fat from roasting pan of Peking duck (see page 42)
4 tbsp chicken stock
2 tsp salt
¼ tsp pepper
6 eggs
1 tbsp ground ham
1 tbsp chopped coriander

METHOD
In a mixing bowl mix 2-3 tbsp duck fat with the chicken stock, salt and pepper and the eggs.

Heat 2-3 tbsp duck fat in a pan and add the egg mixture, beaten and well blended. Scramble over medium heat until set.

Remove and place on plate. Sprinkle with ground ham and chopped coriander and serve.

▶ *Scrambled eggs with roast duck fat.*

◀ *Fancy Steamed Eggs, here garnished with crab meat and peas.*

Pan-Fried Egg Dumpling with Ground Pork and Shrimp

INGREDIENTS *serves 4-6*
6 eggs

MARINADE
1 tbsp egg white (reserved from eggs
   above)
1 tsp salt
1 tsp cornstarch
1/2 tsp sesame seed oil
1/4 lb fillet of pork, ground
8oz shrimp, shelled and deveined
1 medium onion
1 1/4 cups peanut oil
1 tbsp coriander, chopped

METHOD
Break the eggs into a mixing bowl, reserving
1 tbsp egg white for the marinade. Beat the
remainder lightly. Make the marinade in a
separate bowl and mix the pork with half of
the mixture.

Clean the shrimp. Pat them dry and mix
with the other half of the marinade. Keep
refrigerated for 30 minutes.

Chop the onion and set it aside.

Heat the oil in a pan. Add the shrimp,
stirring to separate, and remove them when
their color has changed. Drain and set aside.

Sauté the pork for 2 minutes. Remove
and set aside. Sauté the chopped onion for 1
minute. Remove and set aside.

Mix the pork, shrimp, onion and
coriander with the beaten egg. Heat 1 tbsp
oil in the pan and put 2 tbsp of the egg
mixture in the pan to form one dumpling.
Fry it gently over a medium heat, turning it
over gently until both sides are nicely golden
brown. Make 2 or 3 at a time and continue
until all the ingredients are used. This
simple but effective recipe will make 8 or 10
dumplings in all.

▶ *Pan-Fried Egg Dumpling with Ground
Pork and Shrimp: this is really a type of
Chinese omelet, but with an extra
succulence and delicacy. Patience is the
key to success in this dish – use low heat to
avoid burning the dumplings.*

▲ Preserved eggs with their outer coating of rice husks. To remove the coating, soak in water until the mud softens and comes off easily.

Boatmen's Egg Omelet

INGREDIENTS *serves 4-6*
7 eggs
1 tsp salt
pepper to taste
8 tbsp vegetable oil
1 tbsp finely chopped onion
3 tbsp cooked crab meat
3 tbsp shelled fresh shrimp
3 tbsp peas
2 tbsp finely chopped scallion
1½ tbsp soy sauce

METHOD

Break the eggs into a bowl with the salt and pepper and beat lightly with a fork. Heat 3 tbsp of the oil in a wok or skillet. When hot, stir-fry the onion for a few seconds. Add the crab meat and spread evenly over the bottom of the pan. Pour in one third of the eggs and cook until almost set. With the aid of a spatula, transfer to a heated dish. Re-heat the wok or pan with about 2 tbsp oil and, when hot, add the shrimp. Spread over the bottom of the pan and then pour on another third of the eggs. Cook until almost set, then stack on top of the first "pancake." Re-heat the wok or pan with about 2 tbsp oil and, when hot, add the peas and scallions. Stir-fry for a few seconds, then spread evenly over the bottom of the pan. Pour in the remaining egg and cook until almost set, then stack on top of the other 2 pancakes.

Cut the "triple pancake" into 8 segments. Sprinkle with soy sauce.

Preserved Eggs and Ground Pork

Preserved eggs are sometimes called ancient or thousand-year-old eggs. In fact they are duck's eggs preserved in a mixture of alkali, lime ashes, mud and other materials. After a few months the chemicals penetrate the eggshell, turning both the white and yolk a dark brownish-green color. Normally they are served uncooked.

There are prohibitions on importing these eggs into some countries, and so they are not always obtainable. Moreover, they are an acquired taste, although they *are* a lot more palatable than they look. The recipe below is one example of how they are used.

INGREDIENTS *serves 3-4*
2 Chinese preserved eggs
½lb pork
1 tbsp oil
1½ tbsp soy sauce
1 tsp sesame seed oil

METHOD

Remove the mud covering the egg shells, then clean them in water thoroughly before cracking them. Coarsely chop the eggs and the pork, keeping the two ingredients separate.

Heat the oil and fry the pork. When its color changes, put in the chopped eggs, add the soy sauce and mix well. Finally stir for 3-4 minutes; add sesame seed oil and then serve immediately.

Fried Gluten

Prepared gluten, either plain or ready-fried, is available from Chinese grocers, usually in cans. You can, however, extract your own from flour.

INGREDIENTS *serves 4-6*
2lb flour
1 tbsp salt
2 cups warm water
oil for deep-frying
1 tsp salt
1 tsp sugar
1 tbsp light soy sauce
¼ tsp monosodium glutamate (optional)

METHOD

Sift the flour into a large mixing bowl. Add the salt and the water gradually to make a firm dough. Knead until smooth and then cover with a damp cloth and leave to stand for about 1 hour.

Place the dough in a large colander or strainer and run cold water over it while you press and squeeze the dough with your hands to wash out as much of the starch as you can.

After 10-15 minutes of this hard work, you will end up with about 11oz gluten. Squeeze off as much water as you can and then cut the gluten into about 35-40 small pieces. These can then be cooked either by deep-frying, boiling, steaming or baking.

To fry, heat the oil in a wok or deep-fryer. When hot, deep-fry the gluten pieces in batches – about 6 to 8 at a time – for about 3 minutes or until they turn golden. Remove and drain.

Pour off the excess oil, leaving about 1 tbsp in the wok. Return the partly cooked gluten to the wok, add salt, sugar and soy sauce (and the monosodium glutamate if used), stir, and add a little water if necessary. Braise for about 2 minutes. Serve hot or cold.

Fried "Pocketed Eggs"

Eggs are frequently cooked this way in China. The only preparation you will need to do is to chop the scallion very finely.

INGREDIENTS *serves 4-6*
4 eggs
2-3 tbsp oil
1 tbsp light soy sauce
1 scallion, finely chopped

METHOD
Heat the oil in a hot wok or skillet and fry the eggs on both sides. Add the soy sauce and a little water and braise for 1-2 minutes. Garnish with scallion and serve hot.

Taking a bite of the egg and finding the yolk inside the white is rather like finding something in a pocket - hence the name of this dish.

▶ *Scrambled Eggs with Shrimp.*

Scrambled Eggs with Shrimp

Another name for this dish is *Fu Yung*, in which you are supposed to use the whites of eggs only.

INGREDIENTS *serves 4-6*
¼lb shrimp, shelled
⅓ cup bamboo shoots
1 slice ginger root, peeled
1 scallion
5 eggs including 1 separated
1 tsp salt
1 tbsp rice wine (or sherry)
1 tsp cornstarch
3 tbsp oil
Chinese parsley (fresh coriander) for garnish

METHOD
Marinate the shrimp in a little salt, half the egg white, rice wine or sherry and cornstarch.

Cut the bamboo shoots into small slices, the scallion into short lengths.

Heat 1 tbsp oil in a wok; stir-fry the shrimp and bamboo shoots for 1 minute; remove and mix with beaten eggs.

Heat the remaining oil, toss in the scallion followed by the beaten eggs. Stir for a few seconds until the eggs are set; do not over-cook. Serve with Chinese parsley as a garnish.

◀ *Fried "Pocketed Eggs"*

Stir-Fried Chinese Omelet with Tomatoes

INGREDIENTS *serves 4-6*
4-5 eggs
½ tsp salt
pepper to taste
1 medium onion
3 medium tomatoes
4-5 tbsp vegetable oil
1 tsp sesame seed oil
1½ tbsp scallion, finely chopped
1½ tbsp good quality dark soy sauce

METHOD
Break the eggs into a bowl with the salt and
pepper and beat lightly with a fork. Peel and
finely slice the onion. Cut each tomato into
8 segments.

Heat the vegetable oil in a wok or skillet.
When hot, gently stir-fry the onion for
about 30 seconds, then add the tomatoes.
Spread evenly over the bottom of the pan.
Pour over the beaten egg and allow to flow
over the base of the pan. When the edges of
the egg have begun to set, gently turn and
stir several times, allowing any uncooked
liquid to come in contact with the surface of
the pan. Sprinkle on the sesame seed oil and
arrange the omelet on a heated dish.
Sprinkle over the chopped scallion, with
extra scallion shreds if liked, and soy sauce
and serve.

▶ *Stir-Fried Chinese Omelet with*
Tomatoes.

Stir-Fried Chinese Omelet with Onion and Bacon

INGREDIENTS *serves 4-6*
4-5 eggs
½ tsp salt
pepper to taste
1 medium onion
2 rashers of bacon
4-5 tbsp vegetable oil
1½ tbsp scallion, finely chopped
1½ tbsp dark soy sauce

METHOD
Break the eggs into a bowl with the salt and
pepper and beat lightly with a fork. Peel and
finely slice the onion. Derind and finely slice
the bacon.

Heat the oil in a wok or skillet. When hot,
stir-fry the onion and bacon for about 1½
minutes. Spread evenly over the bottom of
the pan. Pour over the beaten egg and allow
to flow over the base of the pan. When the
edges of the egg have begun to set, gently
turn and stir several times, allowing any
uncooked liquid to come in contact with the
surface of the pan. Arrange on a heated dish,
sprinkle over the scallion and soy sauce and
serve.

Stir-Fried Shrimp "Soufflé"

INGREDIENTS *serves 4-6*
8oz king shrimp, fresh or frozen, shelled
1 tsp salt
pepper to taste
5 tbsp vegetable oil
2 tsp cornstarch
2 cloves garlic
3 scallions
4 eggs
1 tbsp rice wine or dry sherry

METHOD
Sprinkle the shrimp with the salt, pepper, ½
tbsp of the oil and dust with the cornstarch.
Crush the garlic. Cut the scallions into 1in
sections. Beat the eggs in a bowl.

Heat the remaining oil in a wok or skillet.
When hot, stir-fry the garlic and shrimp for
1½ minutes. Pour in the beaten egg and let
the egg flow over the surface of the pan.
Reduce the heat to low, sprinkle on the
scallions and cook for 1½ minutes. When
the eggs are almost set, toss with a metal
spoon. Sprinkle on the sherry and place on a
heated serving plate.

Egg Rolls

INGREDIENTS *serves 4-6*
¼lb pork
1 slice ginger root, peeled
1 scallion
½ tsp salt
2 tsp rice wine (or sherry)
1 cup bean sprouts
4-5 Chinese dried mushrooms, soaked
1 tbsp cornstarch
2 eggs
1 tbsp all-purpose
2½ cups oil for deep-frying
salt and Sichuan pepper for dip

METHOD
Finely grind the pork; mix it with finely chopped ginger root and scallion; add salt, wine or sherry and about ½ tbsp cornstarch. Blend well.

Beat up the eggs with the rest of the cornstarch, then warm up a wok or skillet over a moderate heat; grease the pan with a little oil and pour in half the beaten eggs. Tip the pan from side to side until a thin, round pancake of egg forms (about 6in in diameter). Gently lift the pancake up with a spatula and lay it flat on a plate. Make another pancake with the remaining eggs in the same way.

Mix the all-purpose flour with a little water to form a thin paste and spread some of it on the surface of the egg pancake. Chop the Chinese dried mushrooms into small pieces. Place about half of the pork mixture, bean sprouts and Chinese dried mushrooms on the pancake. Fold up the pancake as though doing up a package, sealing the edges with a little more flour paste, then press them down firmly.

Warm up the oil over a moderate heat; deep-fry the rolls for about 2-3 minutes, then increase the heat to high and continue cooking for about 10 minutes or until golden. Remove and drain.

Serve by dipping in salt and Sichuan pepper mix.

◀ *Egg Rolls with some of the ingredients used to make them – eggs, bean sprouts and Chinese dried mushrooms.*

Stir-Fried Eggs with Oysters

INGREDIENTS *serves 4-6*
5-6 eggs
½ tsp salt
2 tsp chopped fresh ginger root
4-5oz fresh or canned oysters
2 scallions
3 tbsp vegetable oil
1oz lard
1 tbsp rice wine or dry sherry

METHOD
Break the eggs into a bowl with half the salt
and beat lightly with a fork. Mix the ginger
and remaining salt with the oysters and
marinate for 15 minutes, then drain.
Coarsely chop the scallions.

Heat the oil and lard in a wok or skillet.
When hot, stir-fry the ginger, oysters and
scallions for 1 minute. Pour in the eggs and,
when they are almost set, stir a few times
and sprinkle on the wine or sherry. Cook for
a further 30 seconds and serve.

Eggs with Tomatoes

INGREDIENTS *serves 4-6*
9oz firm tomatoes
5 eggs
1½ tsp salt
2 scallions, finely chopped
1 tsp finely chopped ginger root
  (optional)
4 tbsp oil

METHOD
Scald the tomatoes in a bowl of boiling
water and peel off the skins. Cut each
tomato in half lengthwise and then crosscut
each half into wedges.

Beat the eggs with a pinch of salt and
about a third of the finely chopped scallions.

Heat about half the oil in a hot wok or
skillet and lightly scramble the eggs over a
moderate heat until set. Remove the eggs
from the wok.

Heat the wok again over high heat and
add the remaining oil. When the oil is hot,
add the rest of the finely chopped scallions,
the ginger root (if used) and the tomatoes.
Stir a few times and then add the scrambled
eggs with the remaining salt. Continue
stirring for about 1 minute and serve hot.
Note: other vegetables such as cucumber,
green peppers or green peas can be
substituted for the tomatoes.

▲ *Eggs with Tomatoes.*

RICE AND NOODLES

Boiled Rice

The best plain boiled rice is obtained by using only the long-grain rice known as patna. Should you prefer your rice to be softer and less fluffy, use half long-grain rice and half rounded, pudding rice and reduce the amount of water for cooking by a quarter.

INGREDIENTS *serves 4-6*
1¼ cups long-grain rice
2½ cups water

METHOD
Wash and rinse the rice in cold water until clean. Bring the water to a boil in a saucepan over high heat. Add the washed rice and bring back to a boil. Stir the rice with a spoon to prevent it sticking to the bottom of the pan and then cover the pan tightly with a lid and reduce the heat to very low. Cook gently for 15-20 minutes.
Note It is best not to serve the rice immediately. Fluff it up with a fork or spoon and leave it under cover in the pan for 10 minutes or so before serving.

Egg-Fried Rice

To use up leftover cooked rice, fry it with eggs. If you add a little finely chopped scallion and/or green peas, you will improve not only its flavor but its appearance as well.

INGREDIENTS *serves 6-8*
3 eggs
2 scallions, finely chopped
1 tsp salt
4 tbsp oil
1 cup green peas
4 cups cooked rice
1 tbsp light soy sauce (optional)

METHOD
Lightly beat the eggs with about half of the finely chopped scallions and a pinch of salt.

Heat about half of the oil in a hot wok or skillet, pour in the beaten eggs and lightly

scramble until set. Remove.

Heat the remaining oil and when hot, add the remaining scallions followed by the green peas and stir-fry for about 30 seconds. Add the cooked rice and stir to separate each grain. Add the salt and soy sauce together with the eggs and stir to break the eggs into small pieces. Serve as soon as everything is well blended.

▼ Rice: *a staple food throughout China especially in the south and west. White, long-grain rice is preferred to short or glutinous varieties for most meals as long, properly cooked fragrant grains are a perfect complement to other dishes served. To enjoy it at its best, be sure to use ordinary long-grain rice that needs to be washed before cooking in preference to instant or pre-cooked varieties which lack flavour.*

1 Egg-Fried Rice: fry in the beaten eggs until barely set.

2 Add plain boiled rice to the egg.

3 Add scallions and other ingredients to the mixture.

4 Season with soy sauce.

5 Turn and mix over low heat.

Yin and Yang Rice

INGREDIENTS *serves 4-6*
½lb chicken breast
9oz shrimp, shelled and deveined
4 tbsp peanut oil
1 tbsp shredded fresh ginger root
2 eggs, beaten
1 cup cold plain cooked rice
2 tbsp light soy sauce
1¼ cups chicken stock
1¼ cups peanut oil
½ cup peas
1 tsp salt
1 tsp fresh root ginger, chopped
1 tsp garlic, chopped

MARINADE
1 egg white
1 tbsp cornstarch
1 tsp sesame seed oil
1 tsp salt

WHITE SAUCE
8 tbsp chicken stock
2 tbsp milk
1 tbsp cornstarch
1 tsp salt

RED SAUCE
1½ tbsp tomato catsup
8 tbsp chicken stock
1 tbsp cornstarch
1 tsp sugar
1 tbsp light soy sauce

METHOD
Mix together the marinade ingredients in a bowl. Shred the chicken breasts and add to half of the marinade. Set aside.

Clean the shrimp and pat them dry. Mix them with the other half of the marinade in a bowl and refrigerate for 30 minutes.

Heat 4 tbsp oil in a pan and add 1 tbsp shredded ginger. When hot, add the beaten eggs and, when the eggs are partly set, add the rice. Stir-fry for 2 minutes, breaking up the egg with a spatula. Add the soy sauce and chicken stock and keep on stir-frying for 3 minutes. Transfer to a large dish.

Heat the oil in a pan. Add the shrimp, stirring to separate. Remove and set aside. Add the chicken to the oil, again stirring to separate. Remove and set aside. Cook the peas in 8 tbsp water with 1 tsp salt for 5

minutes. Drain and set aside.

Heat 1 tbsp oil in the pan and add ½ tsp garlic. When the aroma rises, return the shrimp and peas to the pan. Add the white sauce ingredients and bring to a boil. Pour over one half of the dish of fried rice, using an S-shaped piece of foil to keep the sauce to one side of the dish.

Heat 1 tbsp oil in the pan and add ½ tsp ginger and ½ tsp garlic and when the aroma rises, return the chicken to the pan. Add the red sauce and bring to the boil. Pour over the fried rice on the other side of the foil. Remove the foil and serve.

▲▲ *Shanghai Vegetable Rice, which includes spicy Chinese sausage among its ingredients.*

▲ *Yin and Yang Rice.*

Shanghai Vegetable Rice

INGREDIENTS *serves 5-6*
2 cups long-grain rice
1lb green cabbage or collards
1½ tbsp dried shrimp
about ½lb Chinese sausages
2 tbsp vegetable oil
1½ tsp lard
1½ tsp salt

METHOD
Wash and measure the rice. Simmer in the same volume of water for 6 minutes. Remove from the heat and leave to stand, covered, for 7-8 minutes. Wash and dry the cabbage. Chop into 1½×3in pieces, removing the tougher stalks. Soak the dried shrimp in hot water to cover for 7-8 minutes, then drain. Cut the sausages slantwise into 1in sections.

Heat the oil and lard in a deep saucepan. When hot, stir-fry the shrimp for 30 seconds. Add the cabbage and toss and turn for 1½ minutes until well coated with oil. Sprinkle the cabbage with the salt. Pack in the rice. Push pieces of sausage into the rice. Add 4-5 tbsp water down the side of the pan. Cover and simmer very gently for about 15 minutes. Transfer to a heated serving dish.

Fukien Crab Rice

INGREDIENTS *serves 6-8*
1 bowl cooked glutinous rice
2 bowls cooked long-grain rice
8-12oz young leeks
3 slices fresh ginger root
2 cloves garlic
2 medium crabs, about 3lb
$\frac{2}{3}$ cup vegetable oil
1oz lard
1 tsp salt
$\frac{3}{4}$ cup good stock
1 chicken bouillon cube
2 tbsp tomato paste
1 tsp paprika
1 tbsp light soy sauce
$\frac{2}{3}$ cup dry sherry
1 tbsp cornstarch blended with 2 tbsp
    water

METHOD
Place the bowl of glutinous rice in a saucepan with 1½ bowls of water. Bring to a boil and simmer very gently for 15 minutes. Add this rice to the cooked long grain rice and mix together. Clean and cut the leeks slantwise into 2in sections. Shred the ginger. Coarsely chop the garlic. Chop each crab through the shell into 12 pieces, cracking the claws with the side of the chopper. Discard the dead men's fingers.

Heat the oil in a wok or large skillet. When very hot, add the crab pieces and turn them around in the hot oil for 3 minutes. Drain. Pour away the oil to use for other purposes, leaving 2 tbsp. Add the lard and re-heat the wok or pan. When hot, stir-fry the ginger and garlic over medium heat for 15 seconds. Add the leeks and salt and stir-fry for 1 minute. Pour in the stock and sprinkle in the crumbled bouillon cube, then add the tomato paste, paprika, soy sauce and sherry. Bring to a boil, stirring, and return the crab pieces to the pan. Cook over medium heat for 3 minutes. Add the blended cornstarch, turn and stir a few times until thickened.

Place the mixed rice into a medium two-handled wok with a lid, or a large flameproof casserole. Pour the crab and leek mixture over the rice. Place the wok or casserole over a low heat, cover and cook gently for 5 minutes. Bring the container to the table for serving.

Ten Variety Fried Rice

The ingredients can be varied as you wish or according to availability.

INGREDIENTS *serves 4-6*
1$\frac{1}{3}$ cups rice
$\frac{1}{4}$lb shrimp
$\frac{1}{4}$lb cooked ham or pork
2 scallions
3 eggs
salt
$\frac{1}{4}$lb green peas
2 tbsp soy sauce

METHOD
Wash the rice in cold water just once, then cover it with more cold water so that there is about 1in of water above the surface of the rice in the saucepan. Bring it to a boil; stir to prevent it sticking to the bottom of the pan when cooked. Replace the lid tightly and reduce the heat so that it is as low as possible. Cook for about 15-20 minutes.

Peel the shrimp, dice the ham or pork into small cubes the size of the peas. Finely chop the scallions. Beat up the eggs with a little salt; heat up about 1 tbsp oil and make an omelet; set aside to cool. Heat up the remaining oil, stir-fry the finely chopped scallions, followed by the shrimp, ham or pork, and peas; stir, adding a little salt, then add the cooked rice and soy sauce. When all the ingredients are mixed well, add the omelet, breaking it into little bits. When everything is well blended it is ready to serve.

Fried Rice Chiu Chow Style

INGREDIENTS *serves 3-4*
$\frac{1}{4}$lb Chinese kale, stem only
4 tbsp peanut oil
2 tbsp shredded fresh ginger root
$\frac{1}{4}$lb shrimp, shelled and deveined
2 eggs, lightly beaten
1 cup cold plain cooked rice
2 tbsp shrimp sauce
$\frac{1}{4}$ cup chicken stock

METHOD
Dice the stems of the Chinese kale into small pieces.

Heat the oil in a pan and add the shredded ginger, shrimp and Chinese kale, stir-frying them for 1 minute.

Add the eggs (beaten for 10 seconds) and, when they are partly set, add the cold plain rice. Stir-fry over a very high heat. Scramble the eggs, breaking them into tiny pieces with your spoon or spatula.

Add the shrimp sauce and chicken stock and stir-fry over reduced heat for a further 3-5 minutes. Serve.

▲ *As Chiu Chow is by the sea, many of the dishes from the area feature seafood, like this local variation on fried rice.*

Plain Cooked Rice Gruel or Congee

Congee, rather like a rice porridge, is popularly eaten for breakfast. It is filling but bland, and often enlivened with strong-tasting savory accompaniments such as salted fish or shredded dried meat.

INGREDIENTS *serves 4-6*
2 cups or bowls long-grain white rice
10 cups or bowls water

METHOD
Wash and rinse the rice, drain well. Place in a deep heavy pot or pan and add the water. Bring to a boil, reduce the heat and simmer very gently, uncovered, for 1½ hours, stirring occasionally. By this time, the rice will be fairly thick and porridgy. Serve accompanied by pickled or salted foods.

Fried Rice-Noodles

Rice-noodles, also known as rice-sticks, are very popular with children.

INGREDIENTS *serves 6-8*
1lb rice-noodles
2 tbsp dried shrimp
¼ cup chopped pork
⅓ cup bamboo shoots
3-4 small dried Chinese mushrooms
1 celery stalk
1 leek
1 tsp salt
2 tbsp soy sauce
4 tbsp stock
4 tbsp oil

METHOD
Soak the rice-noodles in warm water until soft; soak the dried shrimp and mushrooms. Cut the pork, bamboo shoots and leek into match-sized shreds.

Stir-fry the pork, bamboo shoots, shrimp, celery and leeks in a little hot oil; add salt and stock; cook for about 2

minutes, remove.

Heat up the remaining oil; stir-fry the rice-noodles for 2-3 minutes; add the other cooked ingredients and soy sauce; stir for a further 2 minutes until there is no juice at all left; serve hot.

▲ *From top right and running clockwise, the dishes pictured are: Fried Rice-Noodles; Raw Noodles; Ten Variety Fried Rice.*

Shanghai Emerald Fried Rice

INGREDIENTS *serves 4-6*
1/2lb spring greens or cabbage
2 tsp salt
4 1/2-5 1/2 tbsp vegetable oil
2 eggs
2 scallions
1lb cooked rice
2 tbsp chopped ham
1/4 tsp monosodium glutamate (optional)

METHOD
Wash and finely shred the cabbage. Sprinkle with 1 1/2 tsp salt. Toss and leave to season for 10 minutes. Squeeze dry. Heat 1 1/2 tbsp oil in a wok or pan. When hot, stir-fry the cabbage for 30 seconds. Remove from the pan. Add 1 tbsp oil to the wok or pan. When hot, add the beaten eggs to form a thin pancake. As soon as the egg sets, remove from the pan and chop. Chop the scallions.

Heat 2-3 tbsp oil in a wok or pan. When hot, stir-fry the scallion for a few seconds. Add the rice and stir with the scallion. Reduce the heat to low, stir and turn until the rice is heated through. Add the cabbage, egg and ham. Stir and mix them together well. Sprinkle with monosodium glutamate, if using, and remaining salt. Stir and turn once more, then sprinkle with remaining egg.

Yanchow Fried Rice

INGREDIENTS *serves 5-6*
1 recipe fried rice
1 medium red pepper
good 1/3 cup bean sprouts
3oz fresh or frozen medium or large shrimp
2-3oz canned straw mushrooms or 1/4lb fresh button mushrooms
1 medium zucchini
2 1/2 tbsp vegetable oil
2 tbsp corn kernels
3oz fresh or frozen small shrimp
3/4oz lard or butter
1 1/2 tbsp light soy sauce

METHOD
Prepare one quantity of basic fried rice. Cut the red pepper into 1/4in pieces. Wash and dry the bean sprouts. Cut each large shrimp into 2-3 pieces. If using button mushrooms, quarter them. Cut the zucchini into 8 sections, then further divide in quarters.

Heat the oil in a wok or skillet. When hot, stir-fry the pepper, mushrooms, bean sprouts, zucchini, corn kernels and all the shrimp over high heat for 1 1/2 minutes. Add the lard and light soy sauce and continue to stir-fry over medium heat for 1 1/2 minutes. Turn the contents into the pan containing the fried rice. Reduce the heat to low, turn and stir together for 30 seconds.

Vegetarian Special Fried Rice

Vegetarian special fried rice is one stage richer and more elaborate than egg-fried rice and almost a meal in itself.

INGREDIENTS *serves 4-6*
4-6 dried Chinese mushrooms
1 green pepper, cored and seeded
1 red pepper, cored and seeded
2/3 cup bamboo shoots
2 eggs
2 scallions, finely chopped
2 tsp salt
4-5 tbsp oil
6 cups cooked rice
1 tbsp light soy sauce (optional)

METHOD
Soak the dried mushrooms in warm water for 25-30 minutes, squeeze dry and discard the hard stalks. Cut the mushrooms into small cubes.

Cut the green and red peppers and the bamboo shoots into small cubes.

Lightly beat the eggs with about half of the scallions and a pinch of the salt.

Heat about 2 tbsp oil in a hot wok, add the beaten eggs and scramble until set. Remove.

Heat the remaining oil. When hot, add the rest of the scallions followed by all the vegetables and stir-fry until each piece is covered with oil. Add the cooked rice and salt and stir to separate each grain of rice. Finally add the soy sauce, blend everything together and serve.

▲ *Vegetarian Special Fried Rice.*

▶ *Shanghai Vegetable Rice.*

◀ *Yanchow Fried Rice.*

Peking Ja Chiang Mein Noodles

INGREDIENTS *serves 4-6*
1 medium onion
2 slices fresh ginger root
2 cloves garlic
4 scallions
6in section cucumber
1lb wheat flour noodles (like spaghetti)
4 tbsp vegetable oil
8oz ground pork
$\frac{1}{2}$ tsp salt
1 tbsp yellow bean paste
1 tbsp soy sauce
4 tbsp good stock
1 tbsp cornstarch blended with 3 tbsp water

METHOD
Coarsely chop the onion, ginger and garlic. Cut the scallions into $2\frac{1}{2}$in sections (dividing the larger stalks in half or a quarter). Cut the cucumber into matchstick-sized shreds. Place the noodles in a saucepan of boiling water and simmer for 8-10 minutes. Drain. Rinse the noodles under running cold water to keep separate.

Heat the oil in a wok or large skillet. When hot, stir-fry the onion and ginger for 1 minute. Add the garlic and pork and stir-fry over medium heat for 3 minutes. Add the salt, yellow bean paste and soy sauce. Stir and cook for 3 minutes. Mix in the stock and continue to cook for a further 3 minutes. Pour in the blended cornstarch, stirring until thickened.

Re-heat the noodles by dipping them in boiling water for 15 seconds, then drain thoroughly. Arrange them on a large heated serving dish. Pour the sauce into the center of the noodles. Arrange the shredded cucumber and scallion sections on either side of the sauce.

Shanghai Cold-Tossed Noodles

INGREDIENTS *serves 3-4*
2 tbsp dried shrimp
3 tbsp dry sherry
3 tbsp light soy sauce
2 tbsp wine vinegar
$1\frac{1}{2}$ tsp red chili oil
2 scallions
1lb freshly made or 12oz dried wheat flour noodles
$2\frac{1}{2}$ tbsp coarsely chopped Sichuan hot Ja Chai pickles
2 tbsp coarsely chopped snow pickles
$1\frac{1}{2}$ tbsp coarsely chopped winter pickles
$1\frac{1}{2}$ tsp sesame seed oil

METHOD
Soak the dried shrimp in hot water to cover for 5 minutes. Drain and coarsely chop. Add the shrimp to the sherry and leave to soak for 15 minutes. Mix the soy sauce, vinegar and red chili oil together. Cut the onions into $\frac{1}{2}$in shreds.

Place the freshly made noodles in a saucepan of boiling water and blanch for 3 minutes; if using dried wheat noodles, simmer for 5-6 minutes. Remove from heat and leave to soak in the hot water for a further 5-6 minutes. Drain and cool.

Spread the noodles on a large serving dish. Sprinkle them evenly with the chopped pickles, shrimp and sherry, then the soy sauce mixture. Finally, add the scallion shreds and sesame seed oil.

To serve the Chinese way, the diners mix and toss the noodles they require and transfer it to their bowls, adjusting any additional seasonings of soy sauce, red chili oil or vinegar.

Vegetarian Noodles in Soup

INGREDIENTS *serves 4-6*
1 cup water chestnuts
$\frac{1}{4}$lb straw mushrooms
$\frac{1}{4}$lb white nuts
3 tbsp oil
1 tsp salt
1 tsp sugar
1 tbsp light soy sauce
1 tsp sesame seed oil
$\frac{1}{2}$lb egg noodles or vermicelli

METHOD
Drain the ingredients if they are canned and cut the water chestnuts into thin slices. The straw mushrooms and white nuts can be left whole.

Heat the oil in a hot wok or skillet. When it starts to smoke, add the vegetables and stir-fry for a few seconds. Add the salt, sugar and soy sauce and continue stirring. When the gravy begins to boil, reduce the heat and let it simmer gently.

Cook the noodles in boiling water. Drain and place them in a large serving bowl. Pour a little of the water in which the noodles were cooked into the bowl - just enough to half-cover the noodles. Then quickly pour the entire contents of the wok or skillet over the top. Garnish with the sesame seed oil and serve hot.

▶ *Vegetarian Noodles in soup is a quick and easy dish, the nuts and mushrooms complementing the soft egg noodles.*

Chow Mein — Fried Noodles

After chop suey, chow mein (which means "fried noodles" in Chinese) must be the next most popular dish in Chinese restaurants. Try to get freshly made noodles from an Oriental food store or Italian delicatessen, as they taste much better than dried ones. As a rough guide, allow at least 2oz dried noodles per person, and double the weight if using freshly made ones.

INGREDIENTS *serves 3-4*
1 tbsp dried tofu skin sticks
1 tbsp dried tiger lily buds
1/3 cup bamboo shoots
1/4lb spinach or any other greens
1/2lb dried egg noodles
2 scallions, thinly shredded
3-4 tbsp oil
1 tsp salt
2 tbsp light soy sauce
2 tsp sesame seed oil

METHOD
Soak the dried vegetables overnight in cold water or in hot water for at least an hour. When soft, thinly shred both the tofu skins and tiger lily buds.

Shred the bamboo shoots and spinach leaves into thin strips.

Cook the noodles in a pan of boiling water according to the instructions on the packet. Depending on the thickness of the noodles, this should take 5 minutes or so. Freshly made noodles will take only about half that time.

Heat about half the oil in a hot wok or skillet. While waiting for it to smoke, drain the noodles in a strainer. Add them with about half the scallions and the soy sauce to the wok and stir-fry. Do not overcook, or the noodles will become soggy. Remove and place them on a serving dish.

Add the rest of the oil to the wok. When hot, add the other scallions and stir a few times. Then add all the vegetables and continue stirring. After 30 seconds or so, add the salt and the remaining soy sauce together with a little water if necessary. As soon as the gravy starts to boil, add the sesame seed oil and blend everything well. Place the mixture on top of the fried noodles as a dressing.

▲ *A selection of dried and fresh noodles.*

▼ *Chow Mein, which simply means "fried noodles," is still one of the most popular dishes in Chinese restaurants. Any of the dressing ingredients can be substituted – dried Chinese mushrooms instead of tofu skin, for example, or shredded carrots or celery for tiger lily buds – as long as contrasts in texture and color are maintained.*

Manchurian Boiled and Braised Lamb Noodles

INGREDIENTS *serves 6-8*
1lb leg of lamb
2 slices fresh ginger root
1½ tbsp cornstarch
4 tbsp vegetable oil
1½lb mutton or lamb
3 medium onions
3 cloves garlic
¾lb young leeks
1 chicken bouillon cube
1 tsp salt
¾lb wheat flour noodles
1 tbsp lard
2 tbsp soy sauce
½ tbsp yellow bean paste
1 tbsp red chili oil
1 tbsp prepared hot mustard

METHOD
Cut the lamb into 1½×¾in thin slices. Finely chop the ginger. Dust and rub the lamb with the ginger, cornstarch and 1 tbsp vegetable oil. Cut the mutton or lamb into 1in cubes. Slice the onions. Coarsely chop the garlic. Clean and cut the leeks into 1in sections.

Parboil the mutton or lamb in a saucepan of boiling water for 5 minutes. Drain. Place in a flameproof casserole and add 4 cups water, the crumbled bouillon cube, salt and onion. Bring to a boil and simmer gently for 1¼ hours or until the stock is reduced by a quarter. Place the noodles in a saucepan of boiling water and blanch for 3 minutes. Drain and add to the mutton. Mix the two together and then cook for 10 minutes.

Meanwhile, heat the remaining oil in a wok or skillet. When hot, stir-fry the leeks for 2 minutes, then push to the sides of the pan. Add the lard to the center of the wok or pan. When hot, stir-fry the lamb and garlic over a high heat for 1 minute. Add the soy sauce and yellow bean paste and stir-fry with the lamb for 1 minute. Finally, mix the leeks with the lamb and then stir-fry for 1 minute.

Pour the noodles and mutton into a deep-sided heated serving dish. Pour the lamb and leeks over them. Trickle the red chili oil and mustard in a criss-cross pattern over the dish.

Shredded Pork, Black Mushrooms, Celery and Noodles in Sesame Sauce

INGREDIENTS *serves 6-8*
2oz pork
1 medium black mushroom
1 Chinese celery
4 packets dried egg noodles
2 tbsp peanut oil

SAUCE
2 tbsp sesame paste
1 tbsp fish sauce or shrimp sauce
1 tsp sugar
1 tsp Chinese yellow wine
2 tbsp cornstarch
1 cup chicken stock

METHOD
Cut the pork into matchstick-sized shreds. Soak the black mushroom in hot water for 30 minutes. Remove and discard the stem and chop the cap finely. Set aside. Chop the Chinese celery into small pieces.

Bring 10 cups water to a boil. Add the noodles, stirring to separate, and cook for 3 minutes. Transfer the noodles to a large pan of cold water. Return the noodles to boiling water and cook for 1 minute. Drain and place in a large bowl or on a plate. Set aside.

Heat 2 tbsp peanut oil in a pan. When hot, add the pork and stir-fry for 1 minute over high heat. Add the mushrooms and celery, and continue to cook for 30 seconds.

Add the sauce ingredients and bring to a boil. Return the noodles to the pan, stirring, and cook for another 30 seconds.

Transfer the noodles to a serving plate first and place the pork, mushroom and celery on top as a garnish. Pour the sauce over them and serve.

▲ *Shredded Pork, Black Mushrooms, Celery and Noodles in Sesame Sauce: the combination of pork, black mushrooms and celery is common enough in China, but what makes this dish from Chiu Chow unusual is the addition of a sesame sauce.*

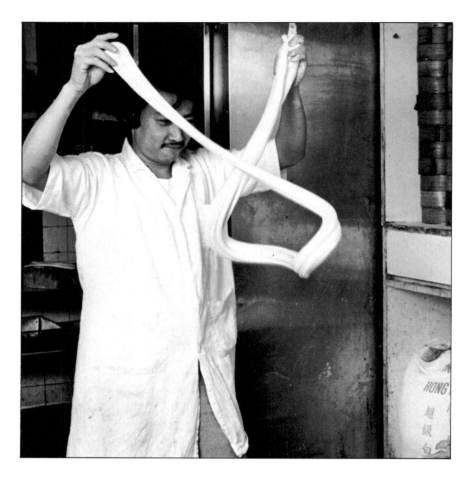

Noodle-making is a highly skilled craft. Years of apprenticeship are required to perfect the skill. The chef (◄) is throwing and pulling the dough to achieve an elastic consistency. The dough is doubled repeatedly (▲) until it falls naturally into fine, thin shreds – the noodles. The whole process takes less than ten minutes. ▼ The finished product – a dish of fresh fried noodles.

Ground Beef, Celery, Chives and Noodles in Soup

INGREDIENTS *serves 6-8*
½lb Chinese celery
½lb Chinese white chives or the white
  part of leeks
1¼lb dried white wheat flour thick
  noodles
2¼ cups chicken stock, boiling
4 tbsp peanut oil
1¼lb ground beef
2 tsp chopped scallion
2 tsp chopped fresh ginger root
2 tsp chopped Sichuan pickle
1 tbsp dark soy sauce
2 tsp chili oil
2 tsp Sichuan peppercorn powder
4 tbsp chicken stock

METHOD
Chop the celery and white chives or leeks
into shavings. Set aside.

Bring 10 cups water to a boil and add the
noodles. Reduce the heat to medium and
cook for 5-6 minutes. Transfer the noodles
to a large pan of cold water, stirring to keep
them separate. Drain the noodles and return
them to a pan of boiling water and cook for
a further 2 minutes. Test with your fingers to
see if they are cooked: they should be firm
but also soft and easy to break. When they
are cooked, remove and drain them and
divide them among four or six bowls.

Add 2 cups boiling chicken stock to the
noodles in the bowls.

Heat the oil in a pan, add the ground beef
and stir-fry quickly over high heat. Add the
chopped celery and chives and, continuing
to stir, cook for 30 seconds.

Add the remaining ingredients, including
an additional 4 tbsp chicken stock, stir and
bring the contents to a boil. Ladle over each
bowl of noodles and serve.

▶ *Ground beef, celery, chives and noodles*
in soup: the proper name for this typical
Sichuan dish is Dan-Da noodles. It
consists of noodles in a clear stock with
stir-fried beef in a savory sauce placed on
top so that the flavor and hotness
permeate the noodles.

Braised E-Fu Noodles with Shredded Pork and Mushrooms

INGREDIENTS *serves 4-6*
2oz fillet of pork
1 tsp cornstarch
2 medium black mushrooms
¼lb chives
1½pts boiling water
¾lb E-Fu noodles
3-4 tbsp peanut oil
1 tbsp shredded fresh ginger root

SAUCE
1 tbsp oyster sauce
1 tbsp light soy sauce
1 tsp dark soy sauce
1 tsp sesame seed oil
½ tsp sugar

METHOD
Mix the sauce ingredients together in a
bowl. Cut the fillet of pork into matchstick-
sized shreds and add 1 tbsp of the mixed
sauce and 1 tsp cornstarch. Mix well and set
aside.

Soak the black mushrooms in hot water
for 30 minutes. Remove and discard the
stems and cut the caps into shreds. Set aside.
Cut the chives into 1½in pieces and set
aside. Bring the water to a boil and add the
E-Fu noodles. Parboil until soft. Remove,
drain and dry the noodles with absorbent
paper towels.

Heat 3-4 tbsp oil in pan. Add the
shredded ginger and fillet of pork and stir-
fry for 1 minute. Add the mushrooms, stir
and continue to cook for a further minute.
Return the E-Fu noodles to the pan and add
the remainder of the sauce. Stir and mix the
ingredients together, simmering over
medium heat until all the water is absorbed
by the noodles.

Sprinkle the chives over the noodles and
cook for 30 seconds. Transfer to a plate and
serve immediately.

Shrimp and Noodle Balls

INGREDIENTS *makes 15*
¼lb Chinese rice vermicelli (beehoon)
½lb peeled shrimp
½ tsp sugar
2oz pork fat
few slices fresh ginger root
salt and pepper
very little, lightly beaten egg white
oil for deep-frying

METHOD
Crush the beehoon finely and leave in a dry
place. Grind the shrimp (use a food
processor for this), sprinkle with sugar.
Grind the pork fat with fresh ginger, add the
shrimp with seasoning and bind together.
Use wetted hands to form into even, bite-
sized balls. Chill well, and roll in crushed
beehoon just before frying in hot oil. Cook
for about 3-4 minutes until cooked through,
or steam in a bamboo steamer over hot
water for 30 minutes.

Ten Treasure Tapestry Noodles

INGREDIENTS *serves 5-6*
2 slices of bacon
$\frac{1}{3}$-$\frac{1}{4}$ cup chopped pork
$\frac{1}{3}$ cup chopped beef or lamb
$\frac{1}{3}$ cup chopped chicken
1 tsp salt
2 tbsp cornstarch
1 egg white
$\frac{1}{3}$ cup canned bamboo shoots
2 sticks celery
2 scallions
2-3oz green beans
4 dried Chinese mushrooms
5 tbsp good stock
4 tbsp soy sauce
8-12oz packet egg noodles or wheat
   flour noodles
4 tbsp vegetable oil
1$\frac{1}{2}$oz lard
1 tbsp rice wine or dry sherry
1 tsp sesame seed oil

METHOD

Shred the bacon. Cut the pork, beef and chicken into similar matchstick-sized shreds. Rub the meats with the salt. Dust with the cornstarch. Coat with the egg white. Cut the bamboo shoots and celery into similar matchstick-sized shreds. Cut the scallions into 1in sections, separating the white parts from the green. Top and tail the green beans and parboil in boiling water for 2 minutes. Drain. Soak the dried mushrooms in hot water to cover for 25 minutes. Drain and discard the tough stalks. Cut the mushroom caps into shreds. Blend the remainder of the cornstarch with the stock and 1 tbsp soy sauce. Place the noodles in a saucepan of boiling water and simmer for 4 minutes. Drain.

Heat the oil in a wok or large skillet. When hot, stir-fry the pork, chicken, beef, bacon and white parts of the scallions over high heat for 2$\frac{1}{2}$ minutes. Remove two-thirds of the contents and put aside. Add all the vegetables and $\frac{1}{2}$oz of the lard to the wok or pan and stir-fry for 2 minutes. Stir in 2 tbsp soy sauce and half the blended cornstarch. Cook for 1 minute. Pour in the noodles, turn and mix for 1$\frac{1}{2}$ minutes until the noodles are heated through. Heat the remaining lard in a separate wok or pan.

When hot, add the green parts of the scallion and the reserved two-thirds meat mixture. Stir-fry over high heat for 1 minute. Pour in the remainder of the soy sauce and stir-fry for 30 seconds. Add the remainder of the blended cornstarch, the sherry and sesame seed oil. Continue to stir and mix for 30 seconds.

Spread the noodle mixture on to a large heated serving dish. Pour over the meat mixture from the second pan.

Sichuan Noodles with Peanut Sauce and Vegetables

INGREDIENTS *serves 6*
1lb fresh egg noodles or dried noodles,
   cooked according to packet
   instructions
4 tbsp oil for frying

SAUCE
2 large tbsp crunchy peanut butter
1 tbsp hot oil and 1 tsp sesame seed oil

GARNISH
a handful of dry fried peanuts, lightly
   crushed
2 scallions, shredded
4oz bean sprouts, blanched in boiling
   water for 1 minute, rinsed in cold
   water and drained
$\frac{1}{4}$-$\frac{1}{2}$ cucumber, cut into small chunks
a few radishes

METHOD

Plunge the noodles into boiling water for 1 minute. Rinse with cold water and leave on one side to dry. Meanwhile prepare the sauce by blending the peanut butter with hot oil and sesame seed oil to a smooth paste. Prepare the garnishes. Now fry the noodles in two or three lots in hot oil. Flatten out on one side and, when hot, turn over and fry on the other side. Keep warm while cooking the other noodles. Pile onto a large platter and pour over the sauce – mix lightly then scatter with peanuts and scallions. Arrange the bean sprouts, cucumber and radishes either around the noodles or in separate bowls.

Chinese Cabbage, Mung Bean Noodles, Dried Shrimp and Shredded Pork

INGREDIENTS *serves 4-6*
1$\frac{1}{4}$lb Chinese cabbage
$\frac{1}{4}$lb mung bean noodles
4 tbsp dried shrimp
$\frac{1}{4}$ cup chopped fillet of pork

SEASONING
1 tsp salt
2 tsp cornstarch
$\frac{1}{2}$ tsp sesame seed oil
$\frac{1}{2}$ tsp sugar
3-4 tbsp peanut oil
3-4 slices fresh ginger root
4 cups chicken stock
1 tsp salt
2 tsp Chinese yellow wine

METHOD

Cut the Chinese cabbage into $\frac{1}{2} \times 2$in pieces. Soak the mung bean noodles and the dried shrimp in water for about 15 minutes until they are softened. Shred the fillet of pork and mix the meat with the seasoning ingredients. Heat 3-4 tbsp oil in a clay pot or a wok and add the ginger slices and shredded fillet of pork, stirring to separate. Then add the dried shrimp.

Add the Chinese cabbage, stir and mix well. Pour in the chicken stock and bring the contents to a boil. Reduce the heat and simmer for 15 minutes. Add the mung bean noodles and simmer for a further 2-3 minutes. Finally add salt and Chinese yellow wine and serve.

Fried Milk Dai Liang County Style

INGREDIENTS *serves 4-6*

2 cups oil (for frying noodles and olive kernels)

$\frac{1}{2}$ cup olive kernels

1oz rice noodles

$1\frac{1}{4}$ cups fresh milk

$\frac{3}{4}$ cup unsweetened evaporated milk

7 egg whites

1 tbsp cornstarch

$\frac{1}{2}$ tsp salt

3 tbsp oil

$2\frac{1}{2}$oz crab meat

GARNISH

2 tsp chopped ham

2 tsp chopped coriander

METHOD

Pour the oil into a pan. When the oil is hot, fry the olive kernels for 5 seconds over medium heat. Remove the kernels and immediately add the dry rice-noodles. As soon as they froth up and float, remove the noodles, drain away the oil on paper towels and put them on a serving dish to keep warm.

In a bowl mix together the fresh milk, evaporated milk, egg whites, cornstarch and salt. Heat the pan until it is very hot and add 3 tbsp oil. Then add the crab meat, olive kernels and milk mixture. Scrape the materials from the bottom and sides of the pan towards the center until the ingredients are set. Remove from the pan and spread over the noodles. Garnish and serve.

▲ *Fried Milk Dai Liang County Style: it is actually the skin of the milk that is fried. Thickened milk is cooked until the skin is thick. The skin can then be skimmed off and fried on its own or used as a rich batter to coat meat or poultry.*

▶ *Mung bean noodles are the basis for a filling soup which is flavored with dried shrimp and shredded pork.*

SOUPS

Bacon and Bamboo Shoot Soup

INGREDIENTS *serves 4-6*
100g/4oz unsmoked fatty (streaky)
bacon in one piece
1 cup/175g/6oz bamboo shoot tips
½ cup/50g/2oz seasonal greens
1 tbsp rice wine (or sherry)
½ tsp monosodium glutamate
1 tsp salt
1 tbsp lard
2½ cups/600ml/1pt water

METHOD
Dice the bacon into small cubes and the
bamboo shoot tips into small triangles.

Bring water to the boil; put in both the
bacon and bamboo shoots at the same time;
add wine or sherry, then reduce heat and
simmer for 10 minutes. Add greens,
monosodium glutamate and salt; increase
heat to high again and when the soup starts
to boil put in the lard and serve.

Deep-Fried Bean Curd and Wooden Ear Soup

INGREDIENTS *serves 4-6*
50g/2oz deep-fried bean curd, or 1 cake
fresh bean curd
15g/½oz Wooden Ears
2½ cups/600ml/1pt water
1 tsp salt
1 tbsp light soy sauce
1 spring onion (scallion), finely chopped
1 tsp sesame seed oil

METHOD
Use either 2 packets of ready-made deep-
fried bean curd (there are about 10 to each
25g/1oz packet), or cut a cake of fresh bean
curd into about 20 small cubes and deep-fry
them in very hot vegetable oil until they are
puffed up and golden. Cut them in half.
Soak the Wooden Ears in water until soft
(this will take about 20-25 minutes) and
rinse until clean.

Bring the water to the boil in a wok or

large pot. Add the bean curd, Wooden Ears
and the salt. When the soup starts to boil
again, add the soy sauce and cook for about
1 minute. Garnish with finely chopped
spring onion and sesame seed oil. Serve hot.

Dried Bean Curd Skin and Vermicelli Soup

INGREDIENTS *serves 4-6*
15g/½oz dried bean curd skin
25g/1oz golden needles (dried tiger-lily
buds)
5g/¼oz black moss
50g/2oz bean thread vermicelli
4 cups/1l/1½pts water
1 tsp salt
2 tbsp light soy sauce
1 tbsp rice wine or dry sherry
1 tsp fresh root ginger, finely chopped
2 spring onions (scallions), finely
chopped
2 tsp sesame seed oil
fresh coriander to garnish

METHOD
Soak the bean curd skin in hot water for 30-
35 minutes and then cut it into small pieces.
Soak the lily buds and black moss in water
separately for about 20-25 minutes. Rinse
the lily buds until clean. Loosen the black
moss until it resembles human hair. With a
pair of scissors, cut the vermicelli into short
lengths.

Bring the water to the boil in a wok or
large pot, and add all the ingredients
together with the seasonings. Stir until well
blended. Cook the soup for 1-1½ minutes.
Add the sesame seed oil and serve hot,
garnished with coriander.

▲ *Dried bean curd skin and vermicelli
soup – a simply made soup but with some
exotic ingredients.*

Good Stock

INGREDIENTS *serves 12*
1.5kg/3-4lb chicken (broiler if available)
or duck carcass or spare ribs
Scant 8 cups/2l/3¼pts water
3-4 slices fresh root ginger

METHOD
Remove the breast meat and the 2 legs from the chicken. Boil the remaining carcass of the chicken in all but ⅔ cup/150ml/¼pt of the water for 20 minutes. Remove from the heat and add the remaining cold water. (The adding of the cold water causes the fat and impurities to cling together, making them easier to remove.) Skim the surface of all scum which rises to the top. Add the ginger and continue to simmer gently for about 1½ hours. After about an hour of simmering, remove the chicken carcass from the stock. Mince the leg meat and the breast meat separately. Add the leg meat to the stock at this stage. Simmer for 10 minutes, then add the breast meat and simmer for about 5 minutes. Strain the stock through a fine sieve or muslin.

Fish-Stock Soup

After the fish is eaten, you can make a delicious soup from the leftovers.

INGREDIENTS *serves 3-4*
head and tail of fish used for other dish
2 cups/500ml/¾pt good stock
1 tbsp onion, finely chopped
1 tsp coriander, finely chopped
ground pepper
1 tbsp vinegar

METHOD
Crush the fish head. Put all the fish leftovers and the stock into a pan and bring slowly to a boil.

Into a large serving bowl put the finely chopped onion, coriander, pepper and vinegar. Strain the fish soup into the bowl and serve very hot.

Chinese Cabbage Soup

INGREDIENTS *serves 4-6*
9oz Chinese cabbage
3-4 dried Chinese mushrooms, soaked in
    warm water for 30 minutes
2 tbsp oil
2 tsp salt
1 tbsp rice wine or dry sherry
4 cups water
1 tsp sesame seed oil

METHOD
Wash the cabbage and cut it into thin slices.
Squeeze dry the soaked mushrooms.
Discard the hard stalks and cut the
mushrooms into small pieces. Reserve the
water in which the mushrooms have been
soaked for use later.

Heat a wok or large pot until hot, add oil
and wait for it to smoke. Add the cabbage
and mushrooms. Stir a few times and then
add the salt, wine, water and mushroom
soaking water. Bring to a boil, add the
sesame seed oil and serve.

Bean Sprout Soup

INGREDIENTS *serves 4-6*
½lb fresh bean sprouts
1 small red pepper, cored and seeded
2 tbsp oil
2 tsp salt
2½ cups water
1 scallion, finely chopped

METHOD
Wash the bean sprouts in cold water,
discarding the husks and other bits and
pieces that float to the surface. It is not
necessary to trim each sprout. Thinly shred
the pepper.

Heat a wok or large pot, add the oil and
wait for it to smoke. Add the bean sprouts
and red pepper and stir a few times. Add the
salt and water. When the soup starts to boil,
garnish with finely chopped scallion and
serve hot.

Pickled Cabbage and Chicken Clear Soup

INGREDIENTS *serves 4-6*
9oz pickled cabbage
9oz chicken breast meat
4 cups chicken stock
1¼ cups water
4 slices fresh ginger root

MARINADE
1 egg white
1 tbsp light soy sauce
½ tsp sesame seed oil
1 tsp cornstarch

METHOD
Soak the pickled cabbage in salted water for
2 hours. Rinse under running cold water,
squeezing several times. Cut into strips.

Cut the chicken breast meat into thin
slices. Mix the marinade, add the chicken
and set aside.

Put the chicken stock, water, ginger and
cabbage in a pot and bring to a boil. Reduce
the heat and simmer for 15 minutes.

Bring 2 cups water to a boil. Add the
chicken slices, stir to separate and remove
immediately. Drain the chicken and transfer
the pieces to the soup in the pot. Simmer for
3 minutes and serve.

◀ *Chinese Cabbage Soup – a homey
everyday soup particularly popular in the
winter.*

▶ *Bean Sprout Soup is an ideal component
in a vegetarian menu, as it is not based on
a meat or fish stock.*

Chicken and Noodles in Soup

INGREDIENTS *serves 2-4*
1/3 cup cooked chopped chicken meat
1/4lb egg noodles
5 leaves cabbage or lettuce
1 1/2 tbsp lard
1 tbsp soy sauce
1/2 tsp salt
1/4 tsp monosodium glutamate (optional)
1 1/4 cups stock

METHOD
Dice the chicken into small cubes; wash and cut the cabbage or lettuce heart into small bits.

Heat 1 1/2 tbsp lard until smoking; stir-fry the cabbage heart for about 30 seconds; add the stock; bring it to a boil. Put in the noodles, cook for about 1 minute or until the noodles are soft; add monosodium glutamate (if using), soy sauce, salt and chicken; stir with chopsticks, reduce heat and simmer for 2 minutes.

Chicken Liver Mousse Clear Soup

INGREDIENTS *serves 4-6*
1/2lb chicken livers
5 egg whites
1 egg yolk
4 cups chicken stock
1 tsp salt
2 tsp Chinese yellow wine
1/4 tsp pepper
1/2 tsp sesame seed oil

METHOD
Finely grind the chicken livers and press them through a strainer. Add the 5 egg whites and the egg yolk to half the chicken stock. Stir to mix well together in a basin. Add the salt, yellow wine, pepper and sesame seed oil, stir and blend thoroughly.

Grease the bottom of a medium-sized soup tureen and transfer the mixture to it to steam over medium heat until set, which will take 7-8 minutes. Heat the remaining chicken stock and place it in a large soup tureen. Transfer the chicken liver mousse to the large tureen, taking care not to damage the mousse in the transfer.

Chicken and Shrimp Ball Soup

INGREDIENTS *serves 4-6*
1/2lb uncooked shrimp
1/3 cup chopped pork fat
1/3 cup chopped chicken breast meat
1/3 chopped cooked ham
1/2 cucumber
2 egg whites
1 1/2 tbsp cornstarch
1 slice fresh root ginger, peeled and finely shredded
2 tbsp rice wine or dry sherry
2 tsp salt
4 cups stock

METHOD
Shell the shrimp and finely grind to a pulp. Grind the pork fat and chicken breast meat. Finely chop the ham. Slice the cucumber thinly.

Mix 1/2 tbsp cornstarch with 4 tbsp water, add the ground chicken breast and 1 egg white, blend well. This is called chicken purée.

Mix together the shrimps, pork fat, the remaining cornstarch, egg white, finely chopped ginger root, 1 tbsp rice wine or sherry and 1 tsp salt; blend well.

Bring the stock to a boil, then reduce the heat and put in the shrimp and pork fat mixture made into small balls about the size of walnuts. Increase the heat to bring it back to a boil. Now add the remaining salt and rice wine or sherry, then reduce heat again and simmer gently for about 10 minutes.

Stir the chicken purée and add it to the soup, stirring all the time so it does not form into lumps.

Add the ham and cucumber; turn up the heat to bring to a rapid boil; serve in a large bowl.

"Three Pearls" Soup

The "three pearls" are chicken, peas and tomato: three contrasting colors, textures and flavors.

INGREDIENTS *serves 4-6*
¼lb chicken breast meat
1 egg white
2 tbsp milk
1½ tbsp cornstarch
½ cup green peas
2 red tomatoes
2½ cups stock
1 tbsp rice wine or dry sherry
1 tsp salt
½ tsp monosodium glutamate (optional)
1 tsp chicken fat

METHOD
Remove all white tendon and membrane from the chicken meat, finely grind it into a pulp, mix it with ½ tbsp cornstarch and milk, add the egg white and blend it all together well.

Skin the tomatoes by dipping in boiling water and cut them into small cubes the same size as the peas.

Bring the stock to a rolling boil, add the peas and tomato, bring it back to a boil then remove it from the flame. Now use a single chopstick to pick up a little bit of chicken mixture at a time and flip it into the stock until all the chicken is used up and you end up with lots of tiny chicken balls the size of peas. Then place the pan back on a high heat and bring the stock to a boil. Mix the rest of the cornstarch in a little water and add to the soup together with salt, rice wine or sherry and monosodium glutamate, if using. When it starts to boil again, all the "three pearls" will float on top; add the chicken fat and serve.

Should you use ham instead of tomato, you will still have the three colors of white, green and pink.

▶ *"Three pearls" Soup in the making.*

▲ *"Three Pearls" Soup. Here we have chicken meat as the main ingredient; its pale color provides a pleasing contrast to the brightness of the green peas, while the third ingredient, the tomato or ham, helps to create an aesthetically-pleasing effect, and adds an extra dimension to the flavor.*

◀ *Chicken and Shrimp Balls Soup, here shown garnished with fresh coriander.*

Chicken, Ham and Mushroom Soup

INGREDIENTS *serves 4-6*

¼lb chicken breast meat
⅓ cup pork fat
¼ cup water chestnuts
⅙ cup bamboo shoots
4-5 Chinese dried mushrooms
⅓ cup cooked ham
1 egg white
1½ tsp salt
2 tsp cornstarch
2 scallions
3 tbsp oil
4 cups thick stock
2 tbsp rice wine (or sherry)
1¼ cups clear stock
1 slice ginger root, peeled and finely
    chopped

METHOD

Soak the chicken breast in cold water for 20 minutes, then remove the white tendon from the meat and finely chop it into a pulp.

Next peel the water chestnuts and parboil for a few minutes, then chop them finely. Finely chop the pork fat as well.

Soak the dried mushrooms in warm water for 20 minutes, squeeze dry and discard the hard stalks, then cut them into small pieces. Cut the bamboo shoots into thin slices of the same size. Cut the ham into thin slices roughly the same size as the bamboo shoots.

Beat the egg white until frothy, mix in the chicken meat, ½ tsp salt, cornstarch, pork fat and water chestnuts; blend well.

Heat 2 tbsp oil in a wok, toss in 1 onion cut into short lengths, after a few seconds discard the onion and reduce the heat to as low as possible. Now wet your hands and make the chicken mixture into small round balls no bigger than cherries; fry them in the oil, turning them round, and press them flat with a spatula. Put the chicken into a bowl, add bamboo shoots, mushrooms and ham, together with ⅔ cup thick stock, ½ tbsp rice wine or sherry and ½ tsp salt. Steam over a high heat for 5 minutes, remove and discard the stock, place the entire contents in a large serving bowl.

Heat up the remaining oil, fry the other scallion (cut into short lengths) for a few seconds and discard, add the remaining thick stock plus the clear stock, salt, finely chopped ginger root and the remaining rice wine or sherry; bring it to a boil then pour it over the chicken.

Serve as a soup for banquets and special occasions.

▲ *Chicken, Ham and Mushroom Soup:*
this dish is so rich that you need only serve
a small portion for each person.

Duck and Cabbage Soup

Traditionally, when duck has been served, the carcass is made into a soup with cabbage. In a restaurant, this soup will be served at the end of a meal since there will always be more than one duck carcass to make the soup with. But at home you will have to wait until the next day as it takes at least an hour to make.

INGREDIENTS *serves 4-6*
1 duck carcass (plus giblets if available)
4 cups Chinese cabbage
2 slices ginger root
salt and Sichuan pepper

METHOD
Break up the carcass, place it together with the giblets, if you have not already used them for another dish, and any other bits and pieces in a large pot or pan; cover it with water, add the ginger root, bring it to a boil. Skim off the impurities floating on the surface and let it simmer gently with a lid on for at least 45 minutes.

About 20 minutes before serving, add the washed and sliced cabbage. Season with salt and pepper, then serve.

Beef Broth Tomato Soup

INGREDIENTS *serves 4-6*
3oz lean beef
1½ tsp salt
1½ tbsp cornstarch
½ egg white
4 tbsp vegetable oil
6 firm medium tomatoes
2 scallions
5 cups good stock
3-4 slices fresh ginger root
1 chicken bouillon cube
1½ tbsp light soy sauce
pepper to taste
1 egg
1 tsp sesame seed oil

METHOD
Cut the beef into very thin slices. Rub with the salt and cornstarch, then toss in the egg white. Heat the vegetable oil in a wok or skillet. When moderately hot, gently fry the beef for 30 seconds, then drain. Cut each tomato into 6 pieces. Cut onions into ½in sections.

Bring the stock to a boil in a wok or saucepan. Add the ginger, crumbled bouillon cube, beef, soy sauce, pepper, scallion and tomatoes. Simmer for 2 minutes and then pour the beaten egg into the soup in a thin stream. Finally, add the sesame seed oil. Stir and serve immediately.

Cucumber Soup

INGREDIENTS *serves 4-6*
½ cucumber
3-4 black field mushrooms
2½ cups water
1½ tsp salt
1 tsp sesame seed oil
1 scallion, finely chopped

METHOD
Split the cucumber in half lengthwise, and thinly slice but do not peel.

Wash and slice the mushrooms, but do not peel.

Bring the water to a boil in a wok or large pot. Add the cucumber and mushroom slices and salt. Boil for about 1 minute.

Add the sesame seed oil and finely chopped scallion, stir and serve hot.

▲ *Cucumber Soup.*

◀ *Duck and Cabbage Soup: a nourishing and delicious soup, particularly at the end of a rich feast. In this picture the chef has added some transparent noodles and Chinese mushrooms, and has garnished the dish with Chinese parsley (fresh coriander).*

Peking Sliced Fish Pepper Pot Soup

INGREDIENTS *serves 4-6*
½lb white fish fillets
1½ tsp salt
1 tbsp cornstarch
1 egg white
2 slices fresh ginger root
1 clove garlic
2 scallions
vegetable oil for deep-frying
4 cups chicken stock
½ tsp salt
¼ tsp monosodium glutamate (optional)
3 tbsp wine vinegar
½ tsp pepper

METHOD
Cut the fish into 1½×¾in slices. Dust with the 1½ tsp salt and the cornstarch, and wet with the egg white. Finely chop the ginger and garlic. Coarsely chop the scallions.

Heat the oil in a wok or deep-fryer. When hot, lightly fry the coated fish for 1 minute. Remove and drain. Bring the stock to a boil in the wok or saucepan. Add the ginger, garlic, remaining salt and monosodium glutamate, if using, and bring back to a boil for 1 minute. Add the fish, vinegar and pepper and simmer for 3-4 minutes. Pour into a heated tureen, sprinkle with scallions and serve.

Roast Duck Bone, Cabbage and Mushroom Soup

INGREDIENTS *serves 4-6*
1 roast duck carcass (from Peking Duck, see page 42)
2lb Chinese cabbage
4-6 medium black mushrooms
1 tbsp peanut oil
2½ cups chicken stock
4 cups water
3-4 slices fresh ginger root
salt and pepper

METHOD
Chop the duck bones into 3in pieces and cut the Chinese cabbage into 2×3in pieces.

Soak the black mushrooms in hot water for 30 minutes. Remove stems.

Blanch the duck pieces in boiling water for 3 minutes. Remove.

Heat the peanut oil in a pan and stir-fry the Chinese cabbage for 2 minutes. Remove and set aside.

Bring the chicken stock and water to a boil. Add all the ingredients and simmer for 1½ hours. Season with salt and pepper to taste. Serve in a large bowl for diners to help themselves.

Crab Meat Soup

INGREDIENTS *serves 5-6*
6-7oz crab meat, fresh or frozen
2 slices fresh ginger root
2 scallions
1 cake fresh tofu
8oz young spinach
2 tbsp vegetable oil
4 cups good stock
1 chicken bouillon cube
1 tsp salt
pepper to taste
2 tbsp cornstarch blended with 5 tbsp water

METHOD
Flake the crab meat, thawing first if necessary. Coarsely chop the ginger. Cut the scallions into ½in shreds. Cut the tofu into cubes. Wash the spinach, removing any tough stems and discolored leaves.

Heat the oil in a wok or saucepan. When hot, stir-fry the ginger and scallion for 30 seconds. Add the crab meat and stir-fry for 15 seconds. Pour in the stock. Add the crumbled bouillon cube and the salt and pepper. Bring to a boil, stirring. Add the spinach and tofu. Bring contents to a boil again, stirring, then simmer gently for 2 minutes. Stir in the blended cornstarch and cook until thickened.

▶ *Crab Meat Soup – a fresh and delicate-tasting dish.*

▼ *The "Egg Flowers" in this pretty soup are made by adding beaten egg in a very thin stream so that it cooks as soon as it meets the hot stock.*

Egg-Flower Soup

INGREDIENTS *serves 4-6*
1 clove garlic
2 slices fresh ginger root
3 scallions
1 egg
1 tsp salt
pepper to taste
4 cups good stock
1 chicken bouillon cube
1 tsp sesame seed oil

METHOD
Finely chop the garlic, ginger and scallions. Lightly beat the egg with a fork for 30 seconds, then sprinkle with a pinch of salt and pepper.

Heat the stock in a wok or saucepan. Add the garlic, ginger and crumbled bouillon cube. Bring to a boil and simmer for 3 minutes. Pour the beaten egg in a very thin stream, along the prongs of a fork, and trail it over the surface of the soup. When the egg has set, sprinkle the soup with chopped scallion, remaining salt and pepper and the sesame seed oil.

Yellow Fish Soup (or Whole Fish Soup)

INGREDIENTS *serves 4-6*
1½lb trout (or sea bass, bream etc)
2 tsp salt
1 tsp ground ginger
1 tsp pepper
5oz leeks
4 slices fresh ginger root
⅓ cup canned bamboo shoots
vegetable oil for deep-frying
5 cups good stock
1 tbsp canned chopped snow pickles, drained
2 tbsp light soy sauce
3 tbsp wine vinegar

METHOD
Clean the fish thoroughly. Rub the inside and outside well with salt, ground ginger and pepper. Leave to season for 20 minutes. Clean the leeks and shred. Shred the ginger and bamboo shoots.

Heat the oil in a wok or deep-fryer. When hot, fry the fish for about 7-8 minutes until beginning to brown and become crispy. Remove and drain on absorbent paper towels.

Heat the stock in an oval-shaped flameproof casserole, wok or similar pan. Lower the fish into the stock. Bring to a boil, add the leeks, ginger, bamboo shoots and pickles, and simmer for 5-6 minutes. Sprinkle on the soy sauce and vinegar, continue to simmer for a further 5-6 minutes.

Ladle the soup and vegetables from the casserole into individual rice bowls and eat immediately. It is best served with rice and fish.

Chinese Mushroom Soup

INGREDIENTS *serves 4-6*
6 dried Chinese mushrooms
2 tsp cornstarch
1 tbsp cold water
3 egg whites
2 tsp salt
2½ cups water
1 scallion, finely chopped

METHOD
Soak the dried mushrooms in warm water for 25-30 minutes. Squeeze them dry, discard the hard stalks and cut each mushroom into thin slices. Reserve the water in which the mushrooms were soaked for use later.

Mix the cornstarch with the water to make a smooth paste. Comb the egg whites with your fingers to loosen them.

Mix the water and the mushroom soaking water in a pan and bring to a boil. Add the mushrooms and cook for about 1 minute. Now add the cornstarch and water mixture, stir and add the salt. Pour the egg whites very slowly into the soup, stirring constantly. Garnish with the finely chopped scallion and serve hot.

Hot and Sour Soup

INGREDIENTS *serves 4-6*
about ¼lb lean pork
⅓ cup canned bamboo shoots
4 medium dried Chinese mushrooms
1 tbsp dried shrimps
1-2 cakes fresh tofu
1 egg
2 scallions
5 cups good stock
3 tbsp fresh or frozen shrimp
1 tsp salt
2 bouillon cubes
2 tbsp peas
1 tsp sesame seed oil

HOT AND SOUR MIXTURE
2 tbsp soy sauce
3 tbsp vinegar
2 tbsp cornstarch
4 tbsp water
pepper to taste

METHOD
Shred the pork and bamboo shoots into 1in strips. Soak the dried mushrooms in hot water to cover for 25 minutes. Drain, reserving the soaking water. Discard the tough stalks from the mushrooms, then cut the caps into slices a similar size to the pork. Add the soaking water to the stock. Cut the tofu into ½in cubes. Beat the egg lightly with a fork for 15 seconds. Roughly chop the scallions. Mix the hot and sour mixture together in a bowl.

Bring the stock to a boil in a wok or saucepan. Add the pork, dried shrimp and mushrooms and simmer for 10 minutes. Add the fresh or frozen shrimp, tofu, bamboo shoots, salt, crumbled bouillon cubes, peas and scallions. Continue to cook for 3-4 minutes, then stir in the hot and sour mixture which will thicken the soup. Gently pour the beaten egg over the surface of the soup in a thin stream. Sprinkle the soup with sesame seed oil and serve immediately.

▶ *Hot and Sour Soup: a typical Sichuan dish which has become popular all over China, and abroad.*

◀ Shark's Fin Consommé: this classic dish
is appreciated by connoisseurs of Chinese
cuisine for its clarity, flavor and the
distinctive glutinous texture of the shark's
fin.

▼ The double boiling technique, as used
for this Squab, Ham and Black Mushroom
Soup, is a favorite Cantonese way of
preparing soup, since it is believed not only
to make the flavor richer but to increase
the nutritional value.

Shark's Fin Consommé

Preparing a shark's fin consommé fit for a
banquet is an extremely time-consuming
and fiddly task. This is a simplified version,
but still involves a long cooking time.

INGREDIENTS *serves 6-8*
1½lb shark's fin
2oz piece ham•
1½lb lean pork
6 cups chicken stock
3 slices ginger
1 cup good stock
1½ tbsp ham, finely shredded
1½ tbsp fresh coriander, chopped

METHOD
Soak the dried shark's fin in 10 cups boiling
water overnight. The next day bring 20 cups
water to a boil and simmer the shark's fin for
6 hours. Remove it from the water and rinse
under running water for 30-60 minutes.

Blanch 2oz ham and the lean pork in 5
cups boiling water for 5 minutes, then place
the meat, the chicken stock and ginger in a
covered china container and steam for 3
hours.

Place the prepared shark's fin on a platter,
add 1 cup good stock and steam for 20
minutes.

Divide the shark's fin into small
individual portions, add the boiling stock
and sprinkle with the finely shredded ham
and chopped coriander. Serve.

Corn and Asparagus Soup

INGREDIENTS *serves 4-6*
6oz white asparagus
1 egg white
1 tbsp cornstarch
2 tbsp water
2½ cups water
1 tsp salt
4oz corn kernels
1 scallion, finely chopped, to garnish

METHOD
Cut the asparagus spears into small cubes.

Beat the egg white lightly. Mix the
cornstarch with the water to make a smooth
paste.

Bring the water to a rolling boil. Add the
salt, corn and asparagus. When the water
starts to boil again, add the cornstarch and
water mixture, stirring constantly.

Add the egg white very slowly and stir.
Serve hot, garnished with finely chopped
scallions.

Double-Boiled Squab, Ham and Black Mushroom Soup

INGREDIENTS *serves 4-6*
2 squab
½lb lean pork
6 medium black mushrooms
¼ cup chopped ham
3 slices fresh ginger root
1 tbsp Chinese yellow wine
2½ cups chicken stock
2-3 tbsp oil

METHOD
Clean the squab thoroughly. Cut out the
breast meat and save it for another dish.
Blanch the lean pork and squab in boiling
water for 2 minutes and rinse under running
water for 1 minute. Soak the black
mushrooms in warm water for about 30
minutes until they have softened. Discard
the stems and cut the caps into evenly sized
pieces.

Put all ingredients in a heavy pot or
casserole with a lid, add the stock and an
equal amount of water, and cover and steam
over medium heat for 3 hours.

Pork and Bamboo Shoot Soup

INGREDIENTS *serves 4-6*
½lb unsmoked bacon in one piece
1lb leg of pork in one piece
2⅔ cups bamboo shoots
8 cups water

METHOD
Place the two pieces of meat in a large pot; add the water, bring to a rolling boil, skim off the scum and reduce the heat to moderate. Replace the lid and simmer for about 2-3 hours, then add the bamboo shoots, cut into chunks, and continue cooking for 20-30 minutes.

When serving, you should be able to pull small pieces of the meat off with your chopsticks or with a serving spoon. The preserved pork or bacon should not taste too salty and the fresh pork should have acquired some of the flavor of the preserved pork. The bamboo shoots should taste fantastic.

▼ *Yin and Yang Vegetable Soup: as with Yin and Yang Rice, different colors are used to form the Chinese symbol of unity in which positive and negative complement each other. The green part is usually made from a green vegetable. The white part is also usually vegetable, perhaps with milk or chicken added.*

Yin and Yang Vegetable Soup

Like Yin and Yang Rice (see page 177), the two different soups should be presented together to form the Taoist yin and yang symbol.

INGREDIENTS *serves 4-6*
1¼lb spinach leaves
1 tsp baking soda
½lb button mushrooms
¼lb chicken breast meat
1 egg white
2 tsp salt
4 tbsp peanut oil
2 tsp Chinese yellow wine
4 cups chicken stock
6 tbsp cornstarch

METHOD
Blanch the spinach for 2 minutes in 2 cups boiling water with 1 tsp baking soda added. Remove and rinse under running water for 1 minute. Drain the leaves before chopping them finely. Set aside. Chop the mushrooms finely. Set aside. Finely grind the chicken breast and mix with the egg white and 1 tsp salt. Set aside.

Heat 2 tbsp oil in a pan. Sauté the spinach for 3 minutes, add 1 tsp Chinese yellow wine and 1 tsp salt and stir together. Add 2 cups chicken stock to the pan having first mixed 3 tbsp of the stock with 3 tbsp cornstarch. Bring the stock to a boil and slowly stir in the cornstarch to make a thick soup.

Place an S-shaped piece of greased cardboard in the center of a soup tureen to divide the bowl into two. Pour the spinach soup into one side of the bowl, holding the cardboard upright by placing a glass of water against it on the empty side.

Heat 2 tbsp oil. Add the mushrooms, sauté for 1 minute and add 1 tsp Chinese yellow wine. Take 3 tbsp of the remaining stock and mix with 3 tbsp cornstarch. Add the rest of the chicken stock to the pan, bring to a boil and slowly stir in the blended cornstarch. When it boils, stir in the ground chicken and mix well.

Pour the chicken soup into the other half of the soup tureen, first removing the glass of water. Take out the cardboard as gently as possible. The one bowl of soup is then presented and served in the two colors of yin and yang.

Top-Rank Bird's Nest

Compared with the other Chinese delicacy, shark's fin, bird's nest is very simple to prepare though it does require a certain amount of patience.

The so-called "bird's nest" is in fact predigested protein from a seaweed used by swallows for building their nests on the cliffs of islands along China's coast (ornithologists might like to know that the swallow is a petrel of the *Procellariidae* family).

Bird's nests, and the Chinese alkali powder used in their preparation, are not usually available in the West. If you do try this dish, be sure to use the correct alkali powder, and do not use more than the quantities given here.

INGREDIENTS *serves 4-6*
2oz "bird's nest"
4½ cups good chicken stock
2 tsp Chinese alkali powder
1 tsp salt
½ tsp monosodium glutamate (optional)
1 tbsp rice wine or dry sherry

METHOD
Soak the "nest" in lukewarm water for about 15 minutes and pick out all the feathers and other bits and pieces with tweezers - this is where patience is required; then rinse very gently in lukewarm water two or three times.

Dissolve the alkali in 2½ cups boiling water, then add the cleaned "bird's nest" and stir gently with chopsticks or a fork. Leave it to stand for 5 minutes, then drain and soak in at least 4½ cups fresh boiling water for a further 5 minutes. Drain again. Finally rinse the "nest" in the same quantity of fresh warm water for 4 minutes more and drain well; by now it is clean and ready for the last stage of cooking.

Bring the chicken stock, salt, monosodium glutamate (if using) and rice wine or sherry to a boil, skim if necessary, then add the well-drained "bird's nest" and serve immediately.

▶ *The bird's nest after cleaning, ready to be added to the chicken broth in the bowl above it.*

Wonton Soup

INGREDIENTS *serves 4-6*
40 wontons
1¼ tbsp dried shrimp
1 tbsp peanut oil
4 slices fresh ginger root
4 cups chicken stock
2 tsp sugar
2 tsp sesame oil
4-6 tsp light soy sauce
2 tbsp scallions, chopped

METHOD

Soak the dried shrimp in 1¼ cups hot water for 30 minutes. Heat 1 tbsp oil in a pot or casserole and add the ginger and dried shrimp, stirring until the aroma rises. Add the chicken stock plus the water used to soak the shrimp. Bring the contents to a boil, reduce the heat and simmer for 30 minutes. Add the sugar and keep warm in the pot.

Use four or six soup bowls and put into each ¼ tsp sesame oil, 1 tsp light soy sauce and 1 tsp chopped onion. Set aside.

Bring 10 cups water to a boil. Add the wontons. Reduce the heat to medium and simmer for 5 minutes. Remove with a perforated spoon and divide them equally among the soup bowls. Add the soup and serve.

▶ *Wontons are used in a variety of ways. Here they are lightly poached in stock to provide a surprisingly filling soup.*

Tripe, Squid and Pea Soup

INGREDIENTS *serves 4-6*
½lb dried squid
3 tsp salt
3 slices fresh ginger root
12oz-1lb tripe
¾lb green peas
4 cups good stock
1 chicken bouillon cube
1½ tbsp cornstarch blended with 4 tbsp water
salt and pepper to taste
1 tsp sesame seed oil

METHOD

Soak the dried squid in warm water to cover for 3 hours. Place the salt and ginger in a saucepan with 5 cups water. Bring to a boil and add the tripe. Simmer for 1½ hours. Drain the tripe and squid, then cut into matchstick-sized shreds. Purée the peas in a liquidizer.

Place the squid in a saucepan with 1¼ cups boiling water. Simmer until the liquid in the pan has been reduced by half, about 15 minutes. Add the tripe and stock and simmer gently for 30 minutes. Add the pea purée and crumbled stock cube. Heat and stir gently for 10 minutes. Add the blended cornstarch and salt and pepper to taste. Stir in the sesame seed oil. Continue to cook for 2 minutes, stirring.

Oxtail Soup

What makes this soup so special is that you make more use of the chicken than the ox tail, so it is really chicken soup with ox tail as the decorative piece. Its flavor also makes it special.

INGREDIENTS *serves 4-6*
1 ox tail
1 boiler chicken
½ lb carrots
½ tbsp crushed ginger root
1 tbsp Sichuan peppercorns
4 tbsp rice wine (or sherry)
salt to taste
15 cups water

METHOD
Trim off the excess fat on the ox tail and cut into pieces. Cut the carrots into thick chunks.

Place the ox tail in a large pot with water, bring to a boil, skim off the scum; add ginger root, Sichuan peppercorns, wine or sherry and chicken. Reduce heat when it starts to boil, simmer for 4 hours or more turning the chicken and ox tail over every hour or so. Add the carrots in the last 20 minutes of cooking time. Discard chicken before serving; add salt to taste.

Fish Soup

INGREDIENTS *serves 4-6*
1 freshwater fish such as trout
⅓ cup cooked ham
3-4 Chinese-dried mushrooms, soaked
1 cake tofu
2 tbsp bamboo shoots
5 cups good stock
1 slice ginger root, peeled
1 scallion
1 tbsp lard
1 tbsp salt
1½ tbsp rice wine (or sherry)
½ tsp Sichuan pepper, ground

METHOD
Clean the fish. Cut the mushrooms and ham into thin strips, cut the bamboo shoots into thin slices and the tofu into small cubes. Finely chop the scallion and ginger root.

Warm up the lard, pour in the stock, bring

it to a boil. Add the fish, followed by the ham, mushrooms, bamboo shoots, wine or sherry, salt, ginger root and scallion. Cook over a high heat for 15 minutes, then add the tofu. Reduce heat and cook a further 5 minutes; garnish with ground pepper and serve.

▲ *Two bowls of Oxtail Soup ready to be served. This is such a rich soup that it is almost a meal in itself.*

▶ *Liver Pâté Soup. The liver pâté is cut into small squares or diamonds, before the stock is poured over.*

Spinach and Tofu Soup

INGREDIENTS *serves 4-6*
½lb fresh spinach
2 cakes tofu
2 tbsp oil
2 tsp salt
2½ cups water
2 tbsp soy sauce
1 tsp sesame seed oil

METHOD
Wash the spinach well, discarding the tough and discolored leaves. Shake off the excess water and cut the leaves into small pieces.

Cut the tofu into about 14 pieces.

In a wok or large pot, heat the oil until hot. Stir-fry the spinach until soft. Add the salt and water and bring to a boil.

Add the tofu and soy sauce and cook for 1½-2 minutes. Add the sesame seed oil just before serving.

Liver Pâté Soup

INGREDIENTS *serves 4-6*
½lb pig's liver
2 egg whites
1 tbsp rice wine (or sherry)
1 tsp salt
3 cups stock
salt and pepper to taste

METHOD
Chop the liver into a pulp; squeeze it through a cheesecloth; mix it with ¼ cup stock and the egg whites; add wine or sherry and salt. Place in a bowl, and steam for 15 minutes; by then it will have become a solid liver pâté; let it cool.

Place the liver pâté on the bottom of a large soup bowl; cut it into small squares (but keep the whole pieces together). Bring the stock to a boil and gently pour it over the liver. Season with salt and pepper and serve.

Tomato and Egg Flower Soup

INGREDIENTS *serves 4-6*
9oz tomatoes, skinned
1 egg
2 scallions, finely chopped
1 tbsp oil
4 cups water
2 tbsp light soy sauce
1 tsp cornstarch mixed with 2 tsp water

METHOD
Skin the tomatoes by dipping them in boiling water for a minute or so and then peel them. Cut into large slices.

Beat the egg. Finely chop the scallions.

Heat a wok or pan over a high heat. Add the oil and wait for it to smoke. Add the scallions to flavor the oil and then pour in the water. Drop in the tomatoes and bring to a boil. Add the soy sauce and very slowly pour in the beaten egg. Add the cornstarch and water mixture. Stir and serve.

DIM SUM AND DESSERTS

Pork Dumplings

INGREDIENTS *serves 6-8*
1 cup all-purpose flour
2 eggs
¼ tsp baking soda

FILLING
3 medium black mushrooms
1¼lb fillet of pork
¼lb pork fat

MARINADE
1 tbsp light soy sauce
½ tsp sugar
½ tsp sesame oil
½ tsp pepper
1 tsp Chinese yellow wine
1 tbsp cornstarch
1 egg white
1 tsp salt

METHOD
Make the wrappers for the dumplings by putting the flour in a mixing bowl. Make a well in the center, add the eggs and baking soda and mix well. Knead the dough on a lightly floured surface until it is smooth.

Roll the dough into a "sausage," approximately 1½in in diameter, cover it with a towel and leave to stand for 20 minutes.

Pull the dough apart and roll the pieces between your palms into small balls approximately 1in in diameter. Flatten each ball slightly, dust with flour and roll out into a thin pancake.

Soak the black mushroom in hot water for 30 minutes. Cut off and discard the stems and finely dice the caps.

Cut the fillet of pork fat into small cubes and mix the pork and mushroom pieces with the marinade ingredients, stirring with a fork until the mixture becomes sticky.

Place one wrapper in the palm of your hand. Put heaped 1 tsp of the filling in the center of the wrapper and squeeze the edges gently together until it looks like a change-purse, but leave the top open. If you wish, trim away any excess wrapper, but this is not essential. Continue until all the wrappers are used. Steam over a high heat for 10 to 15 minutes. Serve.

Cock's-Comb Dumplings

The wrappers are prepared in the same way as for pork dumplings but 2 tbsp chopped water chestnut and 1 tbsp chopped coriander are added to the filling. The dumplings are made and cooked as pork dumplings.

Shrimp Dumplings

INGREDIENTS *serves 6-8*
see Pork Dumplings for wrapper ingredients

FILLING
1½lb shrimp, shelled and deveined
¼lb cooked pork fat
⅔ cup bamboo shoots, shredded
1 tbsp lard
1 tsp sesame oil
½ tsp pepper
1½ tsp sugar
2 tsp salt

METHOD
Put all ingredients for the filling in a mixing bowl and stir until the mixture becomes sticky. Set aside.

Take one wrapper and place 1 tsp filling in the center. Fold the wrapper up, working with both hands to seal the dumpling. Push the upper edge gently towards the left and make ruffles along the top of the dumpling. Steam the dumplings over a very high heat for 8-10 minutes and serve.

Chicken Bundles

INGREDIENTS *serves 6-8*
11oz chicken breast meat (preferably with skin on)
2 tsp light soy sauce
½ tsp sugar
¼ tsp sesame oil
large pinch pepper
2 tbsp cornstarch
¼lb roast fillet of pork
3 medium black mushrooms
2 hard-boiled eggs
½lb Chinese cabbage

METHOD
Cut the chicken into 2×1½in pieces and mix the pieces with the soy sauce, sugar, sesame oil, pepper and cornstarch. Set aside.

Cut the roast fillet of pork into ½in slices and then into 2×½in sticks. Set aside.

Soak the black mushrooms in hot water for 30 minutes. Remove and discard the stems and cut the caps into 2×½in sticks. Set aside.

Cut each hard-boiled egg into eight pieces and set aside.

Blanch the cabbage in 2 cups boiling salted water for 5 minutes, remove from the water, cut into 4×¾in strips and set aside.

On each strip of cabbage place some chicken, roast pork and black mushroom pieces and, at the top, near to one end, a piece of egg. Roll the cabbage up to make a neat bundle. Continue with each strip of cabbage until all the ingredients are used.

Put two bundles into each small dish and steam over a high heat for 7-10 minutes. Serve.

Spring Roll Wrappers

INGREDIENTS *makes approximately 12*
1 egg
2 cups all-purpose flour
$\frac{1}{2}$ tsp salt
$\frac{1}{2}$ cup water
cornstarch for dusting

METHOD

Lightly beat the egg. Sift the flour and salt into a large bowl. Make a well in the center and mix the beaten egg and water into the flour. Stir with a wooden spoon to form a smooth dough. Place the dough on a floured board and knead it for 10 minutes until smooth. Cover with a damp cloth and leave to rest for about 30 minutes. Roll the dough into a 12in sausage, then cut into $1\frac{1}{2}$in pieces. Dust with cornstarch and flatten with the palm of your hand. Roll as thinly as possible, then trim to 6×7in rectangles. Dust with cornstarch and stack them up.

Spring Roll Fillings

INGREDIENTS *serves 6-8*
$\frac{3}{4}$lb lean pork or chicken meat
2 slices fresh ginger root
$\frac{1}{2}$ cup canned bamboo shoots, drained
8 medium dried Chinese mushrooms
2 scallions
3 tbsp vegetable oil
1 tsp salt
2 tbsp soy sauce
2 cups bean sprouts
1 tbsp cornstarch, blended with 2
  tbsp water
beaten egg for sealing
vegetable oil for deep-frying

METHOD

Cut the pork or chicken into matchstick-sized shreds. Cut the ginger and bamboo shoots into similar or finer shreds. Soak the dried mushrooms in hot water to cover for 25 minutes. Drain and discard the tough stalks. Cut the mushroom caps into fine shreds. Neatly divide the scallions lengthwise in half, and then cut them into $\frac{1}{2}$in sections.

Heat the 3 tbsp oil in a wok or skillet. When hot, stir-fry the ginger, salt, mushrooms and shredded meat over high heat for $1\frac{1}{4}$ minutes. Add all the other ingredients, except the cornstarch and stir-fry for 1 minute. Pour in the blended cornstarch, stir and turn for another 30 seconds. Remove from the heat and leave to cool before using as a filling.

Take 2 tbsp of filling and spread across each pancake just below the center. Fold the pancake up from the bottom by raising the lower corner to fold over the filling. Roll the filling over once, and bring in the 2 corners from the side to overlap each other. Finally fold the top flap down, sealing with a little beaten egg. Stack the spring rolls as you make them, placing them so that the weight of the pancake rests on the flap that has just been sealed.

Fry the pancakes soon after they have

▲ *Spring Rolls: the light dough wrapping enclosing a variety of mixed fillings should be crispy and non-greasy.*

been made, as otherwise they may become soggy. Heat the oil in a wok or deep-fryer. When hot, fry no more than 5-6 pancakes at a time for $3\frac{3}{4}$-$4\frac{1}{2}$ minutes until golden brown and crispy. Once fried, they can be kept crispy in the oven for up to 30 minutes. Or store them in the refrigerator for a day after an initial frying of $2\frac{1}{2}$ minutes, then re-fry them for 3 minutes when required. Serve immediately.

◄ *A wide range of* dim sum *is shown in the bamboo baskets in which they are steamed. Recipes for some are given on the pages immediately preceding or following; others appear in earlier chapters.*
(1) *squid stuffed with shrimp;* (2) *steamed pork liver and spare rib of pork;* (3) *chicken in a nest;* (4) *pork dumplings;* (5) *chicken bundles;* (6) *shrimp dumplings;* (7) *cock's-comb dumplings;* (8) *beef and black mushrooms.*

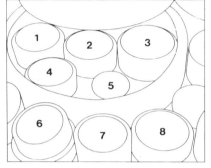

Cha Shao Dumplings

INGREDIENTS *makes 24 dumplings*

PASTRY
4 cups all-purpose flour
1½ tbsp dried yeast
2½ tsp sugar
3 tbsp lukewarm water
1¼ cups lukewarm milk

FILLING
1lb *cha shao* pork
2 cloves garlic
2 tbsp soy sauce
2 tbsp sugar
1 tbsp lard
½ tbsp cornstarch

METHOD
Mix together the yeast, sugar and warm water; stir to dissolve the yeast completely. Leave it in a warm place until frothy.

Sift the flour into a bowl; gradually pour in the yeast mixture and warm milk; stir until a firm dough is formed.

Put the dough onto a lightly floured surface and knead well for about 10 minutes. Leave it in a warm place for 1½ to 2 hours or until the dough doubles in bulk.

Meanwhile prepare the filling. Cut the *cha shao* pork into small, thin slices; crush the garlic.

Heat up the lard and fry the garlic until brown; discard before adding the *cha shao* pork, soy sauce and sugar. Cook for about 2-3 minutes; thicken with cornstarch mixed with a little water, then divide into 24 portions.

Now knead the dough for about 5 minutes, then form into a long sausage roll shape. Slice the roll into 24 rounds. Flatten each round with the palm of your hand, then with a rolling pin roll out each piece until it is about 4in in diameter.

Place a portion of the filling in the center of each round, gather the sides around the filling to meet at the top, then twist the top to close tightly. Let the dumplings rest for 20-30 minutes.

Place the dumplings on a wet cloth on the rack of a steamer, leaving 1in space between each. Steam vigorously for 15 minutes. Serve hot or cold.

Chicken and Glutinous Rice Wrapped in Lotus Leaves

INGREDIENTS *makes 10*
2½ cups glutinous rice
¼lb chicken meat, boned
¼lb pork
¼lb Chinese salami or ham
¼lb shelled and cooked shrimp
3-4 Chinese dried mushrooms, soaked
½ tbsp salt
1 tbsp soy sauce
1 tbsp sugar
2 tbsp lard
1 tbsp rice wine or dry sherry
1 slice ginger root, finely chopped
1 tbsp cornstarch
5 dried lotus leaves, soaked
vegetable oil

METHOD
Wash and rinse the glutinous rice. Add about 5 cups cold water, a little salt and lard; steam vigorously for 20 minutes. Divide

into 20 portions. Cut the chicken into 10 small pieces; cut the pork, salami and mushrooms into small pieces about the size of a thumbnail.

Heat the lard in a wok; stir-fry the chicken, pork, salami or ham, mushrooms and shrimp. Add salt, rice wine or sherry, soy sauce and sugar. Cook for about 5 minutes; add finely chopped ginger root. Thicken with cornstarch mixed with a little water and then divide it into 10 portions.

Soak the lotus leaves in water until soft; divide them into 10 pieces. Grease each leaf lightly with a little vegetable oil. Place one portion of glutinous rice on it, flatten the surface and add one portion of the meat filling with one piece of chicken, place another portion of glutinous rice on top, wrap up the four corners of the lotus leaf like wrapping a package. Steam vigorously for 15 minutes and serve hot. The leaves are not eaten. They may be washed carefully and used again.

◀ Cha Shao *Dumplings, filled with Chinese roast pork.*

▼ *Chicken and Glutinous Rice Wrapped in Lotus Leaves, a steamed dim sum.*

Chicken in a Nest

INGREDIENTS *serves 6-8*
2lb chicken
4-6 medium black mushrooms
1⅓ cups bamboo shoots
1 cup self-rising flour
8 tbsp water
1 tbsp sugar

MARINADE
1 tbsp oyster sauce
1 tbsp light soy sauce
1 tsp dark soy sauce
1 tsp sesame oil
1 tsp sugar
1 tsp salt
1 tbsp Chinese yellow wine
2 tbsp cornstarch

METHOD
Cut the chicken into bite-sized pieces. Mix together the ingredients for the marinade, add the chicken pieces and set aside.

Soak the black mushrooms in hot water for 30 minutes. Cut off and discard the stems and cut each cap into eight pieces.

Cut the bamboo shoots into slices approximately the same size as the mushroom pieces. Add the black mushrooms and bamboo shoots to the chicken, mix well and set aside.

Put the flour in a mixing bowl, add the water and sugar and mix well. Knead the dough on a lightly floured surface until it is smooth, then leave it to stand for 30 minutes.

Roll the dough into a "sausage" and divide it into small balls, approximately 1in in diameter. Flatten the ball slightly with the palm of your hand and work it into a bowl shape, about 2in in diameter. Place the bowl on a piece of paper about 2in square and in each bowl or nest put about 2 tbsp of the chicken, black mushroom and bamboo shoot mixture.

Steam the nests for 10 to 15 minutes. Serve.

▶ *Chicken in a Nest.*

Deep-Fried Crab Claws

INGREDIENTS *serves 5-6*
10 large frozen crab claws
2 slices fresh ginger root
3 eggs
1 tsp salt
½lb peeled shrimp
3 tbsp cornstarch
3 cups dry breadcrumbs
vegetable oil for deep-frying

METHOD
Defrost the claws and chop into half lengthwise. Finely chop the ginger. Beat the eggs. Add the salt and ginger to the shrimp and finely chop, mixing well. Divide the mixture into 10 portions, and press each portion on to the meat of the crab claws. Sprinkle the shrimp mixture with cornstarch, dip each meat side of the claw into beaten egg, and coat with breadcrumbs. Place the filled claws on a plate and chill for 1 hour.

Heat the oil in a wok or deep-fryer. When hot, fry the claws in about 2 batches for 3 minutes. Drain.

Serve hot on a heated dish, garnished with wedges of lemon and sprigs of parsley.

Fried Shrimp Balls

INGREDIENTS *makes 20-25 balls*
½lb fresh shrimp, shelled
1 cup water chestnuts
⅓ cup lean and fat pork (20 per cent fat)
1 tsp salt
½ tsp monosodium glutamate (optional)
½ tsp pepper
½ cup flour
2 cups peanut oil (for frying)

SEASONINGS
1½ tbsp chopped white of leak
1½ tbsp chopped scallion
1 egg

METHOD
Chop and grind the shrimp and dice the water chestnuts and pork into coarse grains.

Put the shrimp into a bowl and stir until the mixture is sticky. Add the water chestnuts, pork and seasonings and mix well. Add the flour.

Heat the oil in a pan until it is smoking hot. Roll the mixture into small balls about ¾in in diameter and fry them until they start to turn brown.

Serve with a dip such as Chiu Chow tangerine jam.

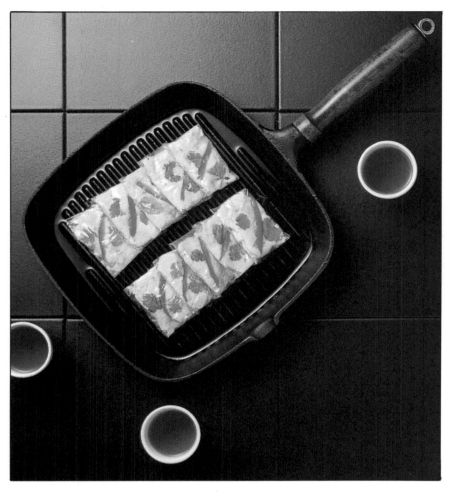

▲ *Sesame Shrimp on Toast: this dish, usually eaten as a starter, is now quite often served in Chinese restaurants abroad.*

◄ *Paper-Wrapped Deep-Fried Chicken: the individual paper envelopes are ready to be brought piping hot to the table and opened.*

◄ *Salt and Pepper Spare Ribs. The leftover marinade can be made into a coating sauce.*

▼ *Braised Tea-Eggs: a very popular snack, usually eaten between meals.*

Paper-Wrapped Deep-Fried Chicken

INGREDIENTS *makes 15 portions*
1lb chicken breasts
5 dried Chinese mushrooms
2 slices ham
2 scallions
2 bunches parsley
15 sheets edible Chinese cellophane paper
2 tbsp sesame seed oil
vegetable oil for deep-frying

MARINADE
3 tbsp light soy sauce
½ tsp salt
1½ tbsp rice wine or dry sherry
½ tsp sugar
¼ tsp pepper
2 tsp sesame seed oil
2 tsp cornstarch

METHOD
Cut the chicken into 2×½in strips. Place in a bowl and add all the ingredients for the marinade. Mix well and leave to marinate for 20 minutes. Soak the dried mushrooms in hot water to cover for 25 minutes. Drain and discard the tough stalks. Cut the mushroom caps into about 6 pieces each. Cut the ham into 2in strips. Cut the scallions into 2in sections. Cut and divide the parsley into about 15 portions. Brush 1 sheet of cellophane paper with sesame seed oil and place a spray of parsley in the middle. Divide and place a little mushroom and ham on either side, lay some sliced chicken on top and a scallion on top of that. Fold the cellophane to completely enclose the filling.

Heat the oil in a wok or deep-fryer. When hot, fry the envelopes for about 2 minutes. Remove. Re-heat the oil and fry again for 2 minutes. Drain. Serve the envelopes arranged on a large heated plate.

Sesame Shrimp on Toast

INGREDIENTS *serves 7-8*
½lb peeled shrimp
⅓ cup pork fat
1 tsp salt
pepper to taste
½ tsp ground ginger
1 tbsp dry sherry or white wine
1½ tbsp finely chopped scallion
1 egg white
2 tsp cornstarch
6 slices bread
4oz sesame seeds
vegetable oil for deep-frying

METHOD
Chop and mix the shrimp and pork fat into a paste in a bowl. Add the salt, pepper, ginger, sherry or wine, scallion, egg white and cornstarch. Mix together thoroughly. Spread the mixture very thickly on the top of the slices of bread. Spread the sesame seeds evenly over the surface of a large plate or a small tray. Place each piece of bread, spread side down, on the sesame seeds. Press gently so that each slice has a good coating of seeds.

Heat the oil in a wok or deep-fryer. When hot, fry the slices of bread, spread-side down (only 2-3 slices of bread can be fried at a time) for 2½ minutes. Turn over and fry for a further 1½ minutes. Drain on paper towels.

When all the slices of bread have been fried and drained, place each piece of bread on a chopping board, cut off and discard the crusts. Cut the coated and fried bread slices into 6 rectangular pieces (the size of fish fingers) or into 4 triangles. Arrange them on a heated serving dish and serve hot.

Salt and Pepper Spare Ribs

INGREDIENTS *serves 4-6*
10oz pork spare ribs
1 egg
1 tsp salt
2 tsp cornstarch
½ tbsp Kao Liang spirit or 1½ tbsp rice wine or dry sherry
½ tsp five-spice powder
1 tsp freshly ground Sichuan pepper
oil for deep-frying

METHOD
Chop the spare ribs into small pieces; marinate with salt, pepper, Kao Liang spirit and five-spice powder for 15 minutes. Add egg and cornstarch; mix well.

Heat the oil until hot; deep-fry the spare ribs for 3 minutes, then soak them in cold oil for 1 minute. Just before serving, crisp them in hot oil once more.

Braised Tea-Eggs

This is actually a national dish with regional variations. The pretty marbled eggs are usually eaten as part of a snack.

INGREDIENTS
12 eggs
2 tsp salt
5 tbsp soy sauce
2-3 star anise
1½ tbsp red tea leaves (the better quality the tea, the better the result)

METHOD
Boil the eggs in warm water for 5-10 minutes. Remove and gently tap the shell of each egg with a spoon until it is cracked finely all over. Put the eggs back into the pot and cover with fresh water. Add salt, soy sauce, star anise and tea leaves. Bring to a boil and simmer for 30-45 minutes. Let the eggs cool for a while in the liquid.

When you peel the shells off, the eggs will have a beautiful marbled pattern.

Red Bean Paste Pancakes

INGREDIENTS *makes 10-12 pancakes*
2 cups all-purpose flour
½ cup boiling water
1 egg
3 tbsp oil
4-5 tbsp sweetened red bean paste or chestnut paste

METHOD
Sift the flour into a mixing bowl and very gently pour in the boiling water. Add about 1 tsp oil and the beaten egg. Knead the mixture into a firm dough and then divide it into 2 equal portions. Roll out each portion into a long "sausage" on a lightly floured surface and cut it into 4-6 pieces. Using the palm of your hand, press each piece into a flat pancake. On a lightly floured surface, flatten each pancake into a 6in circle with a rolling pin and roll gently.

Place an ungreased skillet on a high heat. When hot, reduce the heat to low and place one pancake at a time in the pan. Turn it over when little brown spots appear on the underside. Remove and keep under a damp cloth until you have finished making all the pancakes.

Spread about 2 tbsp red bean paste or chestnut paste over about 80 per cent of the pancake surface and roll it over 3 or 4 times to form a flattened roll.

Heat the oil in a skillet and shallow-fry the pancakes until golden brown, turning over once. Cut each pancake into 3-4 pieces and serve hot or cold.

▲ *Red Bean Paste Pancakes are spread with a sweet bean paste.*

▼ *Red Bean Paste Pancakes, fried and ready to serve.*

Lotus-Leaf Pancakes

INGREDIENTS *makes 24 pancakes*
1lb all-purpose flour
1¼ cups boiling water
3 tsp vegetable oil

METHOD

Sift the flour into a mixing bowl and very slowly pour in the boiling water, mixed with 1 tsp oil, while stirring with a pair of chopsticks or a wooden spoon. Do not be tempted to add any more water than the amount given, otherwise the mixture will get too wet and become messy.

Knead the mixture into a firm dough, then divide it into 3 equal portions. Now roll out each portion into a long "sausage," and cut each sausage into 8 equal parts; then, using the palm of your hand, press each piece into a flat pancake. Brush one of the pancakes with a little oil, and place another one on top to form a "sandwich", so that you end up with 12 sandwiches. Now use a rolling pin to flatten each sandwich into a 6in circle by rolling gently on each side on a lightly floured surface.

To cook, place a skillet over a high heat, and when it is hot reduce the heat to moderate. Put one pancake "sandwich" at a time into the ungreased pan, and turn it over when it starts to puff up with bubbles. It is done when little brown spots appear on the underside. Remove from the pan and very gently peel apart the 2 layers and fold each one in half.

If the pancakes are not to be served as soon as they are cooked, they can be stored and warmed up, either in a steamer, or the oven for 5-10 minutes.

Water Chestnut "Cake"

INGREDIENTS *serves 5-6*
2 cups canned water chestnuts, drained
¾-1 cup sugar
1¾-2 cups water chestnut flour
4 tbsp corn oil
3 tbsp vegetable oil

METHOD

Cut the water chestnuts into matchstick-sized shreds. Place them in a saucepan, add the sugar and 2 cups water. Bring to a boil. Stir in the water chestnut flour and add another 2 cups water. Stir and mix well, then simmer for 5 minutes. Add the corn oil, stir and bring once more to a boil. Reduce heat to very low and simmer gently for 5 minutes. Pour the mixture into a square cake tin or jelly roll pan. Place the pan in a steamer and steam for 30 minutes. Remove from the steamer and leave to cool.

When cold the "cake" is like a firm jelly with streaks of water chestnut inside. Cut into pieces about the thickness of bread slices. Heat the vegetable oil in a skillet. When hot, fry each slice of chestnut "cake" for 2½ minutes on each side. Serve hot or cold.

▲ *Won't Stick Three Ways – so called, because it should not stick on the spoon, on chopsticks or on your teeth! The garnish is crispy "seaweed."*

Won't Stick Three Ways

INGREDIENTS *serves 4-6*
5 egg yolks
2 tbsp cornstarch
5 tbsp water
½ cup sugar
3 tbsp lard

METHOD

Beat the egg yolks, add sugar, cornstarch and water, blend well.

Heat the lard in a skillet over a high heat, tilt the pan so that the entire surface is covered by lard, then pour the excess lard (about half) into a jug for later use. Reduce the heat to moderate, pour the egg mixture into the pan, stir and scramble for about 2 minutes and add the remaining lard from the jug little by little, stirring and scrambling all the time until the eggs become bright golden, then serve.

Toffee Apples

INGREDIENTS *serves 6-8*
3 apples
1 tbsp lemon juice
$\frac{1}{2}$ cup cornstarch
2 tbsp sesame seeds
about 8-10 ice cubes
3 cups iced water
2 cups peanut oil
$\frac{1}{2}$ cup sugar
1 tsp vinegar

METHOD
Peel and core the apples and cut each into six pieces. Cut each piece into three. Sprinkle lemon juice over the apples immediately to prevent discoloration. Coat the apple pieces with cornstarch and set them aside.

Sauté the sesame seeds in a pan over a low heat. Set aside.

Rub a serving plate with oil and set it aside. Place the ice cubes and iced water in a bowl and set them aside in the fridge.

Heat the oil and fry the apple for 10 minutes until nicely golden. Remove, drain and set aside.

In another pan bring $1\frac{1}{4}$ cups water to a vigorous boil. Add the sugar, stirring until it starts to caramelize, then add the vinegar and stir.

Add the apple pieces until they are evenly coated with syrup. Sprinkle sesame seeds over the apple and transfer them to a serving plate.

Dip the syrup-coated apple pieces into the iced water. Remove immediately or when the syrup hardens and becomes brittle. Serve immediately. It is worth practicing this recipe a few times to achieve the correct contrast between the brittle, ice-cold coating of caramelized sugar and the hot, tender apple center.

▶ *Toffee Apples: small pieces of apple are coated in batter and deep-fried. They are then coated again in molten rice sugar and quickly dipped in iced water so that the coating becomes cold and brittle, while the apple inside remains hot.*

Eight Treasure Pudding

INGREDIENTS *serves 6-8*
$1\frac{1}{4}$lb glutinous rice
$1\frac{1}{2}$ tbsp lard
$\frac{1}{3}$ cup sugar
$\frac{1}{5}$-$\frac{1}{4}$ cup nuts, eg, almonds, walnuts, chestnuts or lotus seeds
6 tbsp candied and dried fruits (optional)
about $1\frac{1}{2}$ tbsp sweet bean paste

METHOD
Wash the rice and place in a saucepan. Cover with $\frac{1}{2}$in water. Bring to a boil and simmer gently for 11-12 minutes. Add half the lard and all the sugar, turn and stir until well mixed. Grease the sides of a large heatproof bowl heavily with the remaining lard (lard must be cold). Stick the nuts and candied or dried fruits of your choice in a pattern on the sides of the bowl in the lard, arranging the remainder at the bottom of the bowl. Place a layer of sweetened rice in the bowl, then spread a thinner layer of sweet bean paste on top of the rice. Repeat the layers, finishing with a rice layer. Cover the bowl with foil, leaving a little room for expansion.

Place the bowl into a steamer and steam steadily for 1 hour 10 minutes until cooked. Invert the bowl on to a large round heated serving dish to turn out the pudding. Decorate with extra candied fruits, if liked.

Sa Chi Ma

INGREDIENTS *serves 5-6*
1 cup flour
2 tsp baking powder
3 eggs
1 cup sugar
$\frac{3}{4}$ cup maltose or honey
1 cup water
oil for deep-frying

METHOD
Sift flour and baking powder onto a pastry board. Spread to form a hollow in the center; add eggs, blend well. Then knead the dough thoroughly until it is smooth.

Roll the dough with a rolling pin until it is like a big pancake about $\frac{1}{8}$in in thickness. Cut it into 2in long thin strips; dust strips with flour so they won't stick.

Heat up the oil and deep-fry the thin strips in batches for 45 seconds until light golden. Remove. Drain.

Place the sugar, maltose or honey and water in a saucepan; bring it to a boil over a high heat; simmer and stir until the mixture is like syrup. Add the thin strips and mix thoroughly until each strip is coated with syrup. Turn it out into a pre-greased cake tin and press to form one big piece. When cool, cut it into squares with a sharp knife.

Almond Junket

This junket can be made from agar-agar, isinglass or gelatine. When chilled and served with a variety of fresh and canned fruit, it is a most refreshing dessert.

INGREDIENTS *serves 4*
$\frac{1}{3}$oz agar-agar or isinglass (or 1oz gelatin powder)
4 tbsp sugar
$\frac{1}{2}$ cup evaporated milk
$2\frac{1}{2}$ cups water
1 tsp almond extract
1 can cherries with syrup to garnish

METHOD
Dissolve the agar-agar or isinglass and the sugar with water in two separate pans over gentle heat. (If using gelatin powder, just follow the instructions on the packets.) Add milk and almond essence and pour the mixture into a large serving bowl. Allow to cool for at least 30 minutes and then place in the refrigerator for 2-3 hours to set. To serve, cut the junket into small cubes and pour the canned fruit and syrup over it.

▲ *Eight Treasure Pudding – a sticky, delicious pudding studded with fruit and nut "treasures."*

▶ *Sa Chi Ma – loosely translated as "a stone riding a horse."*

▼ *Toffee Bananas.*

Toffee Bananas

INGREDIENTS *serves 4*
4 bananas, peeled
1 egg
2 tbsp all-purpose flour
oil for deep-frying
4 tbsp sugar
1 tbsp cold water

METHOD
Cut the bananas in half lengthwise and then cut each half into two crosswise.

Beat the egg, add the flour and mix well to make a smooth batter.

Heat the oil in a wok or deep-fryer. Coat each piece of banana with batter and deep fry until golden. Remove and drain.

Pour off the excess oil leaving about 1 tbsp of oil in the wok. Add the sugar and water and stir over a medium heat to dissolve the sugar. Continue stirring and when the sugar has carmelized, add the hot banana pieces. Coat well and remove. Dip the hot bananas in cold water to harden the toffee and serve immediately.

219

INDEX